Published by Semiotext(e)
PO BOX 629, South Pasadena, CA 91031
www.semiotexte.com

Cover photograph: Nancy Campbell

Design: Hedi El Kholti

ISBN: 978-1-63590-202-0

10 9 8 7 6 5 4 3 2 1

Distributed by the MIT Press, Cambridge, Mass., and London, England
Printed in the United States of America

IF YOU'RE A GIRL

Selected Stories 1985–2023

Ann Rower

Introduction by Sheila Heti

Semiotext(e)

Contents

Introduction by Sheila Heti

Legacies, influences, are fragile and disappearing things, like silken threads. The sunlight slants one way, and you can see them just barely. The light slants another way, and they disappear.

One July morning, I woke up to an email from Chris Kraus. She began telling me about Ann Rower, a writer she had long known. "Ann is eighty-five and homebound in a NY apartment," she told me. She hadn't written anything in twenty years, since the suicide of her partner, Heather Lewis. But when Chris told Ann that she wanted to reissue her collection *If You're a Girl*, which was the first book Chris published in her Native Agents series in 1991, the opportunity "unlocked something," in Ann, and she sat down and wrote eight new stories.

"*If You're a Girl* perfectly captured an attitude and pitch of NY bohemian life," Chris said. "Ann's an incredible writer, and for me a powerful influence." I was dead curious. I had to read this writer! In some corner of my memory I'd heard of Ann Rower. I didn't think I'd read her, but I knew I must. For me, it was Chris Kraus who had been "a powerful influence." In 2008, when I was writing my book *How Should a Person Be?*, I came across *I Love Dick* in a summer sublet in New York (at the home of two young academics) and consumed it in a fever. Chris's fearlessness, her nakedness, the strange way her life had given birth to her book, gave me direction and strength. I asked Chris to send me Ann's book right away. I wanted to hear this other voice behind Chris's own voice. I sensed the precarity of female literary history in receiving Chris's email, and the necessity of independent publishing, where the only concern is how badly the editor needs the book in the world. I saw that in publishing Ann Rower now, Chris was slamming this writer into the soil, so that other writers might grow from her, the same way Chris had, and the same way I had grown from Chris. Chris is doing this with Ann in 2023, as she did it before, in 1991. I don't mean to suggest we only grow from one writer, but each writer we grow from adds something unique.

The pages came my way not long after. And when I finished *If You're a Girl*, the expanded edition, I was doubly astonished: not only to discover Ann Rower's buoyant, busy, ringing voice—but to discover that the sound of her today, in her mideighties, layered so musically, so ingeniously, with the sound of her writing at a much earlier age.

In essence, this book is the result of more than three decades of work. The earliest stories were written in the late 1980s. The most recent were written during the pandemic. The book includes excerpts from two Ann Rower novels, *Armed Response* (1995) and *Lee & Elaine* (2002).

Yet this book is not at all that ordinary thing—a "collected works" or a "selected works" or "the essential Ann Rower." It's a completely new book, whole and true, stitched from a lifetime of writing, as if this had always been the point—to come to this book, to present the self as an unlikely harmony of indelible moments, more believable *as* a self because of the unlikeliness of all the parts.

Reading Rower's stark and sobering dialogue about Timothy Leary's parties, next to her delightful Jewish farce about gossipy aunts gathering for their late, great brother's funeral, alongside her elderly efforts at moving her body during the lonely days of COVID, up against the sexy group languor of the St. Mark's Poetry Project—one can hardly believe how many scenes a life can contain! Ann Rower passed through so many great American moments (like Forrest Gump or Zelig, I thought at various points), but that's not even what really matters; what matters is that she was really *alive* for them. And one thinks: maybe it's the aliveness of just one person that makes a scene *a scene*. Her writing gets you excited about being alive at just about any moment at all, for who knows whether this instant is part of History? And isn't everything that is fully lived, *actually and authentically* History? Is this what excited Chris about Ann? This sense of *one's life* as a legitimate Historical moment, as if living it thoroughly and with great attention and even *play* is what transforms it from something that happened and is gone, into Something That Happened?

Unlike writing a memoir at the end of one's life—where the pen flows smoothly, and the retrospective glance colors everything the same color—these stories were written with enough proximity to the times they were lived that each one bursts with a separate flavour, a unique vitality, a texture that seems essential to this stunning portrait of a life.

What is happiness? I thought, reading these stories. *What is joy?* It's a funny question to ask of a book that is so much about pain—the pain of loss, of suicide, of loneliness, of the shambles and cracks of existence. Yet happiness and joy are always there. Reading Ann Rower, I think: Joy is the specific kind of leaping life inside one that finds its way to the page, or the canvas, or the stage, like a dying animal crawling and clawing its way to its home, with the thought that maybe once it gets to its home, it will be safe there, it will live. This is the feeling her stories give me: that a writer's home is the square of the page, and that we crawl to it, we claw our way to it, through whatever pain or dullness we are feeling, because we will be safe there; because there we will live. Maybe, at heart, this is the strength that Chris's book gave me. Maybe it's what Ann Rower's book gave to Chris, and why Chris is giving Ann to us again.

I cried this morning. I've been so sad all week. But seeing the arc of Ann's life-work before me, I have some new hopes about art and being, and about this realest place where some of us live: It's always here waiting for us. We can always come home to it. When we speak into it, we sound like ourselves. We sound like ourselves forever and ever. Just like Ann Rower did.

IF YOU'RE A GIRL

IF YOU'RE A GIRL

(2023)

Story of the Stories

The story of the stories, as I like to think of it—how they fell back into my lap out of a clear blue sky, some after more than thirty years—is a pretty good story in itself. So here it is:

Just after my fourteenth birthday my parents sent me off to a summer camp called Dartmuthe. The name was a smushing together of *dance*, *art*, *music*, and *theater*—the things we did all summer. It attracted a lot of kids from NYC who all went to special high schools like Music and Art, Performing Arts, even a few precocious ones got early admittance to Juilliard, and they all fascinated me. They were so much more interesting than the cashmere-sweater set and pearl-wearing—real ones—girls from my suburban high school on Long Island, especially since I had not yet found my niche with the arty crowd. This was before Francis Ford Coppola (Francie) joined us. Funny thing: Just last night I saw him on the Oscars because it's the fiftieth anniversary of the release of *The Godfather*. I was a little shocked because I didn't recognize him at all. He looked like an old man. That must mean I look like an old lady, though Luis, head doorman and now my roommate, says I don't. Luis is a fox. I love it when he calls me "Mama." Latin culture is not ageist. Anyway, the other kids at that camp had exotic names, they hung out in the Village, some of them, like Margot Lewitin, even lived there. One seventeen

Waverly Place. They smoked and drank wine and went to off-Broadway plays, sipped espresso from tiny demitasse cups in coffee houses and hung out in art galleries and museums and went to movies with subtitles. I took the train in from Great Neck, a thirty-minute ride on the LIRR to Main Street Flushing where I transferred to the subway, which let me off at Lex and Fifty-Ninth right over (yes, it was elevated at the time) Bloomingdale's, which was back then a young store, a cool haven for inexpensive even cheap radical-chic clothes. I always drifted through the store on my way east to my modern dance class on Sixty-Third with Martha Graham—yes, she was actually still teaching—or if it was Saturday I'd take the E and get off at Fifty-Third and Fifth and walk west to "the Modern," as we called it, long before *MOMA* was the word, though I notice the very fancy pricey restaurant now associated with the museum is called the Modern, and probably hardly anyone even knows that used to be the name, where I "took," as we called it, a Saturday-afternoon art class.

I was on sabbatical from teaching at SVA and could afford the cheap winter rental in Chris and Sylvère's yellow house on Squaw Road in the Springs. The town of East Hampton itself in those days was still deserted in the winter, especially the beach, which was beautifully empty except for the dogs who in those days and in that season were allowed there 24/7. Before 24/7 was even a thing.

But back many years before that winter sublet, when I was still in high school, when I came into the city, sometimes I would take the E down to West Fourth and wander around the Village by myself, comfortable among the grown-up artists and writers—they all looked like artists and writers to me because they wore a lot of black. Since I was an aspiring dancer, I always wore black tights instead of the high school–style woolen bobby socks which looked terrible on me because my calves were so big. I even wore a leotard (now called a "bodysuit") under my clothes instead of a bra, which flattened out my teen tits and was infinitely more comfortable than a bra, which I never ever got used to wearing, even to this day. Much to my delight everybody went braless for a while, which was even more comfortable especially if, like me, you had lovely perky fourteen-year-old tits (which offset the more problematic big legs and even bigger ass down below). Until Camp Dartmuthe I'd never really gotten up close to a real… I don't know what to call them—it was too late for *bohemian* or even *beatnik* and much too soon for *hippie*. For me it was life-changing. The camp was in Chatham, Mass., on Cape Cod, mid-Cape on the ocean side atop of a huge cliff overlooking the eternally rough Atlantic way down below and set in these beautiful dark woods that I got to know intimately once I'd befriended Margot Lewitin in theater class… Her passion was directing. She was a big, tall, and big-busted with a big booming voice. She used to invite me to walk with her after supper. We'd sit on a big damp rock by a stream and munch on the Triscuits and little triangles of gruyere cheese my mom would send up to me every few weeks. But that was all. At least until the end of the summer when we'd gotten much closer. One night we went back to my bunk when my roommate, Evie from Baltimore, with that great Baltimore accent, snuck off to be with her boyfriend in the next cabin leaving Margot and me free to snuggle down in my narrow cot bed and figure out what to do next, and we figured it out pretty quickly. Margot had her first-ever orgasm. When the summer was done we wrote passionate love letters full of quotes from *The Little Prince* to each other, when we were not hanging out in her apartment on 117 Waverly Place, while her mother, a handsome Episcopalian from St. Louis, and her lover, Mrs. Campbell, cautiously smooched in the next room, while her father, an Egyptian Jew, painted strange abstract-expressionist canvases that earned him some minor fame in the art world of the day.

Sometimes Margot would come out to visit us in Great Neck. My parents were quite taken with her, at least at first, before "the discovery"—what we would call the big "reveal" these days. She always brought her flute and played Bach, which my father loved until that fateful afternoon my mother snooped in my room, in my desk, and found the erotic letters Margot had written to me, full of those endearing quotations from *The Little Prince*. "The essential is invisible to the eye." Maybe you had to be fifteen to find that incredibly profound. It's opening on Broadway, as a musical, next month, now that Broadway is finally back, though everyone still has to wear masks, at least until April 30.

Margot's letters, tied with a black satin ribbon, were in my desk drawer, which my mother had left gaping wide open. She must have wanted me to know that she knew. Or maybe, in a state of shock, she forgot to close the drawer. I got home late from school that night so I didn't see her when I came in, but as soon as I saw the open drawer I too went into shock. I don't remember what I did. Closed the drawer probably. But I remember clearly how I felt the next morning going down, slowly, very slowly to breakfast, which we always ate together. I can still remember the knot in my stomach. My mom glared at me for a moment and looked away without speaking. Then she delivered the speech any ultraliberal parent at the time would have delivered, her voice quieter than usual but firm. She said of course there was nothing wrong with homosexuality. I guess that's what she called it. I don't think people said "gay" yet and "queer" still had the derogatory connotation. She said some of her colleagues at the children's library (where she was the head librarian) were "that." She said she was just looking out for me, trying to protect me from having a life where I would be subject to criticism, where I wouldn't be accepted or treated right. She probably would have had the same argument if I brought home a Black boyfriend. Remember it was not quite yet the sixties. She asked me never to see Margot or anyone "like that" again. She might have even forbade it, though that was not her way. Not the liberal way. But all I knew was that she meant what she said, and I always did adore my mother—everybody did. Everybody always used to say they wished she were their mother, and except for this one awful, earthshaking thing, she was indeed a perfect mother. But her quiet disapproval scared me straight for the next forty years, into the arms of various men I was not in love with.

Actually, Margot and I did continue to see each other on the sly and eventually my mom relented and let her visit on the condition that we keep my bedroom door open and that there would be absolutely no "funny business" happening. I swore there never would be. Of course, I was lying, but somehow she trusted me. Also the liberal way. I wonder if this is when my proficiency at lying started. Or was it the diet pills? I mean, it was Mom who took me to see Dr. Strax. She went too, but she didn't like the way the pills made her feel, how she always ended up spending hours straightening her dresser drawers. So she gave her pills to me. Can you imagine?

I don't even remember how my father felt about Margot, or if he ever spoke to me about it at all. He was a child psychologist

who specialized in treating what were called "juvenile delin-
quents," which I guess I was, before I became an adult delinquent.
All I know is I had to wait till they both were dead before I came
out. I often think about all that time wasted, waiting, wondering,
wishing, wanting.

When I taught at the School of Visual Arts, in my Journal
class I always put "bisexual" at the top of the list of "100 True
Facts about Yourself" and read the list out loud. And I'd regularly
attend meetings of a group called ILGO at the Center on West
Thirteenth Street. ILGO stood for Irish Lesbian and Gay
Organization. One year Joan Schenkar, brilliant biographer and
dear friend who sadly had a stroke and died in Paris last summer
(she had a friend who arranged for her to be buried in the famous
literary cemetery Père Lachaise where Jim Morrison is buried,
right up the hill from Colette), and I went to an ILGO protest
at the St. Patrick's Day Parade to protest the Hibernian Society
forbidding gays to march. I remember we were standing on the
sidelines in front of the main public library at Forty-Second
Street and when the police announced loudly through a mega-
phone "If you step off the curb you will be arrested," we stepped
defiantly off the curb to join the passing bagpipe players and
were promptly arrested. They cuffed us (possibly in deference to
our age and race and gender, they cuffed us in front) and hustled
us off into a waiting paddy wagon and took us downtown to the
Tombs. Eileen Myles, who was Irish and lesbian and one of my
favorite writers, and, I thought, very sexy (I had a secret crush on
her for years), took her protest further and lay down in the middle of Fifth Avenue and it took four cops, one on each limb, to
drag her off the street. She was charged with a felony and had to
spend the night in jail. Joan and I and the rest of us were put in

a holding cell for many hours along with some of my favorite writers, including Michael Cunningham, whom I idolize to this day. It was thrilling, if a little dank. It was the first and only time I've ever been arrested—at least so far! And when I finally left my dear Vito after twenty-two years, twenty of which were pure delight, I told him, when he asked why I was leaving, that I wanted to be with a woman. He did not seem surprised. He even said I could have stayed and had that too, and that he'd always kind of suspected. But that was not what I had in mind. What I had in mind was a radical lawyer with a Rod Stewart haircut who dumped me after a brief time for the sex queen Annie Sprinkle— who could blame her—though she remained my dear friend for many years. She was also our ILGO lawyer and eventually got us all off, even Eileen.

In the years that followed Margot and I saw each other once in a while, especially when I felt lonely and hopelessly single, as I did after Heather died. If I was probably the love of Margot's life, then Heather was probably the love of mine. Heather Lewis, if you don't know, was a wonderful writer with a terrible history— just my type—and we were together for almost ten years, till 2002 when she took her own life, after which I sunk into a deep clinical depression. Occasionally I'd come up for air and have lunch with Margot on Bleecker Street where I would try to convince her I wanted to be with her again—I just wanted to be with someone, I guess. I wanted her to leave her magnificent girlfriend of many years, Ronnie Geist, with whom she was deeply bonded but whom she did not, I always suspected, love as deeply as she had and probably always would love me. I knew I was tormenting her, though to her credit, of course, she would never leave Ronnie, which was a good thing, since I didn't really mean a word of what I was saying and would not have known what to do with her if she actually had. But I knew she was tempted. It was a terrible thing that I did. In fact, it is a terrible thing I'm doing right now, writing about it for all the world to know. Even for just Ronnie to know. After all, none of this, meaning this book, would even be happening if it weren't for Ronnie.

Fast forward to last summer, 2021. I got a phone call from an old friend of Margot's and mine, Jonathan Ned Katz, brilliant historian of all things queer. Jonny was also at Camp Dartmuthe and went to Music and Art with Margot. He also grew up in the Village, the far-west Village, on Jane Street near the river where he still lives, or lives again, in a brownstone he inherited from his parents. Jonny and Margot and I got very close in those early years because Jonny was my summer boyfriend at the same time as Margot was my girlfriend that first summer at camp. And then also the second summer, at the same time that my boyfriend Allen Ulick—who went to Great Neck High with me where we were a couple—followed me to Dartmuthe. So now Jonny and I were together and Allen and I were together and Margot and I were together. An American teenage version of *La Ronde*. I remember it all climaxed, so to speak, one afternoon when Jonny in a fit of adolescent jealousy ripped off a silver necklace I always wore that had "Ann" engraved on one side and "To my darling, all my love, Allen" on the other, and threw it off the huge cliff hanging over the ocean far below and I have no idea what happened then. All I remember was that Allen at Great Neck High School played the leprechaun in a production of *Finian's Rainbow* directed by Francis Ford Coppola (Francie later made it into a movie at MGM) and Jonny played the same imp in a production at Dartmuthe that summer and both (separately) sang the wonderful

Yip Harburg song "When I'm Not Near the Girl I Love" before either of them knew they were gay. I hadn't heard from Jonny in ages but he'd seen Margot's obit in the *New York Times* and was calling to console me. I didn't even know she had died. It was a very long, loving, complicated, and emotional call. It was in fact a nice way to find out, though I was sorry I never saw her obituary. I never saw Joan Schenkar's either. I keep missing everybody's obits because I never read the *Times* anymore.

I got a phone call out of the blue from Ronnie saying she was going through Margot's things, papers and books, trying to clear out a space for her own things, and she found a collection of my things, papers, books, and writings, all bound and carefully labeled, that Margot had kept over the years. At first, I wasn't even that interested. I couldn't really remember or even imagine what writings she was talking about. But then I had a second thought and said, "Yes, sure, why not? I'd love to see them." This was after she explained that she was planning to come uptown the next day to see her son Daniel, whom she and Margot had raised together, along with Daniel's father, and who lived around the corner from where I had been living with my girlfriend Val on the Upper West Side since 2015, the first time I'd ever lived "above Fourteenth Street," as we used to say, in a full-service building that had doormen and most importantly an elevator, since Val and I both had mobility issues. Ronnie asked if I wanted her to leave it with the doorman. I said, "Why don't you come up for a minute and we can have tea?" I always liked Ronnie a lot. She agreed, though she didn't have much time, she said, sounding a little shy, maybe reluctant, or nervous, but she did come up carrying a large Zabar's shopping bag that looked heavy. She set it down on the floor and took a seat at my '50s cherry-red

Formica kitchen table while I made us some iced tea in my new Upper West Side way—the ice came from the magic ice maker in the refrigerator door just like that and I got the boiling water from the Keurig coffee maker by pressing a certain button that released hot water over the tea bags. This afternoon it was hard to concentrate on all these mechanics and I felt a little shy and awkward myself so I just gave her my glass and sat down.

I'd never been together with Ronnie without Margot and maybe I was a bit distracted by the big bag of my stuff which I hadn't even glanced at because we got to talking very deep and sad. We'd both lost our girlfriends so recently during COVID (but not to COVID) and we both confessed for the first time about how our relationships with our partners had sort of disintegrated toward the end and how terrible that made us feel now. Maybe it had a lot to do with their respective health issues (I learned that Margot had Parkinson's, Val had a million different ailments), which made them miserable and understandably difficult to deal with as they both got sicker, requiring more and more care, which became harder to provide fully and lovingly and willingly, until by the end we were almost relieved to let them go. We confessed how even worse than the grief was the regret, and how, perhaps most significantly, neither of us had ever admitted this before to anyone else, possibly never even had the realization before that moment. There was a sense of us being incredibly close for having shared this terrible secret guilt which left us feeling so awful, as though we'd failed or fucked up really badly. Suddenly she looked at the time and leaped to her feet, saying she was now late for dinner, an appointment with her son, Daniel, and she left. We talked on the phone soon after and even arranged to have dinner together the next time she came uptown.

I suggested my usual treat—Vietnamese dumplings and shrimp summer rolls. She said she'd love to hear me read some of my work to her, which surprised and touched me. It all seemed very charged and unexpectedly easy but then Omicron surged and I misplaced her number and never heard from her to this day.

So anyway, after Ronnie left that night I was so struck by our saying (as everybody now says) "the quiet part out loud," our confessions of guilt, that I almost forgot about the bag of my writing and I just sat there, stunned. Very ashamed. But after a while I pulled myself together and dragged the shopping bag across the floor toward me. It was very heavy. I started to investigate its contents. The first folder I looked in turned out to be a terrible play I had written. It was called *Arcadia General*, which was the name of a mental hospital where it was set—the only decent idea in the whole play. I am not a playwright. Margot must have still been madly in love with me, fifty years after those furtive fumblings—well, they weren't all that furtive—at Camp Dartmuthe, as she had gone on to produce it at her and Ronnie's Women's Interart Center, complete with music, light design, and real actors! Finally, I pulled out a fairly heavy manuscript embalmed in plastic and went into shock. I looked at the address on the title page: 65 Greene Street, my beautiful SoHo loft, two thousand square feet, fourteen-foot original tin ceilings, gigantic windows, the real thing, $300 a month back in 1974 when Vito and I moved in together after his apartment on Jones Street ($33 a month) burned down after a fire started in the junkies' place next door. Anyway, what I was looking at in such complete disbelief was the original manuscript of my first book, *If You're a Girl*, the "pink book" as I always called it. I had decided on hot pink for the cover to complement Cookie Mueller's swimming pool–blue cover for *Walking Through Clear Water in a Pool Painted Black*, also her first book, which was due to be published at the same time. I hadn't seen that manuscript since I submitted it in 1989 to Chris Kraus, who bravely, heroically, started her own imprint to complement and maybe even challenge that of her then husband, Sylvère Lotringer's, well-established series of French theorists: Semiotext(e) Foreign Agents. Chris called her imprint Native Agents. It was all American writers and at first all girls. The pages were a little faded. I handled it gingerly, like it was precious cargo, as I flipped through it, scanning the stories, some of which at first I couldn't even remember writing—a strange feeling, like trying to get back to a dream you just had. But as I turned the pages they gradually came back to me. All thanks to Ronnie. Ronnie Geist. When a story of mine called "Ghost" was published in an East German anthology of new American writing, it was translated as "Geist." But someone else named Geist (whom I called by accident trying to reach Ronnie after I lost her number) later told me that *geist* really means not "ghost" but "spirit." Of course—*zeitgeist*!

Almost half of the stories we'd never used. I didn't remember if they were left out because we already had enough material, or if Chris didn't like them enough to want to include them. I guessed if I got my nerve up to send them over to her, I'd find out. I sat for hours reading all these stories I hadn't seen in over thirty years and I liked them! It was all very weird. Suddenly I was filled with joy and hope. I hadn't felt hope in a long while. Maybe never. It wasn't my kind of emotion. I always seemed to kind of live in the moment (to use an expression I usually can't stand) and had, to quote the Stones, "no expectations." A few days later I got my nerve up and called Chris in LA to feel her out about doing another collection of my stories and essays, some of the ones from the original MS we hadn't used and some that had been published in the interim, in little magazines and journals, and some brand-new pieces. I had scores of notebooks and journals and even a few legal pads I'd filled up scribbling late into the night. Val loved it when I wrote all night. Lying beside her in bed, it was the only time she slept really well, drifting off around 3:00 or 4:00 a.m. to the soft scratching of pen on paper. Lately I'd taken to handwriting everything. It felt really good and I didn't even have to get out of bed. I no longer even remembered how to operate the computer very well since Val always did the typing, even for the Heather book I had been writing, or thought I was writing. She was a very fast typist. She told me the highest praise her mother could ever muster up was to tell people, when she was celebrating her younger brother Brad's brilliant legal mind, how Val had taught herself to touch type. When we first met, I told her I wanted a techie, and so Val being Val struggled and finally succeeded in becoming one.

Back to Chris Kraus. At this point she'd been waiting many years for me to finish the Heather book I'd been working on with Val. It was a bit odd because I was still so angry at Heather for ruining my life by hanging herself, but Val just adored her and really wanted to focus on the love story, even the sex scenes, which you can imagine were not that easy for Val to type up, and even more challenging to help me remember or even invent. We had stopped working on it at the point when Heather and I had left New York City and arrived in Bisbee, Arizona, that afternoon. I just couldn't tell the rest of the story—Heather's breakdown, her suicide back in NYC, my eight-year clinical depression— even though I imagined I'd have a ready-made audience of downtown writers and artists for that, those curious to find out what really happened in Arizona. Though the great Gary Indiana had already taken a fictionized crack at it in *Do Everything in the Dark*. Such a wonderful title, like all his others. But I just couldn't face it. I couldn't write it. I couldn't relive it, especially, I think, with and through Val. It was bad enough just being haunted and taunted by those awful months, almost a full year really, from 9/11 to the weekend of the Kentucky Derby of 2002.

At one point I had called Chris and confessed I was stuck with the Heather book, but she said enthusiastically, encouragingly (?) that she was still interested, and that I should just take my time and finish when I could. And that was that. A few more years passed. COVID. Val died, and after Val died I really couldn't finish writing about Heather's death, when Val's was so recent. And then nothing until this moment, two and a half years later, when I had that old plastic-covered manuscript in my hands. Maybe I didn't even have to write the Heather book. Maybe this would be the new book—my last book, I thought to myself, though I would never stop writing. Could never. It would be a "circling back," as everybody especially media people says these days, but still—a fitting end to my writing... adventure? Dreams, or whatever they are, do come true (last night I had a dream that I lost weight in my feet and was able to wear white sneakers, like everyone else).

But before any of this happened, I had started doing physical therapy, and the way that happened was another bit of serendipity. What happened was this: Alma, my helper in multiple ways, was picking up her kids in a nearby building where their babysitter lived. She ran into a young man helping an old woman down the front steps with her walker. Alma stood aside politely, waiting for them to reach the street and somehow surmised from their conversation in the interim that the young man was a physical therapist and the older woman was his patient. Alma being Alma, and always on the lookout for ways to help me, just went right up to him and started talking and eventually got his card for me. And that was the start of the story of how my life was so profoundly altered that I was charged enough by physical therapy to contact my old friend Chris and send her the stories.

But it took some doing... doing some physical therapy. In fact that was the only kind of therapy I was doing at that point, since both my psychopharmacologist and Jane, my regular therapist, who'd been helping me since right after Heather died, had recently retired. Did I mention that Jane was deaf? This got a giggle out of everyone, but she was a great therapist, very good at reading faces and body language, cheap and queer but also, as of a year ago, ready to retire and spend the rest of her life and energy in her Brooklyn brownstone with her partner and her five parrots. I wonder what it is with therapists and birds?

Funny story. The first time I saw her, I was still shopping around for a new therapist. I'd recently bolted from my former therapist after telling her, strangely, almost gleefully, throwing my arms into the air like a gymnast sticking a landing (I guess I was in shock), that Heather had killed herself the night before. Since then, I learned that people in serious trauma often immediately quit therapy. But the first time I met Jane, I told her the story of how I'd visited another shrink, of the Gestalt persuasion, a few days before, and somehow we got to talking about how I didn't have any pictures of Heather or even my parents displayed anywhere in my apartment. The therapist expressed shock and disapproval. I didn't think you were supposed to do that but then

I didn't know anything about Gestalt! She asked me if there were any pictures, and if so, where they were, and I told her they were in a suitcase in my storage bin in the basement. Or they had been, before Superstorm Sandy washed everything away. And when I told this story to Jane, the deaf one, she was neither shocked nor disapproving, but she told me she had pictures of her family right in her office. She wanted me to see them. I was curious to see what her parents looked like, and followed her to the other side of the room where she proudly produced a beautifully framed photo of herself with her arm extended. On it were not parents but parrots, five of them, each one more wonderful than the next.

It was the first of many misunderstandings because of her deafness, I guess, but it didn't deter me from choosing her over the Gestalt therapist, who was very expensive and who had pictures of her lawyer husband and her parents on the wall. The point being that I was desperately in need of some kind of therapy, especially right after Val died (June 21–28, 2020). And I was definitely sick of regular therapy, so Alma's bumping into this new physical therapist Matt Bauer, by pure chance (especially since his specialty was geriatric physical therapy), was like a dream—not to sound too much like a Disney princess—come true. Come true fast, at that. I've had other physical therapy in my life, especially recently, a lot of it at the Rusk Institute. But I've never gotten high from it. And I mean *high* high. Floating, soaring, thrillingly alive high. I guess it's partly what people call "endorphins," although to me it seemed with this six-foot-two slender imp of a therapist there was a tad of norepinephrine in the mix somehow, somewhere, you know, that can't eat, can't sleep, early spring, almost-like-being-in-love (remember I did say "almost") feeling—and the good news is you don't even have to be newly or madly in love at all. You can be a completely single lady and get the same norepinephrine rush from eating chocolate, cheese, and to my surprise, my favorite, sausage, not to mention from a healthy (and I did say healthy) dose of oxytocin—that warm, fuzzy, purring happiness, reminiscent of a different kind of love, the kind of bond people have with their animals, their close family, what my pussycat, Nuchenuche, gives me to boot. When I got to know Matt a little better, which, as I said, seemed to happen awfully fast, I asked him to explain his "technique" and without missing a beat he said—well, actually, he texted—right back: "It's a mixture of organically chaotic but encouraging energy."

So you can see how I was completely taken, hooked. Another aspect of the Matt Bauer technique—a way with words! And with no words. Maybe a nod, a gesture, a brief demonstration, a glance, in complete silence, except for our occasional chattering about this or that, the war in Ukraine, the Supreme Court hearings, flannel shirts, haircuts, kissing... Anything but the physical therapy we were doing. That just happened. That just flowed, flowered, the rush it left me with lasting long into the evening, ending up all over my divinely—and I do mean, kind of, divinely—hurting body, my whole body, well into the next day. I must have inexplicably cathected to him. *Cathexis*: a word I've always loved, though I seem to be the only person who's ever heard of it. All I know is it comes from psychoanalysis and has to do with the way a patient attaches energy to an object, usually the therapist, I guess. I've always had the image of someone casting a fishing line out over the water with a big barbed fishing hook on the end, which makes it very hard to remove without pain. Maybe that's why, when I looked up the definition of *cathexis* on my phone, it said it was thought to be unhealthy. That was upsetting. I never heard that part. I just thought it was about deep attachment. But hey—what does a Samsung cell phone know? But maybe it's not so inexplicable after all. Maybe because he occasionally touched me, barely, lightly, just with his fingertips, or a brush of palm, only to keep me from falling or losing my balance, partly because a lot of the physical therapy he does involves balance exercises, as falling is such a common problem with older people (and remember his specialty is geriatric physical therapy, to make matters worse... hmm, better?), I often seemed to get dizzy when he came over, but the truth was I loved it. Not the dizziness—the touch. If you can believe it, it's the only touch I've had since Val died. Since before she died. Since COVID. She was terrified of COVID. Terrified of hugging. Especially terrified of kissing. In the beginning, in March 2020, I even called 311 one morning to ask about kissing. "What about kissing?" I asked the operator. There was a long pause. I could almost hear her gulp. Then she said, "I have no idea. Ask your doctor." But I never did.

But I did ask around and found out a lot of gay people I knew did not kiss either. Mark and Paul did not kiss except lightly on the top of the head. Paul told me that one time Mark forgot and kissed him hard on the mouth and Paul went into complete shock. So those occasional light grazes during our physical therapy, or even when he was taking my blood pressure, which was also shockingly, scarily so very high when he came, and even more recently, like yesterday, when it was so high he was afraid he'd have to call 911, were earthshaking for me. At one point Luis came into the room where we were exercising and asked "How was your blood pressure?" "High," I said. "She just gets excited," he said to Matt, like they were in cahoots. Like I wasn't even there! But we had to skip my usual warm up with the walker—four or five laps up and down the long hall—because he feared it would elevate my pressure even higher, so he just had me stretch in multiple ways for the whole fifty minutes. It was the best fifty minutes I've had in years! And to take the blood pressure the real way, like a doctor, with a stethoscope, he'd have to push up my sleeve and touch the flesh of my arm, and just the way he held my arm, kind of hard and tight. It was almost like a shock every time. And just last Thursday, after he was done taking it, he gently rolled the sleeve of my pink shirt back down for me and I found it very sweet, caring, very touching for some reason—like it wasn't exactly part of his job description. I confess that the only reason I'm including this tangential material about doing physical therapy is because of this: touch. And the lack thereof. And he touched me! Somebody touched me! That fifth sense. During COVID, the forgotten sense. The forbidden one. Maybe I'd better cut this part. It's kind of embarrassing. I'm sure Matt, my physical therapist, would be relieved too. When I mentioned to him that I was writing about him he looked kind of terrified. I don't know what's the matter with me. I've completely lost my filter. If I ever even had one. I mean, I remember how delighted I was when Chris Kraus referred to me, in her fun first novel, *I Love Dick*, as "the unshockable Ann Rower"!

As I said earlier, the physical therapy somehow prepared me, with new strength and even grace—call it courage, really—to send these stories to Chris in the first place. Because another thing the therapist did with that "encouraging energy" he described as his "technique" was to treat me like a writer. While walking backward no less. I sometimes mentioned to him that I'd stayed up late scribbling into the night and the next time I saw him he'd ask, "How are your essays?" I don't know why he called them that, but it made me want to write essays. Maybe he was prescient. What I'm writing now—this—feels like an essay. But he and I talked about writing, and he seemed genuinely interested in my writing, long before these stories even found their way back, through Ronnie, through Margot's death, really, into my life. And now I have a book deal. Can you imagine!

It was not the first time the death of someone I loved very much ended up bringing new joy into my then-sad life. The other time, in 2002, the death of a profound love of mine, Heather Lewis, by suicide—the worst thing that had ever happened to me—turned, eight years later, into the best thing that ever happened to me. Because it was Heather Lewis who actually brought Val to me, as Val and I would always say with a wink, or sometimes even with a tear. Because Val got to know Heather, then Constance Jones's girlfriend, when Val was researching *For the Love of Friends*, the book Connie was writing at the time. She'd go to Connie and Heather's huge apartment on Seventh between First and Second to drop off her latest findings, and then spend as much time as she could squeeze in with Heather, and it seemed like Heather too was always excited to spend time with Val. They were great pals. When Heather heard her come in, she would roll into the living room on her desk chair with a big happy smile. It sounded to me that each had a little crush on the other. But then Connie's project was done. Val left NYC and went back to DC where the rest of her family lived—her mother and younger brother, Brad, who was teaching at the law school at GW there. Val had no real contact with Heather until one afternoon eight years later she had arranged to have lunch with her old friend, Louise. As they were strolling through the Audubon Room at the New York Historical Society, the recorded sounds of the beautiful creatures chirping cheerfully away in the background, at one point Val asked Louise how Heather and Connie were. Louise pulled back. "You didn't know? About Heather?" I guess Val shook her head. So Louise proceeded to tell her that Heather had killed herself years ago, back in 2002. It was now 2009. How could she have not known, not heard, in all that time? Val fled in despair. And then tried to figure out how to get in touch with Connie—even though Louise did say Heather and Connie had split up—but Connie didn't tell her that Heather was with me. So Val, not to be deterred in her search for the person she must give her condolences to, like that was a crucial spiritual act or something, and more crucial, the person with whom she could share her grief, finally landed on the idea to look at Heather's latest book, to see if there were any clues in the acknowledgements. Lo and behold her intuition was correct. I was in there. Val was always a brilliant researcher. That's how she came to be working for Connie in the first place, how she then met Heather, whom she always liked better. Didn't everyone? Strange how things work, though. After I did finally meet Val, I called Connie to ask about her. All Connie said was, "Stay away from her. She's crazy," which only made me dislike Connie more.

The dedication at the start of Heather's book was to her mother, who had recently died. Heather had the most peculiar relationship imaginable with her, especially since her husband, meaning Heather's father, had been regularly raping Heather since she was a child of ten. Heather's mother must have known (don't they always know, somehow, deep down?). But it was very touching that Heather did dedicate the book to her. I do think they loved each other, but Heather had been so alienated from the entire family for so long that only at the very end—literally the end of her mother's life—did they reconnect. The next time Heather was taking the train up to Bedford, to the big mansion the Lewises occupied (but couldn't afford), she arrived a little later than promised and when the housekeeper, who had always looked out for Heather since she was a child, came to the door, she had to tell Heather that her mother had died an hour ago, while Heather was still on the train. On her way to say goodbye. (I think this happens a lot. I remember when my friend Amy Scholder was flying out to see her dying mother in LA, her mother died while Amy was still in the air. And when my beloved Ron Vawter, the brilliant Wooster Group actor, was being flown home to die in NYC, and I'd been designated to meet him at the airport and bring him back to his partner Greg in Greenwich Village, someone called me when I was already on my way to the airport, a few hours before his plane was supposed to land, to say he'd died midflight, not from AIDS as predicted, but from a sudden heart attack at exactly the same age as his father had—forty-five—young! And all I really still remember was how relieved I was, because I was so scared about actually having to meet his plane and deal with him in his current state, which we all knew was demented for sure. The only other thing I remember was Vito breaking down, seeing Ron in his open casket, and flinging himself over the body, sobbing his sweet heart out at the funeral home on Fourteenth Street where so many other gay actors ended up being laid out.)

But back to Val's search for me in Heather's second novel. She found my name on the acknowledgements page, so now she had the important clue and had only to find who Ann Rower was, and how she could be reached. Luckily for me, I'd stood up for myself for once in my life, because in the original acknowledgements for *The Second Suspect* Heather had listed her therapist, her astrologer, her agent, her editor, her trainer at the gym, and somewhere buried among them, me. When I saw this, I was enraged. Furious. Slighted, insulted, so mad I couldn't contain it, had to express it, told her even to my chagrin and embarrassment at sounding like a selfish spoiled little baby—I said, "No." I didn't want to be embedded in a long list, between Gloria, the astrologer in Santa Fe she called three times a year, and Nan Talese, her bigshot editor at Doubleday who didn't even read the damn book but handed it over to her assistant. I wanted my own special dedication, on my own special page, or at least my own paragraph. I wanted to be first, just me, me and nobody else, and of course, Heather being a brilliant writer and a great lover, and greatly in love with me for sure (everyone used to say things like they'd never seen her this happy), came up with the most spectacular solution imaginable.

"The author would like to thank Ann Rower for the grasp and the grapple—for hoisting the wreckage." Rereading it tonight to get the exact quote right, I get turned on all over again, as I always did when I read her words, especially when they were about sex, even tangentially. Even after all this time. "The grasp" and "the grapple" were our erotic private codes because we thought they sounded sexy when Flight 200 from JFK to Paris crashed off the coast of the Hamptons and they brought in the two rescue vessels *The Grasp* and *The Grapple*. For weeks there was nothing on TV but the blue waters of the Atlantic depths and these two rescue vessels looking very tiny against the sea and sky and finding nothing. But "hoisting the wreckage" was and still is such a turn-on and so that's how Val Clark came to find me, who was already impatient to meet up in person after weeks of back-and-forth emails and phone calls between DC and NYC. The meeting was going to take place in the community garden next to my East Village apartment on Seventh Street between C and D. Val at this point had never been east of Avenue A in Alphabet City, so the trip east on Seventh was terrifying for her, so many gardens, until finally she got to the last garden on the block, and peeped in through the iron gate just as I was giving up all hope that she would ever even show up. Somehow, when we saw each other in that instant, we both know this was it. I rose to meet her and she fell into my arms, sobbing for Heather, whom she had loved, and then we pulled back a little and gazed into each other's eyes. We fell madly in love. So whenever people would ask "How did you two meet?" that's when we'd shyly, slyly look at each other and say, in unison, "Heather."

But anyway, I found some other stories that were recent and some really new stuff and finally got them all together. Alma took them down to Columbia Copy and I extravagantly FedExed them to Chris in LA a few days later. The guy said they would arrive five days after that, and the very next day Chris and Hedi, the managing editor of Semiotext(e), emailed my contracts for *If You're a Girl*, the expanded edition, without even seeing the manuscript! What if they hate it? But they didn't, don't, and now I have a book coming out, much to my delight and amazement. How thrilled Val would have been, but for some reason I think maybe none of this would have happened if Val were still here, and we were still mostly lounging around in bed and watching TV. I couldn't help telling people, and for some reason all they ever asked was what was I going to call it, and everybody had their own different ideas for what the new book should be called, and I just this minute remembered that the original "pink book," the first edition of *If You're a Girl*, began with a discussion of that title, and how everyone had strong, conflicting opinions about it. The girls—and I listed them—all liked it then. But what about now? So much has changed with how we talk about gender. Not just how we talk about it either. Maybe now it might be more of a question, and not just a statement. But Chris's choice was *If You're a Girl*, expanded edition. I don't think I ever even talked about it with Val. We always called it the "pink book," and besides, it was so long ago. And how could I even begin to discuss it with her? I mean, c'mon. She always referred to herself as "gender inconsolable." My new friend (she was Val's good friend) Irene said "How about: *If You're an Old Girl*," thinking of the British expression used fondly. My cousin Scott, who loves to edit my writing, had many suggestions, like *If You're a Sophisticated Girl*, then *If You're a Sophisticated Woman*, which I changed to *Sophisticated Lady*, because there's a song like that, and he said he liked that (he thought I was serious). And then I told a few more people about having a new book, and again they all asked "What are you going to call it?" and this time I joked nervously, I guess, and said "Not *If You're a Girl*, but *If You're an Old Lady*," and everyone burst out laughing really hard, but it scares the shit out of me, the "old lady" thing, and I quickly added "Of course, I'm kidding," but I almost said "It scares me to death."

And that would've been that. I was going to end my foreword, the story of the stories, with that: the word "death," even though it did seem like a bit of a downer, until, that is, last night. Sometime a little after five in the evening, Dr. Matt came by for a late session, the latest we'd ever gotten together to exercise. I thought it might work out well for me, because the usual time when the vertigo would hit would be long passed, but my head started spinning like mad as soon as he walked in the door. For a moment I felt kind of ashamed, as always, for being so out of control, but it was a beautiful time of day, early April and still light out. April. I think of reading T. S. Eliot in senior English class in high school. You know, "April is the cruellest month, breeding / Lilacs out of the dead land, mixing / Memory and desire," as he rolls up the sleeve of my pink linen shirt and takes my blood pressure which has shot up through the roof again and I look down at my arm and see my wrinkled skin. "Did I tell you my new theory of aging," I ask. He says, "No. *My New Theory of Aging.* That would be a great title for your new book." He's so smart about language, as I've noted before, and I nod in agreement. "So tell me. What is your new theory of aging?" He is not self-conscious about this subject like I am. In fact, he once told me most of his patients are older than I am. "Well," I say. "You know how everyone always says that with old age comes wisdom?" He nods. "Well, even if that's really true, if you do the math, you then have to subtract short-term memory issues and, even worse, wrinkles." This makes him laugh. "It would be a great title," I say, "but Chris, my editor, wants it to be *If You're a Girl*, expanded edition, to match Cookie Mueller's *Walking Through Clear Water in a Pool Painted Black*, expanded edition," although Cookie's book is due to come out in June and mine not till 2024 (I won't tell you what I'm thinking!). It makes me think of our two books coming out together way back in 1990, just after Cookie died of AIDS, and how bittersweet the big celebratory reading-party at a downtown disco was, and how Richard Hell and Sharon Niesp had to read for Cookie, which they did beautifully. And then, last but not least, my physical therapist and I did some beautiful hamstring stretches, my favorite stretches, especially since he does them too. But this time—meaning last night—I noticed that he didn't straighten his knee completely, and I inappropriately pointed it out. "I pulled something yesterday," he said. He's training to run in some special race, maybe the half marathon in May, which had to be cancelled for the last two years because of COVID—but as I was saying, if you do the math and subtract the annoying memory problems and all the hideous wrinkles, you pretty much break even, or as my dear dyslexic Vito would say, "Break out even." Once again, another silly little joke at Vito's expense. "Yet another full-circle moment," I say, while we're stretching, "I hate that expression." "Why do you hate it?" he asks. "Oh, it seems like it's so Oprah-speak." He laughs. "Anyway," I say, "I keep having these full-circle moments. No wonder I'm always getting dizzy!"

Notice

The other miraculous thing about Hedi and Chris agreeing to do my book unseen was that the package also included a second contract, a contract for *Notice*. *Notice* was technically Heather Lewis's last book. But she had actually been thinking about how to write it for years, maybe even before her first novel *House Rules*, and definitely way before *Second Suspect*, which was more her editor Nan Talese's project, and even more so her new agent's, who was really only interested in a big movie deal. The closest he got to fulfilling that fantasy was to set up a meeting between Heather and the great director Alan Pakula, right after Thanksgiving. Alan was driving out to East Hampton for the holiday when a huge improperly secured steel beam slid off the truck behind him, through Alan's back window into his brain, killing him, not to mention the dreams of so many around him, including Heather. Alan was also the uncle of Heather's dear friend Jennie Livingston, who had also been waiting for him to arrive for a festive weekend in the Hamptons. Jennie was a great director herself (*Paris Is Burning*) and had been planning to join Alan and Heather for lunch that next Monday to make things easier and possibly help things along, especially since Jennie was a great fan of *Second Suspect*, a sexy thriller. *Second Suspect* was intended to follow up Heather's magnificent first book, *House*

Rules, which was not a gigantic commercial success but generally considered to be a masterpiece debut novel by all who knew literature, especially queer lit.

It's peculiar how things work sometimes. In those early days (I got the contracts on February 12, 2022, Lincoln's real birthday), as much as I was completely over the moon at the idea of having another book at this stage—at this age—what seemed so great was the *Notice* part, the other contract, and the prospect of deepening my bond with Hedi, Chris's Semiotext(e) partner. Because since I held the copyright to *Notice* after Heather's death, it was Hedi who had approached me for permission to reprint it, an entirely new place for me to be in the literary world. It made me feel powerful, like I could make a real connection between Heather and Hedi, like I could make a difference.

Not that working again with Chris Kraus, my first editor from back in the nineties, wasn't thrilling all by itself. Chris and I had our own special history that went way back. Way way back. Back to the Poetry Project at St. Mark's Church in the early eighties, where Chris and I kind of bonded because neither of us were poets. And Chris at this time was not even a writer. She was a filmmaker who projected her early black-and-white movies like *How to Shoot a Crime*—a brilliant title which perfectly combined film and murder language—onto the rickety screen at the church on Monday nights. I was intrigued partly because Chris's first films were intriguing and also because I had gotten into filmmaking myself, with my cheap little Super 8 camera. Super 8 was as close as you could get to video in those days, and I was hooked. I had my own editing space in the huge front room of Vito's and my loft on Greene Street. I loved editing because editing is a kind of writing. And shortly thereafter Chris and I started writing screenplays together for real. Aside from Vito, with whom I wrote songs, Chris is really the only person I ever seriously collaborated with, and since writing is normally a very lonely process, writing, especially screenwriting, with somebody else is fun, exciting, and comforting too. We worked endlessly on an adaptation of Erje Ayden's odd spy novel *Sadness at Leaving* and almost got it made. We then made a script from a real-life country crime in New Hampshire, where I spent many summers in Margot Lewitin's beautiful beat-up, run-down farm house in Center Sandwich on Squam Lake, the actual lake where they shot *On Golden Pond*. It was a plucked-from-the-headlines story we called the *Chipper Murder*, where the villain killed a girl and ran her corpse through a woodchipper. They have one every winter in Tompkins Square Park in the East Village and everyone drags their expired Christmas trees over to turn them into mulch. But instead of spewing little bits of tree trunks and branches, our woodchipper sent little pieces of the victim's flesh high into the air and all over the countryside. Fortunately the local sheriff picked up the bits of flesh, but nobody picked up the script—maybe a good thing for our screenwriting careers, our writing careers period.

But that was not the end of our working together. Chris did so many great things for my life, my well-being, and my writing. In the late 1980s, she found me the perfect apartment for the next almost three decades, especially perfect for a basically starving artist whose only income came from a position as an adjunct at the School of Visual Arts. They didn't call us "adjuncts" there because it was assumed that the talented faculty were all part-time teachers by choice—it was really so they didn't have to give us health insurance. The apartment was a cheap, lovely studio on East Seventh Street, which looked out on a beautiful garden, the Firemen's Garden, named after a firefighter killed trying to save some local squatters back in the late sixties. It had an amazing huge weeping willow tree, which was almost better than an ocean view. The building was between C and D, right across the street from Chris and Sylvère's apartment. My mother had recently died and left me some money, so I could pay cash upfront—which in 1989 was only $47,500—and move right in without even having to paint or pay rent (except for a very modest maintenance), even though I did put the rest of my inheritance up my nose.

The second favor Chris did was to include me on a tour she and Sylvère organized for the East German press Galrev, which had just published an anthology of contemporary American writing called *AM LIT*. It was published right after the Berlin wall came down and the East Germans we stayed with were still very loyal to the Soviet Union and very sad about losing their government health insurance when West Germany took them over. They were not at all pleased when they listened to Reagan, who cried out "Mr. Gorbachev, tear down this wall!" When we were there, they kept pointing to empty spaces, saying fondly: "Ze vall vaz zere. Zere vaz ze vall." At first we all stayed in different places around town (in cities like Hamburg, Frankfurt, Cologne, and Berlin). I remember Eileen Myles and I ended up being the only occupants of a huge government-arts-council Soviet-style-architecture building and though it had many many rooms, we shared one of them, a tiny space which rekindled my old Eileen crush from back in the '70s at the Poetry Project, but of course nothing happened, except in my mind—I was much too old for Eileen anyway, so probably just would have gotten hurt. It was a great group Chris and Sylvère assembled: besides Eileen there were Lynne Tillman, Kathy Acker, Chris and Sylvère, Richard Hell, and me. Lynne fell in love with the cute guy who chauffeured us around in a big VW van and she ended up broken-hearted. Chris was uneasy with Kathy trying to hit on poor Sylvère (they'd been an item years earlier). Kathy tried to show off riding a motorcycle way too big for her to handle, especially on the Autobahn, though I admit she looked awfully cute in the expensive white sailor suit she bought in Cologne and it was a nice change from all the leather she usually wore. Of all of them I was possibly the eldest, except for Sylvère, and did not own any leather clothing at all. I was definitely the least, well, to quote one reviewer who admired my reading but was concerned about my outfit—a black jersey-print shift dress with multi-colored blossoms all over it that my mother and her oldest sister got me to wear on the tour—"Nicht gerade 'hip.'" I don't know German but that I understood. Truly the most crushing review I ever got.

But some of the most revelatory and life-changing weeks of my life were during a stay upstate in the Adirondacks, when Chris got a NYFA teaching grant and brought me along for the wonderful ride. Our job consisted of teaching three very diverse ninth-grade high school writing classes in the middle of October, the middle of fall foliage in the land of mountains and lakes and trees, so many trees in so many colors. I'll never forget what it was like waking up that first morning, after coming in on the bus from Port Authority late the night before in the pitch dark and then stepping into the big living room with its big picture windows gazing out into this raging magnificent bath of mid-October color the next day. Deep-blue morning sky, reds, purples, oranges, golds, browns, many kinds of green near and far down the sloping mountainside into a lake reflecting everything plus the sun and clouds from above. It was great. The kids from Warrensburg, a poor little village populated by hunters, young and old, only wanted to write about the deer they killed and how that felt—good for them, not for us—and all we wanted was for them to tell us about it. And thus, our journal workshop, which we both coasted on for the rest of our teaching lives, was born. The second school was in a town called Bolton Landing. I remember my parents talking about visiting it in their youth, an arty country-vacation spot for urban villagers (Greenwich Villagers), writers and painters trying to get away from the city they loved, at least for a while. Those kids were the happy off-spring of hippies and bohos who loved writing and enjoyed the oddball "prompts," as they call them. And lastly Lake George High School, in a very upscale, conventional community. The kids were excellent, disciplined, bright students who didn't quite know what to think of Chris and me, but who were fine with everything. Until the last night. It wasn't meant to be our last night, but what happened was this: the parents were impressed at having guest artists from New York City in their midst and arranged for a night of student performances culminating in a reading by us, or maybe just me, as the finale. Chris, brilliant as she was, was also kind of innocent and idealistic about the ways of the world. She suggested I read a new story I had just finished called "Cherry," which was not a reference to anyone's virginity, at least not consciously, but the color of the café curtains my mother sewed for my bedroom to match the cherry walls. Perfect for a young girl's room. There was nothing too shocking to us about the story if you don't count the references to my learning to masturbate for the first time with the long, thick tail of a stuffed lion I had won in Atlantic City with my father standing behind me for luck. When I placed a quarter on the square called Lucky Jack and the car stopped right there I won this beautiful huge stuffed animal. I carried him home, named him Leonidas, and though I was too old for toys, I was not too young for that toy, I eventually discovered. A miraculous period of discovery for pubescent thirteen-year-olds everywhere, come, so to speak, to think of it. I guess that's why Chris thought it was appropriate for Lake George High adolescents. Well, maybe not their parents. Because it was about a certain aspect of the junior high school experience and oh, yes, there were some references to the diet pills I was taking at the time, green and white—not Dexedrine, maybe Dexamyl—and all I really remember was that the parents were called in the next morning to vote us out and how quickly they hustled us onto the next bus out of town. I don't think they made us give the money back. But maybe they did. All I remember was Chris saying plaintively, and very upset, "But you had a prescription for those pills, Ann!"

Oh, Chris, I am so looking forward to our new adventure. But back then, in February, I was looking forward to working again with Hedi too. Because doing the new edition of *Notice* was not really Chris's passion. It was Hedi's, one that he and I definitely and absolutely shared. I hardly knew Hedi El Kholti, but I clearly remember how I felt about him at our very first meeting in New York when Chris arranged for us to have lunch in some diner on the Upper West Side. We were meeting to discuss the possibility of Semiotext(e) publishing my new, next book: a novel about Heather's story and especially its tragic ending which at that moment I still felt a strong pull to write about. Chris knew that Hedi was a big fan of *If You're a Girl*, the "pink book" that came out so long ago. Lately, it seems that time has speeded up, which everyone says as they age, but it feels like everything I believe happened twenty years ago was really thirty years ago, or even more.

Part of the charm of the original Native Agents books was their colorful covers, in contrast to the Foreign Agents books of French theory, which were all black, like Sylvère's leather clothes (there was a period when he'd show up to teach philosophy at Columbia wearing a black leather vest over his otherwise naked chest—trying to be sexy for his graduate students, I suppose!).

When Hedi became managing editor of Semiotext(e), the press got bigger and better due to his brilliance and diligence. He started a new journal called *Animal Shelter*, a great mix of writing and visual content, ranging from the exquisite to the really raunchy. See, for example, Gary Indiana's "My Hole."

But back to that lunch on the Upper West Side, which must have been when I recovered from my depression after Heather's suicide, around 2009, the wonderful year I met Val. But no—Val and I didn't move uptown until 2014 (after Val's hip surgery made even two flights of stairs impossible). But my point is that when Hedi and I had lunch on the UWS it was because Val and I were living up there for real, in a magnificent building, the Manchester, from the twenties, in which her family owned and maintained a beautiful one bedroom, much as I resented no longer being able to claim the East Village, downtown, as my hometown. But Hedi seemed perfectly comfortable there. Anyway, Hedi is irresistibly charming and easy to talk to. We hit it off immediately and by the time the check came it was clear that Hedi was going to say "Yes, let's do it," meaning the Heather book, which was at this point just a sketchy narrative concept, a couple of rough chapters, a story idea—admittedly a pretty intriguing story, if a little gruesome. And that was all there was between us, except for a flurry of emails around *Animal Shelter* publishing a section of it a few years later. Hedi and Chris ran the magazine in their own special style, or lack of it. I remember them asking me to submit something, which I did, and then never hearing back. I kept saying to Val, "I wonder if they like it, if they want to use it…" And Val would try to be encouraging, reassuring: "Of course they want to use it." "But," I'd say over and over, "but I never heard anything back from them." And then it came out and of course there was my story, a version of a chapter from the Heather book, which by now was almost half-done, thanks to Val. At first, Val was just typing my scribblings, but that led to a real collaboration, and also a big conflict: Val wanted to focus on how much in love Heather and I were, early days, the love story, and I wanted to write about her breakdown, her illness, the abuse and my rage, which at that point was all I was left with.

But that was really all of my contact with Hedi, except for one lovely, purely coincidental moment, also on the Upper West Side, standing behind him and his boyfriend in an endlessly long line at a French bistro for the ever-popular UWS Sunday brunch. It was thrilling to meet this way, especially since Val was with me, still with me, so they could actually meet in person after hearing wonderful things about one another for years, and as it was with Val and so many people, an instant warmth passed between them. The next time, around Valentine's Day, when Hedi and I did actually speak, instead of just texting about his wanting to reprint Heather's book, *Notice*, his first words were not about the publishing business, but heartfelt condolences about my losing Val and how much he liked her, as so many, but not all, did. And then, only then, we began to share for the first time, I think, our love for *Notice*, which so many, but not all, did not. Love, I mean.

Because *Notice* was a problem. Heather famously shopped it around to eighteen editors. They all turned it down. "Too dark, much too dark," they all said. Even some of her biggest fans and dearest oldest best friends (even Val, to name one) didn't like it, could hardly stand to read it, had to put it down, couldn't finish it—not just because the sex was so rough, to put it mildly, so violent, but worse: because the tone was so flat... Heather's genius creation was the voice of a horribly abused young woman who spoke dispassionately about the shocking scenes of her own abuse. For this, many hated it, though Sapphire loved it. Of course she did... Sapphire and Heather went way back, both "survivors," as you know from their books, back to the days when they attended the same incest and abuse meetings, and both ended up knowing how to write about it spectacularly well. Heather's heart broke at the almost universal rejection of *Notice*, but she tried to repair it with the next book, *Second Suspect*, by sticking the amazing and erotic opening chapter of *Notice* at the front of *Second Suspect*, to seduce readers and salvage the best part of *Notice*, presenting it in a place where everybody could finally see it... But the reception of *Second Suspect* was not considered enough for her fans or the market. Heather died, by her own hand, as most know, thinking of herself as a failure. She always wanted to straddle the cool downtown world and its community of writers, which she was too late for, and the uptown six- or seven-figure advances of the mainstream publishing world where she never really fit either. *Notice* was finally published posthumously, to everyone's surprise, in a generous gesture by my other beloved editor, Amy Scholder, at High Risk / Serpent's Tail. Amy certainly took a high risk publishing a book the whole New York publishing world would have none of, was even repulsed by, which made me love and admire her even more than I already and always did. Do.

But years before Heather's death, when she was just beginning to shop *Notice*, her masterpiece, as she (correctly) thought of it, around, I remember reading a draft of the book in bed with a terrible cold, and Heather and I had just fallen in love for real, just kissed for the first time under a pink sodium street lamp on the corner of First and Seventh Street after the dyke march earlier that day, which Eileen Myles and Heather and I had attended together. I admit, I even secretly wondered which one I would end up going home with—of course neither, I told myself, silly me. But that didn't stop my hungry imagination from secretly panting for something, someone, after so many pleasant creative years in the loft with Vito, followed by a few more years of nothing. At one point Eileen leaned over and smiled that crooked devilish Boston Eileen smile and said, half-snide, half-affectionate, "So, Ann, are you gay now?" The three of us went to the dyke-march after-party on Avenue A that night, and once "Ain't No Mountain High Enough" came on, and I discovered what a terrible dancer Heather was, and that it didn't even matter, we flopped back down on some ratty couch and started to kiss. I discovered she was a great kisser and that did matter. A lot. I remember Eileen came up and stood behind us on the couch and interrupted our tentative advances, asking "So what are you two guys up to?" The answer was now clear to me, if not to Eileen, that we couldn't really stop what we were doing to answer. So she slunk away, I guess… Heather and I walked home across Seventh Street as far as First Avenue and we kissed again, this time for real. Hard. I remember taking hold of her long hair and pulling her toward me to seal the deal and then let go, uncertain how or where or what to do from there, so we said goodnight, and I continued eastward and Heather went up to her apartment above Miracle Grill. I don't remember feeling sick at that point, but the next day I awoke with the most awful cold dripping out of me by any means necessary, so Heather and I had to wait days to fully (for the first time of an infinite number of amazing times) consummate our new, or at any rate newly acknowledged, attraction, which had been bubbling beneath the surface since we were both sent out on the High Risk book tour at least a year before. We jokingly called it "The Bitches of High Risk Tour," or alternately, more politely, "The Girls" or "The Women" or sometimes "The Ladies," because it was an all-girls group—me, Heather, Lynne Tillman, one Canadian, and the High Risk wrangler who literally got us on and off the trains from city to city (Philly, DC, Baltimore, and of course the Big Apple). I always felt they (someone) made sure that Heather and Catherine (and not me) shared a room and Lynne and I the other. It was fun spending time with Lynne, though. I remember one hotel where the tub was in the room where we slept and Lynne was taking a hot bath one night and as she got into the tub, with her back toward me, lifting one leg and then the other, I remarked, "You have a nice ass." Which she does. "David said that's why he married me," she said. Lynne didn't come to LA and San Fran with us, but I remember the night before we left, Amy and I cabbed it uptown together to Malaga Baldi's (Malaga was Heather's agent, both for *House Rules* and *Notice*). I can still hear Connie's vaguely threatening farewell to me, standing at the door after the party, the night before Heather and I and Ira and others were flying out to LA. She looked at me hard, and said, putting her arm around Heather's shoulder, "Take good care of my girlfriend." The "girlfriend" she had already broken up with, I happened to know. Malaga threw a huge party to celebrate the paperback release of *House Rules*, which ended up being published by Ira and Amy at High Risk after Nan and Doubleday lost interest. Poor Heather. She was so counting on that big advance to pay off at least some of her Amex bill. But then she wouldn't have had such a spectacular Rex Ray cover. Those two beautiful sexy crossed riding crops.

So it was a year after that that Heather and I first kissed and when I woke up sick the next day, she gave me *Notice* to read, probably partly as a means to seduction, something she knew how to do well, maybe almost too well, I sometimes thought. The only other thing I did that whole time I was sick in bed was speak endlessly on the phone with Eileen and Gary Indiana for advice about whether I should take the plunge and really get involved with Heather Lewis. I recall that Eileen had reservations. The first thing she said was "You know, Ann, she has a terrible history." Heather did have a terrible history to be sure, which was, I admit, part of her attraction, which is, I admit, kind of crazy of me to admit. Like now, here. In print. Gary, on the other hand, was thrilled. He adored Heather in every way possible—he always blurbed her books. I went with Gary! The rest of the time I practically sucked *Notice* up through my terrible stuffy nose. I couldn't get enough and there just was not enough of it. That's how much I adored it. And how much it turned me on. I've given up asking people if they thought *Notice* was the sexiest book they ever read, or even sexy at all, because they all looked at me like I was crazy or a pervert, so turned off in some way or other by it—by the tone, the theme, the story, the characters, possibly the cover, even the title, though I have noticed, ahem, that when I am congested, especially with fever, I am easily aroused. What is that?

It would have thrilled Heather to know that the celebratory first reading of *Notice* was at Bob Holman's Bowery Poetry Club, the quintessential downtown venue. The reading was a small, intimate event. I don't even think I read, either because Amy knew I was in bad shape, or because I was still being treated like the spouse at a funeral, sitting in silence, but in the front row. Allen Gurganus, whom Amy had asked (or "tasked," as they obnoxiously now say) to write the afterword, came up from North Carolina and went out with us all to Noho Star afterward. Noho Star, yet another COVID casualty. I remember Mary Dorman was there plying Kirsten Skrinde with drinks. Kirsten was one of Heather's former devoted students, one of the only people, another being Anne Lopatto (and of course me), who stayed loyally and firmly dedicated to Heather in the eight awful months between Arizona and her suicide. Through the mania— which vanished in the middle of the summer once the Bisbee, Arizona, police had locked her up. I guess jail made her feel safe: four walls and three squares a day, after months of lonely craziness, left to her madness in the high desert, free to paint the house doorways with her own shit as a magic protection, or to blow pot smoke into her cat Whoopi's mouth to calm her down. But back to the *Notice* reading—I think the only thing Kirsten remembers was that at the end of the night she went to the bathroom and when she came out we had all left. The event was small, intense, perfect, moving, moving people to tears. Even me—I say this only because I hardly ever cry. Whenever I used to say this, Val would say, "You do so cry." I don't know why. I haven't cried for Heather. I haven't cried for Val. The only time I came close was watching John Lewis's funeral. And also, once, watching him dance. He was such a great dancer.

Anyway, Amy ran the evening flawlessly. It was one of the many things she does impressively well. It was memorable, even to me, who couldn't remember anything at this point and wouldn't until at least five or six years later when I finally rose to the surface of my deep depression and came up for air. Depression, the real clinical kind, is a strange beast. My face on my SVA photo ID, which I had to take at that point, looks nothing like me. But the depression took a while to kick in. Right after Heather's dramatic exit I was running on a kind of almost manic energy, which was a blessing, because right after that I was scheduled to fly out to the West Coast for a book tour for my new novel, *Lee & Elaine*, which came out at that exact same time. I remember someone told me (I don't know who) that Heather died on the weekend of the Kentucky Derby, which is always the first Saturday in May, next weekend actually—oh no, another anniversary. Heather, who had been a talented horse rider, watched it every year. We never could figure out whether she killed herself before, during, or just after the Derby. Also, that weekend the Sunday *New York Times* book review of *Lee & Elaine* by my neighbor Catherine Texier was scheduled to come out. I heard that Heather ran around frantically to every newspaper store in the West Village looking for a copy. She apparently was so thrilled, so proud. Funny combo. It wasn't a great review. It had a big BUT right in the middle. You know, very positive at first till it turned. I can't remember what the BUT was about, and of course, since it was such a weird time, I didn't save it. And besides, all I cared about was that the *Times'* Sunday Book Review reviewed it at all. Heather died shortly after, though the review was not so terrible it would cause anyone to off themselves. High Risk arranged a fabulous West Coast book tour, just me and the remarkable Mary Woronov, who was reading from her new book *Niagara*, a wonderful book. But the high energy didn't last. By the time I got back to New York I was crashing for real. The only thing I could handle was teaching and I'm sure I wasn't great at that. And the depression lasted a long long time. Years. Somewhere in the middle of it *Notice* came out, and until that night in 2004, at Bowery Poetry Club, I didn't even know that Amy had given me the copyright to have and to hold. So last February I could say to Hedi, when he asked for permission to reprint the book we both loved so much, "Yes."

Anyway, Hedi and Chris wanting to redo *Notice* at the same time as my new book miraculously changed everything, completely changed how I'd been feeling about Heather since she hung herself in Paul and James's back bedroom on Eighth Street, where she'd been staying since I bought her back to NYC from Arizona shortly after 9/11 (because the people she knew in Bisbee all believed the bombing of the Twin Towers was the work of the Devil. Seriously). So I flew out to Tucson two days after— no one but a few other desperate souls was even flying yet, I remember Dr. Isaacs just saying "Be careful" when I told him I was going out there, even though I lied and said Kirsten was coming with me—and when I brought her back she was very fragile, emaciated and postmanic (now deeply depressed), and naturally she wanted to stay with me on Seventh Street, but I would not allow it, to protect my own mental health, for once. So I scrambled around and finally found a place for her to live nearby, in the West Village. It was Paul and James's wonderful apartment with a great terrace on Eighth Street, which they hardly ever used since they had moved up to Woodstock. I got them to agree to this arrangement (reluctantly, because they knew all about Heather's Arizona breakdown) by assuring them that she was no longer manic, merely somewhat depressed, but basically reliable as a tenant, and I kept assuring them that nothing bad would happen, and that of course, if it did, I would take full responsibility, whatever that meant, not of course knowing what the future held in store for Heather, for all of us. But somehow they were convinced it would be OK. Perhaps through loving Heather and wanting to help her, and also loving me and wanting to help me—protect me, basically—they agreed. So from September 17, 2001, to the weekend of the Kentucky Derby, 2002, she lived there. I would come over on weekends to hang out (oops, I did it again!). It was hard. She wasn't really eating, just smoking a lot. Once a day her father, who was sending her $3,000 a month, would call. It was always around dinnertime. I guess we always ordered in. She would pick up, answer monosyllabically, and hang up, shaking but somehow relieved. I insisted she take her Xanax when I came over for the weekend because it miraculously restored her to sanity. Of course, I had to get it for her from my own doctor—good thing he was what Burroughs would call "a writer"—because none of her shrinks would allow her to take it because they all agreed (assholes!) it was addicting, even though it was clearly the perfect drug for her, the only one that worked. Zoloft only made her ill and even more depressed, and worst of all, numb.

Until one night she confessed that she wanted to hang on to the full bottle (oh no, I didn't mean to say it) she'd just gotten, in case she couldn't take it anymore and decided to swallow the contents and die. Well of course I went into full panic mode and the minute she left the room I grabbed the pills and stuffed them into my shirt and took them home to Seventh Street and tucked them at the very back of my white filing cabinet drawer. It was almost like she let me, was relieved to have them out of her sight, especially since I agreed to dole them back out to her on an "as needed" basis. She eventually convinced me that the suicide idea was a passing thought, and swore that she would never do it for real, and for some crazy reason I brought them back and gave them to her. Again. Of course the threat came up again, and this time I grabbed a big smooth stone that was part of Paul and James's décor and started furiously smashing the little blue tablets into a fine powder as she watched, sobbing and crying that I was ruining her only way of keeping her sanity, that when she took them she felt normal and that's really the only reason she needed to have them in her possession, and I, oddly, felt terrible. I believed her, and actually helped her pick out the remaining uncrushed pills and the larger intact fragments. We worked together in silence in a calming quiet. It was so intimate. I swept up the powder, of which there was a lot, into a baggy and tucked it away to take back to my apartment on the East Side. That night was the one time we had sex after she returned from Arizona. Though the sex was hot as ever, we never did it again. I just didn't want to.

She killed herself a month later. I became furious at her for ruining my life and sank into a deep clinical depression which transformed me into a zombie. I remember hearing that someone in my boss's office at SVA had said "We've lost Ann." Six years later I was found, or I somehow found myself. I changed back and everybody noticed. The only thing that didn't change was how angry I still was at Heather. I carried that rage along with my recovery and only when Chris and Hedi sent me the contract for the new version of *Notice*, along with the one for my new book, on February 12 (Lincoln's birthday), just a few months ago, was I able to let it go, love her writing and feel connected to her once again, but in a new way, a beautiful way, which is how I feel now. It's almost the first Saturday in May, Kentucky Derby day. Heather's death day. I just put her picture up on my bedroom wall, a Xerox of the picture Hedi and Chris used to accompany my story in *Animal Shelter* back in the spring of 2015. I wonder whose idea that was. The caption reads: "Heather Lewis holding her kitten in Arizona. Photograph by Ann Rower." Another step in the right direction. Another release. Whenever I use the word "release" I think of Joni's beautiful line: "Laughing and crying / You know it's the same release."

I Think I Was on That Ferry

The only trouble with this story is that the punchline comes at the very beginning, which complicates the storytelling process. So either it'll have to be a very short story or I'll have to figure out some other way to tell it, or maybe just the old circle-back routine. We'll see. The other thing is that Heather and I really "first met" twice. Once, when we first saw each other at her debut at the Drawing Center, for Linda Yablonsky's great NightLight series, in the fall of 1996, where Heather read wonderfully from her first book, *House Rules* (which was much talked about and attracted me to her and her "work" before I ever even laid eyes on her). And at least two years after that we met again on the High Risk tour, during which we read and traveled together—the camaraderie often bordering on intimacy—sharing multiple meals, motels, medications, and adventures, from Baltimore's aquarium and Poe's cottage and Cookie's old stomping grounds to A Different Light in LA, Santa Monica, the Rex (in honor of Rex Ray, who designed all our covers) Hotel in San Francisco. Serious glorious fun. Plus neither Heather nor I drank. And drinking, especially after readings, was a big part of the touring shenanigans, as most writers know. It was just another element that brought us even closer, something we alone seemed to share. I had given up alcohol, along with spices, smoke, coffee, all kinds of acid, because I had GERD (gastroenteritis reflux disorder), and Heather because she was an alcoholic. She used to confide in me that Connie, her ex-girlfriend, would regularly threaten to leave her if she ever took even a tiny sip of a drink, so Heather obeyed and didn't ever drink, not even one tiny little sip. Ever. And though I no longer had a boyfriend, everyone (especially Heather and maybe Eileen) was somewhat confused about where I was with all that.

Our first kiss coincided with Heather having just gotten a new high-powered agent, Mort Janklow, who in turn got her a six-figure advance from Nan Talese at Doubleday for her second novel. So she was in love and in the money simultaneously. The very next week she rented a house on Fire Island so we could play full-time. We even planned to invite our dear friend Amy out for the day later in the week. We were living—or soon would be— the extremely high life. And of course, being so deeply, madly, and finally in love was at the very core, the base, the basis of it all.

But H wanted to go out to Fire Island alone first, though I remember at the time thinking, a tad resentfully, Why don't we just go out together? I was probably in the right, as usual, but she went out first anyway, ignoring my advice, as usual. I was to take the Saturday 11:00 a.m. ferry from Bayshore to Fire Island, which she would meet. We would find each other on the dock— *whatever she wants*—and we'd just take it from there. How perfectly and absolutely romantic. And the most exciting part wasn't even part of the plan (as it never is—how could it be?). On the dock just ahead of me, waiting in line to board the boat, was standing, one hip thrown out, in tiny cut-off denim shorts and a tight black tee shirt and flip-flops, with newly shining blond curls, my very favorite weatherman, ABC's Sam Champion. A very young, very pretty, very gay, very out (unusually for mid-nineties daytime TV) lovely Sam Champion at the beginning of his long career—he's still on. How much more perfect can you get at the very start of the deepest, most perfect love story of your life? I was deliriously happy the whole ride out (ferry rides can do that to you—the ferry from Boston to P-town also does it every time), so delirious in fact that I was so anxious for it all to begin, to meet Heather at the dock—and maybe even a little distracted from ogling Sam Champion's adorable daytime-TV ass—that I got mixed up and got off the ferry at the first stop, the wrong stop, at the Pines instead of Cherry Grove, partly because I was such a Fire Island novice at the time, and of course there was no Heather anywhere to be found, to meet me, as we had so enthusiastically planned, at the dock... In fact, there was no dock.

I was frantic. Really. I doubted for a moment that I would ever even see her again. My distress must have been so obvious that a few random people came up to me and offered suggestions. One, the most appealing, but out of the question economically, was to take a water taxi to Cherry Grove, which I didn't even know how to do even if I could afford it. Others convinced me that I could just walk through the woods and out the other side, which seemed scary and iffy... How could I even expect H to still be there waiting, and how would she even ever find me, or I her, even if she did? In the days before cell phones. But that seemed like the only real option, so I shouldered my duffel bag which suddenly seemed impossibly heavy—what was even in there? The only thing I remembered packing was my leopard-print Bettina Riedel jumpsuit which H had specifically requested I bring so we could try to reenact the scene from my story "Baby"—as if we needed any extra turn-ons in our lovemaking.

But anyway, I walked, trudged, through the tangled brambles of those woods, full of large curious deer those woods were known to be full of, still curious after years of watching gay boys and girls getting it on atop of the pine needles where they could find some privacy for their lust (sharing with four or five roommates was common—the only way people could afford the exorbitant Fire Island rentals). I walked and walked. Some places there wasn't even a path to follow. Scared and discouraged, sweaty and out of breath, on and on until finally—at last—the forest got thinner and there was light through the trees. I parted the branches and stepped out onto the long wooden walkway that led down to Great South Bay and there, to my amazement, was a very small figure in the distance, looking out over the water. It was my darling Heather. Waiting, as if she had been waiting there forever. For me. I ran down to meet her. What a rush. What an embrace. "Did you bring it?" she said, grabbing my bag chivalrously off my shoulder and placing it in the little red wagon, which came, she later explained, with the house. "Of course," I nodded, suddenly shy, but I wouldn't be for long.

I couldn't wait to tell Heather, after describing the arduous trip through the scratchy woods with the big-eyed deer watching, about my delight at seeing Sam Champion in his cut-offs the minute I stepped on the ferry. It was such an unforgettable moment. Still is to this day! And then there were those awkward moments of bumping into the landlady on the stairs—she lived on the second floor—wondering if we would keep her up all night with our noisy antics. Heather's noises really. She was terribly loud. But I didn't really care about the landlady. After all, we were on Fire Island. And paying a lot of money to rent the house for an entire week. And I must admit the whole week went swimmingly, as they say, from the initial sighting of Sam Champion in his teeny cut-offs and flip-flops to the eventual cutting with scissors, as a last resort, to remove my $200 SoHo jumpsuit. Except that there was no swimming involved (because Heather was afraid of the ocean and I was reluctant to go in by myself, though the beach was a mere hundred yards from the house). No swimming, that is, until the penultimate day of the whole visit, when Amy came out, as planned, though I couldn't have planned her prelude to swimming any more dramatically if I had fantasized it myself. Soon after lunch on the deck Amy rose to her feet, unceremoniously unzipped her jeans, and carefully stepped out of them completely and lo and behold revealed a pair of swimming trunks (I'm sure she had been waiting for this most titillating moment the whole time). Then she removed her tee shirt (she always swam topless, as I already knew) and began to slather her body inch by careful inch with 50-SPF sunscreen as we, Heather and I, observed the process in fascination, understanding that the ritual, the way she was taking such precaution, was not vanity or showing off, but because she had had a melanoma years earlier, so when I joked "You missed a spot," her initial alarm wasn't a laughing matter, and I apologized profusely. She handed me the sunscreen and I did a much less thorough job on myself, but for her sake, I tried. No one could compete with Amy Scholder in the thoroughness department in any endeavor— her editorial fastidiousness was truly a beautiful thing. She then asked Heather if she wanted some, but Heather shook her head, saying "I'll just stay here and make the drinks," which I took to mean soft ones. Amy and I spent a good amount of time in the delicious water. When we came back and plopped down in the deck chairs, exhausted and exhilarated from the swim, I noticed a drinks tray with beautifully arranged Triscuits and cheese and three martini glasses, one of which seemed to be sparkling—water, I assumed, for Heather, who of course didn't drink. Heather could be surprisingly domestic on occasion. She even seemed to remember that Amy took three olives. We raised our glasses, which I realized by now looked identical, took sips, smacked our lips in satisfaction, and sat back in our deck chairs. It was only after we'd emptied our glasses and Heather picked up the tray and took it back inside for refills that Amy and I looked at each other, hard, perplexed. "I thought Heather wasn't supposed to drink," she said. "She's not," I said, a little shaky from the shock of it, of seeing my brand-new girlfriend Heather Lewis take a drink after not having a drop of alcohol over so many years of hard-won sobriety, supervised so perfectly, so strictly by her former boss and girlfriend for over a decade, Constance Jones. When she returned with three more full martini glasses, I left mine on the tray and was silent. But Amy was not. "So are you drinking now?" she asked, bravely. It reminded me of the way Eileen had said "So are you gay now, Ann?" Heather just shook her head, waiting a few beats to gather her reply maybe, and said, sort of sweetly, maybe even sadly, "I just wanted to be like everybody else." She even choked up a little bit. So there was nothing I could say. And never did. Never ever. To this day! Just not my style. To be the substance police.

So anyway, that was the story except for one more thing. The thing I started to say about the punchline of the story coming so early. But here it is now—at the end. Exactly where it belongs. Soon after I came back to the city my friend Kirsten—who, incidentally, had been Heather's student and was still, to this day even, madly in love with her (she referred to Heather as her "pretend girlfriend," which always got on my nerves)—and I were having lunch to catch up. She was dying to know everything about Fire Island, of course. And, as I did whenever I talked about the Sam Champion part of the story, I got excited, but this time—I don't know what happened or how it happened—I must have described my own delight so vividly that Kirsten, when I was finished, actually clapped her hands together with pure adult joy. You know how they sometimes refer to a story or narrative as a "vehicle"? Well Kirsten hopped right on and was transported. And to this day I still think no writer or storyteller could receive higher praise. She said, her own voice full of excitement, "I think I was on that ferry!" High praise indeed!

Heather and Hobe

The strangest thing. Until this very moment while making a few small edits on this piece (so that it would fit the word count Clem required for her magazine), it never occurred to me to even wonder, not even for a moment, what would have happened if Heather and I had not decided to abandon NYC. Forever, we thought at the time—exactly one year to the day before 9/11 changed everything anyway for us all, all us New Yorkers anyway—to move out to this funky little high-desert town in the southeastern corner of Arizona on the Mexican border. Would Heather never have had a complete, devastating breakdown, practically taking the whole town down with her? Would she have returned to New York right after 9/11 to hang herself? Would we have been celebrating instead of grieving? Would Heather still have been whole? Was she ever?

Looking back, I can remember exactly when it started. Heather and I and Peyton and Frank were out at Adam and Tim's ranch in the valley, near where Peyton lived. Peyton is Peyton Smith, great star (and a little bit the great diva) of the Wooster Group, who had abandoned the theater and New York City the year before we did and was our inspiration for going out there. Before dinner, Heather and Frank went off for a long walk through the tumbleweeds. When they came back Heather was beaming with happiness. She was so happy that night. All through the lovely evening meal we had (I have a photo I took of the five of them—Heather, Frank, Peyton, Tim, and Adam— with their backs to the camera, looking out as the sun was setting over the high desert still in full spring bloom). I'll never forget Heather saying, as we were driving back home to our little miners' shack on Moon Canyon, "You know, for the first time in my life, I really think I could be happy." But this happy dream was the beginning of a manic episode, just starting to rise up from the dark place where it had been lurking, a monster waiting to pounce. "Oh no, you won't," it growled. "You cannot be happy. Never be happy." What we had thought was happiness was the mania talking. It was the beginning of the end.

Frank was a great cook, a gorgeous man whom Heather had a huge crush on. That last night in Bisbee, just a few months later, Frank cooked. He made pasta puttanesca, without garlic (in deference to my stomach). After dinner I remember going out the side door to have a cigarette—yes, I'd started smoking—and soon Amy came out to join me. "Can I bum one?" she said. Apparently she'd started smoking too. Amy was there because I'd called her to come out and rescue me from the effects of Heather's full-blown mania. The sun was just setting over the desert I had fallen in love with. We sat on the low concrete stoop. Amy put her arm around me as I started to cry. "I can't believe I'm just leaving her all alone in the middle of the desert, a raving lunatic in the midst of a nervous breakdown."

The next morning when I got dressed, I tucked my white shirt into my jeans. I never did that before. "You look nice," Peyton said. I couldn't believe I was going home. Heather was so manic that she actually told Amy and me that she thought it was a great idea that we were leaving her and going back to New York City. Amy is a great packer. I still have a little sample-sized bottle of Creme de Corps body lotion from Kiehl's with duct tape around the cap so it wouldn't explode on the plane!

Later in the summer, I was back in New York, bouncing around from one secret location to another to keep Heather from finding out my whereabouts. Anything to keep her from reaching me when she was at her craziest, painting the window and door frames of the great house on Nighthawk in Bisbee with her own shit—you know, classic crazy. She finally got herself arrested for some dumb thing with our Saab and some woman poet she met in the mental hospital. But the strangest thing happened. As soon as Heather went to jail, the mania vanished. Completely disappeared. I was working behind the scenes, but Amy was really trying hard to deal with the staff at the jail and the nearby hospital in Tucson along with our friend Adam who had a lot of personal experience with mental hospitals. We tried to see if we could get her transferred directly from the jail to the hospital long-term. Of course, this meant getting in touch with her "real" family, as opposed to her local gay "family"—Amy, Adam, and I. As soon as Hobe was informed, he wanted to come out to Bisbee to see her, though he was blind as a bat. He wanted to help her. He still loved her, of course, in his fashion. Hobe, of course, is Hobart Lewis, CEO of *Reader's Digest*, and, of course, Heather's father. The grand villain of the piece—of all the pieces she ever wrote, every interview she ever gave, every thought she had, every breath she took—who tried to stick his tongue as far down her throat as he possibly could every chance he ever got. At least until the mania kicked in. As soon as he found out she was in trouble, he started sending her money immediately, much to the rest of the family's dismay and disapproval. And of course we had to call Tim, Heather's next of kin (her baby brother), but he refused to bring Hobe out to Arizona, wisely I suppose, despite Hobe begging him. Tim, along with Amy, ended up spending a lot of time on the phone to the jail and the hospital shrink, alas, to no avail. The process brought them close together. I remember hearing, from Amy I guess, that Tim said to her (after sharing that he too was gay): "It's such a shame that we're meeting like this. Under other circumstances, we might have been great friends."

When the summer was over, after the mania, after the Twin Towers collapsed—I always thought of Heather as the Third Twin—I brought her back to New York. We made a few trips up to Bedford to visit Hobe. It was very difficult. He was now living in a nice little condo by himself. I guess at a certain point the Lewises had to give up the mansion they could never afford. This was all after he retired from running *Reader's Digest* in the nearby town of Pleasantville, which always struck me as darkly hilarious name for such a creepy place. At least I always thought it was creepy. Actually, I think I must have gotten that from my father, who was (until Stalin invaded Poland—some things never change) a bit of a Red, and I don't mean a Republican. My father always said he thought *Reader's Digest* was a CIA front. It wasn't just commie gossip, I'm sure. My father knew about things like that.

Incest was not Hobe's only crime. He was President Nixon's confidant and bagman. I remember Heather told me he carried millions of dollars in a suitcase to Cambodia for Nixon during Watergate, a time when no one was allowed to enter Cambodia because of the threat of the Khmer Rouge. He brought Heather back a painting of two horses on a gold background by a local

Cambodian artist. It was beautiful, kind of primitive. Painted on wood. Hobe had always been proud of Heather's horse riding, especially her jumping. He followed her riding career faithfully and intently. The painting was an acknowledgement to say he knew how much she loved horses (as you know if you read *House Rules*). It was small and could easily fit in the suitcase once the cash had been transferred to God-knows-whom. And why Cambodia? We always wondered, but of course we couldn't really ever ask. The painting is sitting right over there on my shelf where I can see it from my bed, right next to a lovely old snapshot of Heather at sixteen in full-dress riding gear, complete with velvet hat and a beautiful leather riding crop. Hobe was one of the few Watergate participants who never got exposed. Heather researched his involvement in the whole thing and his relationship with Nixon. I remember she told me Nixon once came to visit the Lewis family in their big house in Bedford. Hobe insisted on dressing Heather (who was maybe nine at the time—almost ripe!) in a white sailor suit. She had stood proudly at the door to say goodbye to the not-yet-disgraced president of the United States and saluted! Heather found tapes at the library—I guess the famous Nixon tapes—and any number of recordings of Hobe in conversation with Nixon. Her favorite was the one of Hobe and the president chatting away, which must have happened right after that visit to Bedford, in which Nixon signed off fondly (referring to the little girl in the sailor suit) "Give my regards to the admiral." Maybe because he was sending her money every month, Heather felt obligated to try to have some contact with Hobe, so we rented a car a few times. Until her breakdown Heather had always done the driving, whenever we went anywhere in the blue Saab convertible we bought for

$7,000. She would often take off in the car by herself, heading to Sierra Vista to shop at Target. But by now she was too weak, too unsure of herself, or too scared to do almost anything, let alone a navigate a big heavy Swedish car. The saddest part was that we never even put the top down. Not once. We sold it to friends for a meager thousand bucks before we left that time we both flew out to Bisbee for Thanksgiving in November 2001 with Peyton and the gang. Heather may have even pulled herself together enough to make her specialty sweet potatoes and marshmallows—the only time she ever did anything remotely like that in all the time between 9/11 and her death. Maybe it was because we were back in Bisbee. Maybe it was for Frank's benefit. I remember when I tried to get everyone in Bisbee to read *House Rules* and Frank confided in me that he was repulsed by the lesbian sex scenes, which made me despise him. The only one who loved *House Rules* was Bonnie, Peyton's brother's wife, who was actually the first of the whole group of New Yorkers to discover Bisbee, because she was allergic to the city and Bisbee was famous for its clean air. Now that I think of it, one of my regrets about moving us both out to the sweet little high-desert village was that by bringing our craziness to it we polluted Bisbee for good. I felt terrible guilt for that. Bisbee used to be a prosperous mining town (the Copper Queen was the name of the mine, and then the hospital, and the hotel that Heather's ex-student Kirsten stayed in and the library and the high school and every other damn landmark left once the mine shut down and wiped out prosperity once and for all—at least until the hippies finally moved in and set up shop: health food stores, cafés, bookstores, dress shops, and the like). There's a wonderful quote from the great film *LA Confidential*, in which Kim Basinger says she plans to move home to Bisbee, Arizona, after her life in LA, uttering the immortal words "I grew up there. I'm going back in a couple years, open up a dress shop. The girls in Bisbee need a little glamour."

But to return (to "circle back," as Jen Psaki, former Biden press secretary, used to say—she quit just today) to our visits to see Hobe, back in the fall and winter of 2001, as soon as we got there, Heather would shut down. Even with Xanax. She barely said a word. But Hobe and I bonded in an odd sort of way. I remember he had food for us and I helped him serve it because he couldn't see. Once we left, Heather would perk back up, but she was always left shaken. It was very hard to be with him. Who knows what was going through her mind. Either of their minds. We never talked about it. But Hobe tried valiantly to keep the contact going. In addition to the $3,000 monthly checks, he called her every single evening.

When Kirsten and Anne Lopatto "found" Heather (they wouldn't take me with them, as they knew how upsetting it would be for me if our suspicions were confirmed), we waited till the next morning to call the family—Paul actually, the older stepbrother, rather than Hobe. Just today, in fact, twenty years almost to the day later, it's another Kentucky Derby weekend. It was a wonderful race, I made myself watch it for Heather, and I backed a surprise winner at eighty-to-one odds. A "dark horse," as they say.

But as soon as Paul was informed, the family took over and made all the arrangements, like it were any ordinary death, and soon after that I flew out to LA for my book tour, as if it were just an ordinary book tour, and then I came back to the city. And then I collapsed. For years. But the very dark place I found, or rather lost myself in, had really started back in Bisbee. The book tour was a brief respite from the darkness, a lovely few weeks during which I saw a lot of Amy, who was living in Malibu at the time, and also a lot of Anne-christine d'Adesky, who had also moved west by then. They both came to all my readings. Anne in particular had devoted herself to my care as soon as she found out that Heather had killed herself. I must have called her that night. I don't remember. At this point she was still living in Brooklyn, Clinton Hill. She was very active in ACT UP for years and knew what to do when someone you loved had died. She got on the subway at two in the morning and was at my apartment by two thirty and we just lay there side by side by for a few hours till I fell asleep. I was still in that dark place a few years later when *Notice* came out. When I opened the book for the first time I saw on the copyright page my name next to Hobe's. It was at the Bowery Poetry Club in 2004, a mere two years after Heather's suicide.

As Amy explained to me just yesterday, since Heather died without a will, the copyright for *Notice* would automatically go to the next of kin. That would be Hobe, Heather's father, and then after he died, to her older stepbrother and sister from his first marriage. But Hobe didn't want anything like that, knowing as he must have the animosity that existed between Heather and her step siblings. He wasn't about to share the copyright with any of them. He loved Heather too much. And, to be clear about a very cloudy subject, he really did love her. Always had, though he sure had a dreadful way of showing it. She usually called it "rape." And we'll never know. Maybe Tim knows. Tim and his partner showed up at Heather's memorial service at a packed St. Mark's Church that summer, much to my surprise. We had never met.

We embraced and never saw each other after that. Val and I even tried to find him. We planned a very unlikely scenario, to barge in on him one Sunday up in Westchester when he was playing the church organ, but we never did. I for one believe that it happened. With Hobe, I mean. The drunken assaults, night after night, year after year, from before Heather was ten to when she was in her twenties. I did not believe the manic ravings that came out of her mouth when she was full-blown crazy, when she denied that he ever touched her. Like her stories of befriending Nico of the Velvet Underground, which started backstage at some little club somewhere in Jersey. Nico was wearing a brown silk dressing gown which inspired Heather to search high and low until she found one just like it. Years later she used the belt from that brown silk robe to hang herself—that really did happen. For years I had that robe hanging, beltless, in my closet. I guess the medical examiner took the belt away with her that night as evidence, maybe still wrapped around Heather's long neck.

After Amy published *Notice* she must have sent Hobe a copy. Soon after that he wrote a long flowery letter which he sent to everyone he knew praising the genius of the book and of his beautiful daughter. There was something so totally strange to me about the letter, considering he was blind, and it left me wondering how he could possibly read the book in order to praise it so fulsomely. I couldn't see Hobe asking any of his children to read it to him. Maybe he had someone record it for him, but that seems creepy too. All the references to his abuse. Can you imagine?! I couldn't help wondering what his dear friends, the Wallaces— Lila Acheson Wallace and her husband DeWitt—thought about all the gossip. Maybe they never discussed it. It hardly seems like good pillow talk. DeWitt was Hobe's boss. He was the publisher of *Reader's Digest*, and chief spy, if my own father was right, and Lila was a world-famous philanthropist. Some of her charities were also connected to the *Digest*. There was a wing at the Metropolitan Museum of Art named after her. She was also Heather's godmother. Heather told me she used to fantasize about running away from her terrible home life to Lila and climbing up onto Lila's lap and begging her to adopt her forever. By the time I met Hobe he was an old man, without, I'm quite sure, a lecherous bone in his body. Well, if you don't count the time—shortly after I got the letter about *Notice* he sent to everyone in his world—when two dozen red roses were delivered to my East Village apartment door. He had sent me flowers many times before, all from the same fancy florist in Rockefeller Center. But never before was there a little card enclosed in its own little envelope. I opened it up. It said, "All my love, Heather."

IF YOU'RE A GIRL

(1990)

Vito in Europe

1

The phone is dead. The man is coming to fix it between nine and six. Usually Vito is at home anyway or we share domestic chores but today I'm home alone. He is in Europe, on tour with Creation Production Company. I hate the thought of having to sit home all day without the consoling possibility of a transatlantic phone call from Amsterdam but at least it will force me to write this story. It seems weird how all these embarrassing female-type stories seemed to be popping into my mind, and then into my writing, since V was away: stories about sex, abuse, rape, abortion, marriage, divorce, infection, kids. I want to make a collection of them and call it *If You're a Girl*.

What a great title, say all the girls: Louise, Andrea, Rose, Eileen, Vicky, etc.

Is it about prepubescence? said Paul Cherry snidely.

No, I said, immediately on the defensive, it's, you know, a state of mind.

Yes, said Paul, nodding. Passive. No, he said, taking the pipe out of his mouth and waving it in a professional way. No, I like it. You could have an asterisk—he jabbed at the air with his pipe stem and a parenthesis—*For Girls and Fairies*.

I nodded happily. How about *For Girls and Other Fairies?*
But some straight men didn't like it.

And some gay girls.

How about *In a Man's World?*

No answer.

No doubt about it. Touchy subject. But then all the interesting subjects were touchy. Or taken. This one was about drugs, not sex, but just as touchy. And related in my mind because it always seemed women took drugs to make them feel more like what society calls a man: self-motivated. At least I did.

This story was one I had been trying to bury but it wouldn't stay buried. I had tried to write it once before but found I couldn't tell it in the first person. So I invented a character, named Candy, inspired, no doubt, by Cookie Mueller, so I could tell it in the third-person, but I canned that approach too and put it back in the drawer. But suddenly it popped up again last night in a strange way in one of those long wonderful strong intimate conversations one can have with Lewis Warsh.

It was Tuesday, the second Tuesday Vito was away. I had agreed to work for the Poetry Project benefit which was organized around the opening of the Larry Rivers show at Marlborough Gallery on Fifty-Seventh Street. I knew it would be fun to watch. Minkville. And I love that kind of work: setting up chairs, hanging up coats, taking tickets. Mindless. Like collating. Occupational therapy. I didn't even care about hearing the reading: Ted Berrigan, Allen Ginsberg, Anne Waldman, the usual. I was there for the social rub.

So I was glad when Rose Lesniak didn't show up and I was drafted on the spot to work at the door with Helena Hughes even though I had been assigned the lower job of setting up upstairs.

It was fun working with Helena. Helena was very hard. She wouldn't let anyone in without paying.

You see, Larry's opening at Marlborough Gallery was a benefit for the St. Mark's Poetry Project but Larry neglected to tell all his rich friends that they'd have to pay $30 to get in. And Helena wouldn't let anyone in unless they really paid the money or really were on the guest list she had in her fist.

Larry said I could get in, one tearful guy said. We were in Mexico together. Look! He jabbed at his cheek. It was deeply tanned. It was in fact the exact color of Larry's but Helena was firm. Vague but firm. She wouldn't let Prince Michael of Greece up or was it her chauffeur. She made one man who said he had a message for someone leave his wife downstairs as ransom just to prove he wasn't trying to sneak in.

The have-nots definitely had the night sewed tightly up. We got in free. There were so many volunteers that by the time the guests began to arrive there was no room on the rented coat racks for the guests' coats. When I came down from upstairs the coats were beginning to pile up on the wet floor, all except the minks. They kept them on, though it was roasting. The floor was wet because it was raining which it hadn't been when the volunteers arrived three hours earlier. Not only were there no hangers for the guests, there was hardly any more wine 'cause there were so many volunteers and everybody drank it during the three hours we gave ourselves to set up.

That part was fun. There was a lot of drift after the red-velvet folding chairs for the poetry reading had been set up in part of the room. Also Larry's musicians were setting up over there and his beautiful teenage daughter was running around in a gown that looked like the one I wore to my senior prom.

I ran into Lewis by the bar. I had only had one other conversation with him in my life, but I could tell he was a master of that art. It had been a week earlier, also at a bar. It was after a Wednesday-night poetry reading. Vito had been away for two days then but we hadn't talked about it.

We had talked about fucking students, because Michael and Frank had dropped over the night Vito left and had to spend the night because Michael had had too much to drink at an SVA gallery opening and passed out on the bathroom floor and Frank and I sat on the couch watching TV until I pulled myself together and went to bed. How problematic. Impossible to even imagine being in the classroom the next morning after, as Lewis put it, breaking down all those barriers to intimacy.

Besides, I said to Lewis, they tell.

Lewis and I had our second conversation that night at Marlborough. Vito had been in Europe for six more days. I felt more separated. Less part of an androgynous couple. I was feeling more female, more open to others. We talked about being alone.

Everyone said when we moved back to the city, we'd start going out by ourselves. But when Bernadette was away for three days this summer I was at a complete loss, Lewis said.

It takes a while, I said sagely.

It had been eight days. The novelty had not worn off or the loneliness set in. I could speak of the joys of a long relationship and the pleasures of separation. Vito in Europe. My boyfriend was finally, to fulfill a fantasy, on the road.

When Vito and I met, I told Lewis, he used to say he couldn't wait until we'd known each other five years. I thought, ugh, or argh. I never knew anyone that long. It never lasted that long.

Who even wanted it to? But now it's ten years. It seems like I'm never gonna get tired of it. I used to think three was my limit.

I can't wait till it's twenty years and my children are grown.

I bet you can't, I said cynically.

I didn't mean it that way.

I guess you have a different time sense when you have children, I said.

Do you ever think of having children? Lewis asked.

Whenever I thought of children I thought of my husbands. It never seemed possible to conceive of a relationship lasting long enough to make children seem possible.

I never liked the men I was married to in that way enough, I said.

Oh, were you married?

I held up two fingers…

…There they were, the two of them, my future husband and his twin brother standing at the end of the long hall. The place: City Hall, New York, New York. The day: July 1. The light was coming in filtered through the unclean panes behind them. I couldn't tell which was which.

They looked alike although one of them was moderately brain-damaged which affected his expression in a way that made them look different. Their bodies, too, though of identical handsome parts, seemed put together differently. It wasn't so bad. The brother could make change well enough to hold down a job as cashier at Sam Goody to this day and father two normal daughters. He was a real nice guy. He just had no sense of spatial relations or something. Couldn't get a chair through a doorway.

The family looked at the tragedy this way, making the other one, Jim, the slow one, come out the hero. By coming out first, he ran interference for brother John, even getting messed up in the process, a kind of cross between Hercules, Jesus, and a mildly retarded clerk who suffered that his younger perfect brother, whom he loved with all his heart, could have it easy. I wonder if he thought it was so worth it when it turned out the younger one, the perfect one, was sterile. The one I was marrying. Brother Jim was clumsier, looser. The other, the one I was marrying, was the opposite. "Muscle-bound," I think they call it. Still muscle is muscle. He had a tighter grip on things. Me. The first time John touched me, I was sitting on the bottom of his double bed in the apartment on Amsterdam and 103rd Street and he came over and grabbed me and kissed me and, gripping me tightly, said I've been wanting to do that for so long, which was something I thought people only said on TV like…

Just hold me.

From this distance the two brothers looked identical and they could both tell she didn't know which was which. They watched her with different emotions. John could tell she had had her hair done that morning though he could tell she must have fought with the stylist insisting that he make it look like she had not. It didn't surprise him. He and she had been fighting all week but he heard that was typical, even lucky, like in the theater a bad dress rehearsal is said to mean a great opening night. She looked especially beautiful to him, though, that day. He had taken the afternoon off from work. They had fought about that too. She looked beautiful partly because, as he knew, all women look beautiful on their wedding day and partly because she had been up for days and had that tight, thin, hollow-eyed transparency she also took on when she hadn't slept, though he didn't know the reason. She wore white, a double layer of chiffon tube, silver and crystal bugle beads hand-sewn to the collar and cuff. She looked like an angel. No underwear. She had fought with her father about that. No lipstick, either. She had fought with her mother about that. But she gave in and got new shoes and so now she could hear her heels clicking, feel her feet dragging. She got closer. Finally there he was, coming into focus, the one tightly holding the flowers. They were for her but he looked like a bride for a second.

What am I doing? I thought. Walking into a trap? Click. Click. My feet hurt. It was taking too long. Did I really want to end life like this? I knew the answer but when the assistant deputy mayor asked me I said, I do.

I could hear the prison door clang shut. When at the wedding dinner my glamorous cousin Ranny rushed in late, very late, and embraced Jim, the retarded one, and congratulated me, I knew they had thrown away the key.

One time during John's first acid trip, he confessed, not just to me, not even to me but to the nine other people there, that while he and his twin brother Jimmy were growing up, were teenagers, every Saturday night before they went out on their dates they would fuck. He said it and looked around. Then he looked down and buried his head in his hands for a moment.

No, he corrected himself, not we. I used to fuck him. In the ass. I never gave him any choice. I always did it to him. He sobbed, filled with guilt. It was just getting light. They had all been up all night, all naked, until it had gotten cold. Everyone rushed to him to console him and congratulate him for revealing his guilty secret. Everyone but me. My main emotion was rage, not shock. Not sympathy. I was furious that I had to hear it along with the others, at not being told first, privately, as was my right as wife. His wife. My husband. Our secrets. Marriage made me feel things like that. I hated every moment of it.

Crash... the next thing I knew I was wallpapering the inside of the closet on diet pills, and waking up on a bed of broken glass—wedding presents.

I was making this marvelous clear-glass sculpture out of them, piling them up in different ways. Pure balance. No glue. Look ma. No hands. Tinkle tinkle little star. Crash.

Everything all right sweetie? Yes honey.

What happened? For God's sake, it's three in the morning! I dropped a glass.

Come to bed. I want you.

Be right in...

I didn't remember falling down. And I wasn't cut when I woke up on the kitchen floor the next morning. I had spent the night asleep on a bed of broken glass and I wasn't even bleeding. Something funny was going on. Something was being done to my head. It had to do with being married. I knew it.

After the incident of waking up on broken glass, I didn't black out for a month. Then it happened again. Each time I lost track of time. Each time the unaccounted-for periods got longer. And darker. He even started liking my having these mysterious attacks. I even started liking them. It seemed like my only escape from being married, like the lace and ribbons and all the feminine compulsions, like the kleptomania, it was mysterious to everyone but me.

At first, the sicker I got, the better the sex got. The husband liked nothing better than nursing. He was a great nurse. He liked to have me where he could get at me, in bed, and then close the bedroom, I almost said "deadroom," door and get back to his writing. He had at all times six carefully sharpened pencils on a diagonal in the front-right corner of his precious fucking desk.

Once he confessed that he fantasized fucking paraplegics, but real sickness, even when it's a faked real sickness, is a turnoff and it did turn me off.

They took me to doctors.

Are you taking anything? Narcotics? Downs? Sedatives?

Nope, I always said, and it was the truth.

There was a test to see if one was coming on. One of the neurologists showed John how to do it himself. One of the signs would be a tiny trembling of the eyes so I couldn't follow focus. The condition is called nystagmus. It's a symptom of epilepsy. Whenever John suspected one of my fits was coming on, if I started getting deeply engrossed in intense graphic or written projects, started getting out my collection of colored thread, or manifested any evidence of being creative, he held up his finger right in front of my eyes and moved it left and right. Follow my finger, he would say in an authoritative voice. The thread came from Bloomingdale's. That was the first time there were witnesses. The other times I was alone or he didn't notice, or pretended so as not to deal with it. We were all great pretenders.

Like the time I was in the middle of one of these attacks and time came to go to my aunt and uncle's fiftieth-wedding-anniversary party out on Long Island. They were getting married again. It's traditional.

I was making them a fabulous wedding card out of the sequins and ribbons and colored thread and dried flowers and gold papers I had left over from my wedding announcements.

Actually the main reason I got married was to have an excuse to make something out of all those materials I had acquired while speeding and spending. That and to have a good reason to stop therapy. No one thinks you need therapy if you're getting married.

Anyway, the card wasn't finished. I wasn't dressed. It was time to go. I threw on some weird outfit, no doubt, and packed all the materials, scissors, glue, tape in a suitcase and took it in the car with me. I sat in the back seat with my anguished mother. My father sat in the front, grim, husband in the driver's seat, the LIE speeding by. The big lie.

There was the time in Bloomingdale's. I told everyone after I must have been getting the flu and had passed out in the ladies' room but in fact I was in the store primarily in the Food Department and then, more extensively, in Notions.

That was the time my husband had invited his whole class for dinner and I hadn't shown up by ten. He had panicked and called the police. I arrived home with four hours unaccounted for in which I had charged seventy-five dollars' worth of colored threads and ribbons to my mother and also a pound of Bloomingdale's best pâté. A pound is a lot of pâté. I got it so that we could teach the students how to live. Somehow, though, I had sat on the pâté in the taxi when I finally came down enough to come downtown so it was smeared all over me when I walked in.

You look terrible, he said, rushing to me. He put his arm around me and steered me through the room full of anxious young eyes. My skirt was covered with pâté but at this point it just looked like liverwurst. It was the worst. At least that's what I thought at the time.

But I was wrong. The last time was the worst, of course.

It started innocently enough. I was to present a graduate-seminar paper on Aristotle to my Sixteenth-Century Literary Criticism seminar at Columbia. Come to think of it, that was another reason I married John. I thought he'd help me study for my orals.

He was also a graduate student. He had a cubicle in Low Library. Before we got married he got up every morning at six and went up there to write his dissertation. He used to call it "to diss out." He had all these cute little speech mannerisms at a time (the '60s) when cute was not popular like now. Like "US of A" and "NY of C" and "tooners" for martinis which were also not hip to drink then, and "drant" for fire hydrant which he said a lot because he had a car which he spent a lot of time trying to find a place to park on the street.

After we got married he waited till nine and then sometimes had to drag me with him. Sometimes I would sit in the library and read. Sometimes I would sit in the library and sleep.

This particular morning he was being very particular and I was obviously coming apart already. It was happening again. We both knew it. But instead of dealing with it we pretended it wasn't. Excellent.

Run along, I said.

OK, he said, wanting to get out of the house as fast as possible, I'll see you up there.

I was already beginning to lose control, verbal and motor, and was already beginning to nod out a little. I packed my papers and notecards into a huge bag and got on the subway, boarded the express by mistake, fell asleep and didn't wake up till 125th street. Got off, crossed over, got on the downtown local, fell asleep, got off at 96th street, crossed over, took the uptown local and got off at 116th street, walked in halfway through the class and volunteered to do my report. They had been waiting for my Aristotle paper. I extemporized for forty-five minutes. On Plato.

So they tell me. I don't remember and nobody in that class would ever tell me about it. They all went into shock. The last thing I remember was the trains. And afterward, Dora and Lillian walking me over to John's cubicle but not him taking me over to Saint Luke's Hospital.

I was out for about twelve hours. At one point I woke up for a little while. They, no, someone was shaking me. Making me wake up. No, more than one person. I opened my eyes. A blinding double row of klieg lights was shining directly into my eyes, figures, five or six, three on each side, faces in white caps and sterile emergency room gowns were bending over me. One of them spoke. I thought it was a man; his words swam toward me.

How's your marriage?

I must have looked blank, because he repeated it.

How's your marriage?

This time I got the words but they didn't register. Why was he asking me this funny question? What did my marriage have to do with anything?

Someone else bent forward into the light.

What did you take?

How's your marriage?

Fine.

Are you having trouble with school?

No. No trouble with school.

How many did you take?

What?

How's your marriage? the doctor asked again.

Again I struggled with the question but before I could answer it, it drifted off.

Enter John, the husband. Wearing a jacket and tie, though it is Wednesday afternoon.

Hello, doctor.

Has your wife been under any strain lately? Any problems? No, doctor.

Any reason she might want to try to take her own life?

I don't know what you mean, doctor. What do you mean?

You having trouble with your marriage? No, doctor. Why do you ask?

Is she on anything?

On, Doctor?

What's she taking?

She doesn't take anything.

How do you know?

I'm her husband. I would know.

She seems to have taken an overdose. She exhibits signs of barbiturate poisoning.

It's impossible. I'll call her half brother. He's a neurologist. He'll tell you she's not on drugs. It's outrageous. I would know. There must be a test. Can't you give her a test that'll prove I'm right?

We gave it to her.

Oh, good. Well...?

We won't know the results for twenty-four hours.

Twenty-four hours!

It's a holiday. The lab is closed.

It was Thanksgiving the next day. Why do people always get sick on holidays when all the doctors go on vacation?

She's been having these fits, John continued to explain. They called it "pseudoepilepsy."

Never heard of it, said the doctor.

She just usually goes to sleep for a few hours and she's OK. Can't she just rest here and I'll pick her up later and take her home?

No.

Why not?

You have to commit her.

Commit her? Why?

All ODs have to be committed.

But I tell you. She didn't OD.

The only place you can sleep it off is in the psychiatric unit.

Why?

All ODs are considered potential suicides. And all people who try to kill themselves go to psychiatric. The only way to get to psychiatric is if someone commits them.

That's ridiculous.

That's the way it is.

I'm not committing her. She's my wife.

What are you going to do?

I'm taking her home.

You want to take her home in this condition?

I'll take a cab.

She can't even stand up. How are you going to get her home?

She can't be taking anything.

You can't be sure.

I'm her husband.

These dope addicts can be very sneaky. The doctor pulled out a white form and looked up.

John looked at him. He didn't say anything. He looked at the white form, then back into the doctor's face.

Where do I sign…?

The next time I awoke it was dark. At the time I guess I thought that was the darkest night of my life but there was still one more hell to pass through, no, two. I was lying in a hospital bed that had the bars up. I got scared. I couldn't remember anything and didn't have any idea where I was. The bed had bars on it. Why did the bed have bars? The door had a window with bars on it. There was light coming through. I started to get up out of bed, when I heard something crackling beneath me. I felt underneath my back. It was sharp and thin and smooth. It crunched as I tried to move off it. It was a piece of folded paper. I unfolded it. It looked like a letter. I sat up and held it to the light in the door. Fortunately it was written in large black letters, the writing of a child.

Dear Mommy,
How are you? I hope the doctors will make you better soon. When are you coming home? I miss you.
Especially at Thanksgiving.
Love,
Cindy.

I got scared. If I was here, where was Cindy's mother? Where did they take her? They must not have even changed the sheets. Did she die? Where was I? Somehow I was losing it again, drifting and dreaming. To sleep again. When I woke up again, it was morning. My half brother had already called. He explained to the doctor that I shouldn't be there, that I wasn't on downs but subject to these as-yet-undiagnosed episodes and that I shouldn't have to stay there. Turned out they went to med school together, lucky for me.

Turned out the reason the bed had bars on it and the doors all locked from the inside was that there was not a single free bed on the general psychiatric ward, so they had to put me in maximum security for the night. This was St. Luke's Hospital which serves the Columbia University community. It was Thanksgiving recess. Gee. I always thought students went home for the holidays.

The last thing I remember was checking out just as the attendants were bringing around the trays with the turkey dinner on it. With all the trimmings. They brought me a tray too and were surprised that my brother had gotten me out that fast. Most of the patients didn't know it was Thanksgiving. The little baskets shaped like turkeys and full of goodies confused them. Except one old man. He knew it was Thanksgiving. It's just that he thought Harding was president. (I guess that's why they always ask you who the president is if you've been hit on the head. I guess you can also get hit from the inside.)

Can I have your nuts? he said as I waved goodbye.

This was the last of my "fits," as my husband called them, "your episodes," in the terminologies of each and every neurologist who examined me and there were many. I referred to them as "my attacks." There's this "my" shit again. My wife! My husband! My attacks!

I only know that I survived Christmas without having another. But after New Year's, everyone was so upset about them that I let myself be persuaded to enter the hospital for a week of tests. I mean, my mother and father were destroyed with grief and worry, my husband was desperate. Even my half brother David, with whom I'd only recently been reunited after a twenty-year separation, seemed genuinely concerned. Yet I was prepared to let them think I had some terrible brain disorder rather than admit I might be crazy enough to use drugs. I mean, by now I realized there was a connection to my pills but since no one asked me if I was on speed, and since no speed had ever affected me like this before, I remained silent. Like a POW, I never admitted anything.

The tests consisted of a spinal tap, where they drain some spinal fluid out of the spine and analyze it. They said it wouldn't really hurt but they didn't say only if I lay absolutely still for two hours afterward, so I bounced up and it was like I smashed into this headache and was knocked out all day.

The brain scan was scary but painless if you could forget about the nuclear energy involved. They didn't find anything really. The scan showed that I had a slightly abnormally large brain stem, which is like the low-brain, at the back of the head and neck, but it was probably always like that, they said.

They gave me something like sodium amytal which is like sodium pentothol, what they call "truth serum," and I almost told the doctor then. I did admit using speed in the past but I said it fast and he didn't pick up on it.

One morning they said I was to have a glucose test I guess to see if it had something to do with my blood sugar. The nurse woke me really early. I remember the orderly was mopping the room and he had a radio. It was playing "Mellow Yellow." I remember thinking did he know that song was really about drugs? The glucose test involved getting up every hour, drinking a glass of pure dark-brown glucose marked with the time and then leaving a sample of my urine and labeling it to correspond, and then putting the samples back on the window sill. As the day wore on my urine got darker and darker. The first was at 6:00 a.m.

I walked into the bathroom. There was a note attached with surgical tape to the mirror. I rubbed my eyes sleepily and took it off and sat down on the toilet. It said:

Dear Ann,
Please leave a specimen of your urine in this glass.

I obeyed, stood up, and almost threw the scrap of paper the note was on away. Instead I dreamily turned it over. It was torn from some larger sheet that had writing on it. What had it come from? Always the detective. I guessed that the original must be some kind of patient sheet that hangs by the nurses' station, listing patient's name, her doctor, her diagnosis. By coincidence the corner that the nurse had torn off had my name on it.

Ann Rower. Doctor: Bill Berman.
Diagnosis: BRAIN TUMOR.

I stared at it for a long time. I looked up and stared at myself in the mirror. The light was horrible and harsh. It was 6:15. The doctor didn't make rounds till nine. I was trying to be cool but my heart was pounding as if I had only minutes to live. All this while I thought I had been fooling them, they were lying to me. Of course. It seemed so simple.

When Dr. Berman did come in I was so afraid that I almost didn't say anything. But just as he was leaving, I called him back and told him. At first he turned red but acted offhand.

Oh that. We do that all the time. The only way you can get a bed in this hospital is if you say it's an emergency. We always do that. But I could tell he was upset about me seeing it. Either that or he was upset about me finding out.

Of course you would tell me if I really had a brain tumor? Yes, yes, he said, pushing me back down. Relax. You don't have a brain tumor. But maybe he was upset because he was lying to me. I didn't quite believe him. Still don't.

Later I heard that he had been furious with the nurse who had been so careless as to let the patient see the nurse's chart, and had her fired, and for a second I loved him. But then you always love them somewhat. All that lying around in bed waiting for them to come.

That night my brother came. It's great having a doctor as a relative when you're in the hospital. There's an electricity he brings into the sickroom. That night he brought in (strictly illegal) splits of champagne to my bedside before explaining the final test, the pneumoencephalogram, which I was to have in the morning. The champagne should have been a tip off. But you're never ready for that much pain.

A pneumoencephalogram is a variation of the spinal tap only they empty spinal fluid out of your spinal column so they can then pump air up through your spinal column into your brain so the air bubble will fill your lobes and they can photograph them. It's very irritating to the brain to have air rushing around in it and the brain lets you know it is the king of pain but they can't give you anything because you have to be conscious so the doctor can say...

Tip this way, turn that way, tilt forward. To the side. Other side. Now slide all the way up to the edge of the table and let your head just drop back off the end of the table.

I screamed. It was like something broke. My neck? The dam. A shot of searing agony of pain rushed over me from my head to my toes. My head was aching sort of like after the spinal tap only worse and also like it was never gonna stop and it didn't.

The "pneumo," as it's called in the trade, was negative, but the headache lasted for seven weeks. It's what they call a "positional" headache. That is, if you change your position from horizontal to vertical you get this excruciating splitting headache which goes away when you lie back down. So you have to stay lying down for seven weeks. I was always cold. It was January. The atmosphere was tense and frigid. I was really an invalid. John was sweet. He was getting a lot of work done.

I found that aspirin helped for a little while so I could get up now and then but I took too much of it, a habit of mine, a lot of it, more and more until one day my ears started buzzing. I kept taking aspirin and it buzzed more until it was just buzzing. The next day I couldn't hear anything, not even the buzzing. I was frantic again. This wasn't anything I ordered. My brain tumor must be getting worse. My heart starts to pound now as I think how scared I was then. Fortunately an old friend, David Diamond, came by and mentioned that taking too much aspirin can make you go temporarily deaf but he didn't know how long they said is temporary.

While I was deaf I had this ringing in my ears. I would think it was the phone all the time and kept getting up to answer a dead instrument. No wonder my headache didn't go away. Eventually I brought the phone into bed with me and lay there with it under my hand so I could feel it vibrate if it rang. Helpful hint.

The doctors concluded it was either nothing or pseudo-epilepsy, maybe, so they prescribed Dilantin which is an anti-seizure drug that makes you sleepy so they mostly ended up in my top drawer, but then of course I didn't need them. But only I had figured that out. It never happened again because I switched to a different kind of speed, though they were pretty little tablets, one layer pink, one white, and one speckled pink and white in between. They looked like miniature wedding cakes, but unbeknownst to me they each contained a whole Nembutal, which is a strong sedative, so taking five or six ups (as was my habit) at a time was giving me barbiturate poisoning but I told everyone the reason it never happened again was 'cause I got divorced...

Well, do you? said Lewis.

Do I what?

Ever think about having children.

Only when I'm pregnant, I said.

It was pouring afterward and everyone who worked the benefit also got invited to Larry Rivers's daughter's party she was throwing for him at Studio 54, the doors of which didn't even open for two hours.

In the driving rain a few of us crossed Sixth Avenue and ran into Wolf's Delicatessen to pass the two hours: me, Eileen Myles, Helena Hughes, Allen Ginsberg, Peter Orlovsky, their friend from upstate, and a few others.

Allen had matzo ball soup. Eileen and Helena each had a teeny bite of my tongue sandwich. After all that Helena and I were the only quitters. Everyone else decided to go to Studio but even with Vito in Europe I didn't feel like being bombarded by bodies.

It was still pouring. No cabs. We took the subway. It was ghastly. I got off at West Fourth Street to change for the local. The guy on the platform played with his big Black cock right in front of me. No one said anything. It was almost too close to move but finally I had to. It was all I could to do keep from making eye contact. All I could do was look at his cock flopping around, not really even hearing a word of his doubtless justified torrent of rage.

II

Don't expect me to call, Vito said before he left for Europe.

So I didn't. I really didn't. But when he called me after three days, out of the blue, blue, homesick, and said he'd call back in a few days but he never did, I decided to try and send a cable to him in Amsterdam. I called Western Union and found out it costs twenty-six cents a word. That sounded too cheap. Especially just three little words. So I tried to put it out of my mind. You have to or you go out of your mind.

Luckily my friend Richard Hell, another World Class Conversationalist, came over for dinner and we talked about it, about being separated from someone. We were trying to remember the title of a Borges story about how there really was nothing stored in the brain, no memories, nothing. I thought about my singing a song I wrote: *Nothing out there, all inside you...* and having an argument with Frank about if it is in there or out there. Frank saying it's all out there, there's nothing inside you, two weeks before.

Richard told me about this commune he heard about where you can come if you're pregnant and have the kid and leave it at the commune AND have it back whenever you want it. That sounded strange. There were other strange things. Everyone at the commune had long hair, he said.

It must have been a rule, he said, or there would have been one exception.

You're always so rational, I said.

The commune was down south somewhere. But not Stephen Gaskin's, or whatever his name was. This was different. Richard got it from a book this girl had given him called *Spiritual Midwifery*. The last time I saw him he was reading *Executioner's Song* and another time *A Distant Mirror*, which I ran out and bought. He said the midwives called the contractions "rushes." I guess pain is a rush.

Which reminds me, I have to make an appointment to have my IUD changed. The pain of having an IUD changed is the pain of a single birth contraction. Very Zen. Very painful.

Rich said he was terrified of all bureaucrats and professionals. Like lawyers. And doctors.

I haven't been to a doctor in ten years.

I gasped and shot him a look like the one he gave me when I said until Vito went to Europe a week and two days ago I hadn't been alone this long in ten years.

If you're a girl, at least you get some medical attention every couple of years for your ten-thousand-mile checkup, and pap smear, not counting getting infected or pregnant.

We swapped abortion stories. Nothing like having a good heart-to-heart talk with the son of a feminist, as Joan described him. I told the story of my first abortion. The stories, and there had been a lot of funny ones or so I remember thinking at the time. I used to tell them regularly, it was my abortion routine, but I never wrote any of it down. But I hadn't told them or even thought about them in so many years I wondered if I remembered how to tell them or if they were funny anymore or if what used to be funny was the little shake of terror at the back of my voice, the experiences being so fresh and basically so unfunny.

I told him the part about my having the address wrong. I thought she said 270 Park Avenue so I went there. It was the Union Carbide building. I think Union Carbide moved out of the city down south a few years back but back then, in 1964, it was there, complete with this huge display visible from blocks away, all lit up and flashing of these giant neutrons and protons spinning and working their giant gears in a grinding display of force. And rising above it this giant steel and glass tower, before Park Avenue was all like that then. Somehow, it just didn't look like a doctor's office, much less an abortion mill.

Remember back then abortions were illegal, so finding a doctor you could even talk to about it was a tricky business. Stories of friends being blindfolded by some matron, taken in the subway to somewhere, and then being taken back and left still anesthetized in a daze on an unfamiliar street corner hung in my memory, like dark clouds. Standing in front of the building I knew it was impossible and yet I was so desperate I went inside and looked for the doctor's name on the building directory under *A* for "abortion."

When I called Barbara Cohen back she told me 1070, not 270, dummy.

I cabbed it up Park into the 80s, hope once more in my heart. This was more like it. I was almost not scared anymore when the first thing that happens is I enter this cool dark lobby somewhat tentatively, reassured that there was no doorman when I see the doorman. But he's on the house phone. Good. I tiptoe past when his conversation catches my attention. My full attention.

Hello, Doc? Listen. The cops are here. They say if you're not out of there in five minutes they're gonna take you away.

Oh my god. I saw my abortion go slithering down the drain. What was I gonna do? They were gonna take my abortionist away and probably me with him. In panic I backed out of the building back out of the cool marble floors out into the blinding light and the hot concrete. My heart was pounding. I had to hang on to one of the awning's brass rails to catch my breath. The doorman came out. I knew I would have to move soon. There was a police car at the corner. A man came out. He was carrying a bag of golf clubs which he slung into the trunk and shut it. The car had MD plates. It was double-parked.

Richard chuckled. I was glad to see the story still worked. Still I think it used to be funnier.

I could have gone to Florida if it had been earlier but I was too far gone. I had to fly to Puerto Rico. First time I had seen the Pan Am International Terminal at JFK, which was called Idlewild then. My husband (#1) didn't want to fly with me for (bullshit) reasons: economy. On the plane the stewardess handed me a copy of the *Post* with a headline, ABORT DOC NABBED, and a picture of a Doctor Lothringer, a Queens gynecologist who did abortions, and also a picture of his drain in his driveway which had backed up and spit up little pieces of the cut-up bodies of fetuses and also a couple of parts of grown women. Overgrown. Got me off to a flying start.

Richard told me that when the abortion law first went into effect in 1971, or '72, whenever it was, some girl got him a job in an abortion clinic uptown. He said the doctors were all sadists. He said that while the women were out cold and they were performing the abortion they used to joke around with the girl's genitals and make little puppet mouths out of their labia and have conversations like

Hello, Doctor Steve.

Hi there, my dear. How are you feeling?

I'm feeling great, Doctor Steve. How are you?

I'm fine. Wanna go out?

I just took out the garbage, said Richard and left.

Afterward I felt very lonely for some reason so I went out too even though it was freezing. At M&O's I bumped into the couple who live in back of us coming out with another couple carrying six packs. I couldn't believe it. We've lived a hundred feet apart for ten years and this was the first time I'd ever seen them on the street.

We came close to speaking but didn't. What is there to say? Where would we begin? I mean, we've seen so much and yet know so little. I can never figure out if the man, an artist, can really see into our windows or not and it drives me crazy. I drive Vito crazy.

I run into the room wrapped in a towel which I drop accidentally, and automatically look across to see if he is looking. He is looking.

Oops. I say, OK, so what, free show. Bending down to pick up the towel I turn to Vito, who is reading *Billboard* intently.

Do you think he can see in here?

Oh, Ann. Why do you ask me these ridiculous questions? How am I supposed to know if he can see in here?

What do you think?

Not that there's that much to see but lately I seem to think I see him looking this way more and it makes me think twice about dancing around in the kitchen by myself. Sometimes I look over and he's just sitting there in a straight-backed chair, staring straight into our windows. Maybe he's just meditating. Sometimes it looks like he sees me looking, but like I say, it's not clear.

Last summer I was just out of the shower. V was sitting at the kitchen table reading. I ran into the kitchen for a second without any clothes on, put my arm around Vito's shoulder in a friendly wet way. He turns his head and gives a kiss to my left tit which happens to be at lip level. It feels nice. I throw my head back a little with pleasure and look out and catch the man across the way looking straight at me. To make it worse I double up with embarrassment. I only hope he had looked away by then. Once right after we first moved in, we saw her take a swing at him with something like a pole or a long cardboard tube. They had a big black dog back then. It was barking. They were screaming.

It's just a funny distance I guess, not near enough for definition and detail but close enough for outlines and movement and arousal of curiosity. A typical city distance, perfect for that urban interplay of exhibitionism and voyeurism you can't help getting into. At least I can't.

So, to legitimate my obsession I say I'm writing a story about it. In the story the writer is writing a story about a photographer who lives across the way who is photographing her life, when she's dancing alone in the kitchen to her reflection in the back of Vito's guitar on the brown chair, when she drops her towel, like that. He pins the pictures of her doing all this onto his wall with clear pushpins but she can't tell they are of her.

Last Halloween I was fantasizing about the story to Vito. I said the girl plans to get a pumpkin and carve it and face it back on Halloween. Just to see if there's any response. Then the next day I drove up to Mountainville to see the sculpture at Storm King and the autumn leaves with my mother and brought back a pumpkin.

I'm going to carve it and face it back, I said to V.

You know, Ann, you don't have to do it. You just have to write about it, he said. But you do. I even lit it.

Is he gay? Ron Vawter asked one day.

I looked across the way, surprised somehow. I never thought so. He lived with a woman. Then I saw he had hired a new assistant I never took a good look at and I guess he might be, though, like I said, it's just the wrong distance to be able to tell. Maybe Ron has better vision.

In the last six months he's set up a photography studio in the back too. Brilliant silver white-white umbrellas and lights against the pink-gold fluorescents all the time now. There's so much light coming from their loft till all hours we had to put up shades by our bed. Then they put up these huge twelve-foot window blinds. The spring is so powerful when she rolls them up each morning, I don't need an alarm clock. She gets up at nine thirty every day to go to work. I don't know when he gets up but he stays up working till at least 2:00 a.m.

What does he do? asks everyone who ever comes here at night 'cause it's always lit up and he's always there working, either in the shop, making something like frames, maybe, or in the studio, sculpting or photographing. He must paint or draw too but he must do that in front. But he brings the pictures into the back and tacks them up on the wall opposite me, along with his photos, and sits with his back to the window for hours looking. He talks on the phone a lot. The phone is by the window. Once we waved and smiled but mostly we look, then look away.

The night Frank and Michael were here, the night Vito left two and a half weeks ago, I took some film of the man across the way talking on the phone. I felt very dangerous. I hid behind the plants. Today I got the film back. It's five seconds of grainy grey stuff of a fuzzy man in a window talking on a phone but when I look at it I get a funny feeling in my stomach like I've done something wrong. I must remember to give the man that feeling while he's taking pictures of the woman in my story.

Even with all these windows though we don't get any direct sunlight. When it's grey the enormous windows let in tons of it, like now. Now they're dirty which makes it worse. Frosted gloom. We used to wash them twice a year but it's such a big job and we lost the strap Vito used to use to hang himself out the window. Usually we start talking about it in March, when spring comes, and then do it by May or June. One year we didn't get to them till August. It was the year of the bicentennial.

We had spent all morning arguing about washing the windows and who should, and when, when it started to pour. The storm got so wild that we went inside to the couch in the room I couldn't dignify by calling it the "living room" because all we do there is watch TV (Vito calls it the "parlor") to have sex to be one with the wild storm, and we did and it was, except you came and I didn't and you got blown away and I left you and walked into the bathroom. I sat on the edge of the cold tub in the dark. I was frustrated and undecided. Should I forget it, let it subside? Should I just do it myself?

I couldn't decide so I tiptoed back inside and stood over you. You hadn't moved a fraction of an inch since I left you. You were damp and rosy and a million miles away. I sat down on the edge of the couch. You opened your eyes for a second and smiled beatifically. Then you closed them. That made it easier.

I want you to do something for me, I said. I had to raise my voice above the storm and that made it harder.

What? This time you smiled without opening your eyes, like you didn't hear me, so I repeated it.

I want you to do something for me.

I'll do anything you want. What do you want me to do, wash the windows? No, jerk me off.

It's funny how stories get written. Here are three stories I've been talking about writing or thinking about or trying not to think about writing for so long—the pills story, the abortion monologue, and the one about my voyeuristic relationship with the guy across the way—and now I'm writing about them together because they come together, come up, in life, in real life. So now I have a story. Except I still hadn't figured out how to end it.

There were endless variations. In one recent version in which Ann and Vito are preparing to audition at the Public Theater, I made the guy across the way the man they auditioned for: Joe Papp.

You would know if that was Joe Papp, said Vito.

I don't know, I said, and I didn't. And I never solved the mystery of how much he knows until now, when again the themes became entwined in reality.

It's the third Tuesday Vito's in Europe. He's coming home soon. I had two doctor's appointments that day, appointments I'd been putting off as much as I'd put off writing these stories. One appointment was to have my IUD changed, already a year overdue, and one to have my new contact lenses checked. I bought them the day after I got an NEA grant for $12,500 and never wore them. I was supposed to come back in three months. It had been four. He called. Today was the day. The two doctors are five blocks apart. The two appointments are five hours apart.

I try to get to the gynecologist late. But even late, the office is full of expectant, impatient patients. Obviously the doctor has not arrived. He is still at Roosevelt Hospital. The nurse is talking to one of the patients about how filthy the hospital is. That's where I had my second abortion, the legal one, and I must say of it that the abortion was even better, in terms of togetherness, than the sex that necessitated it. Maybe it had something to do with being legal.

Finally the doctor arrives. He has been up all night, attending a difficult delivery. He looks like a wreck. He calls me in then makes me wait some more. Carmen tells me to undress and wait in one of the examining rooms and I wait some more. I try to think of some way to retaliate. Like stealing something. I think about the pink robe they make you wear but it's gross. It doesn't stay closed. I check out the sterile instruments. I've stolen enough of those stainless forceps. They make great roach clips. Remember roaches? On the table next to the instruments is my folder. I slip off the table, and as I approach it, my heart starts pounding, I don't know why. This is a no-no. Looking in your folder.

All the stuff in it is old. Yellow even. It's from Dr. Chabon, my real gynecologist. He was well known for a book he wrote on natural childbirth called *Awake and Aware*. He had an autographed picture of Bobby Kennedy in his office. For a year, everyone knew he had stomach cancer. It's weird going to a doctor you know is dying.

I turn the pages. I even find the notes to my old abortion. It's called a "procedure," though, I suppose, to distinguish it from surgery. I remember coming to see him after my abortion, the next day in his office. It was as usual, full of beaming natural-childbirth candidates. It felt funny coming about an abortion.

After he examined me we talked in his outer office. I tried to ask the $64,000 question.

What can I do? I mean when can I... (suddenly you don't know what to call it)

You can do anything you want, he said, smiling—

He paused and I can't help grinning lewdly back until he finishes his sentence.

—so long as you keep a piece of paper between your knees.

I wondered if he knew I was a writer.

For some reason I can't stomach looking at all these old notes from when Dr. Chabon was alive, in his handwriting especially. There's an old note to the effect that my payment is seriously delinquent. Another about a bounced check. There isn't anything from the last few years. It must be the wrong folder. Typical. It feels wrong to be looking. I start to turn the page when I hear footsteps and the knob starting to turn. I bounce back up on the examining table. The pink paper that's supposed to be under me gets all fucked up. My robe slips open. The doctor walks in and I try frantically to cover myself while he tells me...

Lie back and relax.

I inherited my new gynecologist when Dr. Chabon died. He's Italian. From Italy. He refers to everything in an old-world way. He calls my cunt "down there," like it's Sardinia.

Click. He turns on the light. I feel something cold.

Just try to relax, he says.

I relax my sphincter, a trick I learned first at the dentist.

That's wonderful, he says. So you have your PhD in English literature, he says.

He must have looked in my folder.

How are old you?

I feel he should be able to know that from looking.

I tell him.

We're the same age, he says. It's hard talking to the gynecologist when he's examining you. It's sort of like trying to converse with the dentist with a mouthful of metal, only the opposite. He stands up, pulls off one rubber glove, then the other.

You have an infection. It has the impact of "You're pregnant."

Is it VD?

No.

I feel better. He gives it a long name and tells me he can't do anything about my IUD till after the infection is gone. This is some consolation. I wasn't looking forward to the pain. He even makes me get off the examining table, take my feet out of the stirrups while trying to keep the paper slippers they give you from slipping off, to look at my infection under his microscope. First he adjusts it then helps me look.

See those two little round ones next to each other?

He stands up. I bend over and look.

That's the bacilli.

I look again.

Get dressed and come into my office and I'll tell you what to do. Suddenly I flash on the last time I had this infection. And how it saved me from being actually raped. I even wrote a story about it called "Midnight Flash."

There was a funny story about the story. It was the first thing I wrote that I ever took anywhere. It was years ago when the *SoHo News* was around the corner. So I took it to the *SoHo News*. I remember it clearly. I walked in. The founder Michael

Goldstein was still actively editing. He looked up. He had been actively making goo-goo eyes at me and every other female on the street for years but now inside the office there was no recognition in his eyes. I stammered that I had written a story his paper might be interested in.

What kind of a story is it? He didn't look interested.

I don't know. What do you mean what kind of a story is it?

Is it news or fiction?

I'm not sure.

Well, what's it about? He was impatient already.

It's sort of a rape story.

Oh, were you raped?

Well, not really.

Then it's fiction.

Not really.

Then you weren't raped?

You have to read it.

He didn't look like he wanted to. I knew I should be trying to make eye contact, throw him a little heat like on the street, but I couldn't. After an excruciating pause he held out his hand. I held out the envelope. He took it, sniffed it, looked full into my eyes as he held my story to his nose and said

Love your perfume.

I get dressed and go into the doctor's office as opposed to the examining room. He makes me wait more. When he finally comes into his office I'm anxious to hear what he has to say but first he lovingly tells me the details of his up-all-night delivery. He has a funny little lisp as well as an Italian accent.

Is there a *meester*?

A what?

A *meester.*

He's in Europe, I explain.

He gives me instructions but I'm so upset and he's so exhausted that now I can't remember whether we have to wait to have sex seven days after I start taking them or after he takes them or if it's sex or liquor I can't have, is it twenty-four hours before or after I start taking them, or stop. I must remember to call in the morning and check.

I don't know if I would have told anyone about having this infection but after the gynecologist I had a lot of time to kill even with all the waiting. Gimbels East was empty. I was empty. No desire. Nothing like having a yeast infection to take away your desire even to shop.

So I stopped into Magi Film Productions to bullshit with Jeff Cahn and his assistants, Michael and Randall.

Hi, Randall, I croon. I feel better already. Hey, Randall. How come you're smooth as silk one minute and little fragments of glass the next?

It's called "acute schizophrenia," says Michael.

Just then the studio phone buzzes. A voice says:

Amy, for Randall.

Randall picks up, lights a cigarette. Lights another. Crashes the receiver down.

Who's Amy? asks Jeff of Michael. Jeff is Randall and Michael's boss. Years ago he was my student.

Old friend, says Randall. She was in town a few days. She just came from the doctor. She has some infection in her tubes. She may have given it to me.

And now you gave it to your true love too, says Jeff. Randall is about to tie the knot.

Oh, God, Randall says, genuinely clutching his hair.

You have to tell her, Jeffrey says. He's serious, paternal.

So, of course, I feel I have to tell everyone I have one too. I guess I had to tell someone and Vito's in Europe.

And I have to, I say, take these little pills and can't drink and can't fuck for a week.

That's just as well, says Randall.

Good thing Vito's in Europe, says Jeff.

He has to take the pills when he comes back, I hang my head sheepishly.

He has to take the pills? He's gonna love you, says Jeff.

That's four little words I thought, thinking of him. Maybe, I say to Jeff, I can dissolve them in his coffee and put it off.

For seven days? You mean you can't fuck?

Not without a condom.

He's really gonna love you.

That's five little words.

I go out. I've still got an hour before the eye doctor. Back to Gimbels' bathroom. I want to put my lenses in early. I'm supposed to come in wearing them. I'm supposed to have been wearing them for the last four months. I'm afraid they'll irritate my eyes. I slip into the ladies' room on 11 to slip them in. They go in like silk.

It's nice walking around and being able to see without wearing glasses. I don't usually wear glasses inside except in the classroom where I need to see people's expressions from far away. On the street I wear prescription shades but usually the lenses are gangster green and I have to take them off inside. So it's a novelty to be able to see clearly distant things inside.

The eye doctor was pleased with my progress which I lied about. You think doctors can tell but they can't.

Vito's been away three weeks, almost. I didn't really feel like going home to an empty house but I said to myself maybe Vito will call and anyway I'll get some writing done. I still have the contacts in and they feel comfortable. I feel wonderful. I can see.

The phone rings. It's Richard again, calling to reciprocate for the first dinner with some guest of the night before's leftover lasagna. I guess they weren't hungry, because it was delicious. He brought some extra sauce along in a plastic container I thought I recognized. On the phone he said she had made it but he admitted it was store-bought. I told him that the sauce I served last time was store-bought too.

It's true confessions time, he said.

And so it is.

I found the answer, I said to him, enthusiastically.

We had been discussing life's depression the week before.

What? he said.

Contacts.

He laughed, so I was glad I came home anyway to wait for Vito's call which didn't come.

By the time he leaves, it is late. The contacts are still in but starting to annoy. I flick off the light. I can't get over it. I can see. See near and far. I realized that I always take my glasses off when I come home, never put them on inside the house since I don't need them for reading or anything close, just for distance. On the street, driving, etc., but never in my own kitchen.

I look back across the way. The woman was coming home from the store with beer, like the other night. The man is in the studio filing a dowel. The woman is opening the refrigerator and taking out a milk container. I can't believe it. All these years I'd been so wrong. There was no metaphysical or existential doubt involved here about the distance, who can see what, too close to ignore, too far to see, as I'd been running on at the mouth about for years. This vague feeling part paranoia, part obsession that someone is watching you but you don't know what they can see. I just couldn't see. Period. Things were blurry at that distance. I see now that he wears glasses too. She looks like the type who's been into contacts for years.

The phone rings. I try to tell from the way it's ringing if it's transatlantic. My pulse is racing up in my throat. It's a lady, calling to invite Vito to attend some abortion rally.

Vito's in Europe, I say.

Imagine asking an orphan what he thinks about abortion.

The phone rings. She answers it. He is now in the shop, sanding a strip of molding. The light is on in the studio part where she is talking. I can see everything. Even his photographs, how they're pinned with clear-plastic push pins to the back wall of the studio. Before they looked like dark, blurry rectangles. Now I see they are of me.

Amore

What is *hoochie coochie?* asks Ernesto Bazan, still pretty fresh off the boat from the "Boot," quick and eager to perfect his I-hate-it-when-they-call-it-English, slang especially. We'd been listening to the Muddy Waters's song "I'm Your Hoochie Coochie Man."

He looks at Nydia. Nydia is older than Ernesto and the rest, except for the teacher (me) and possibly Marva. Marva's short for Marvelous. She looks like she lived in a good middle-class Baptist neighborhood in Brooklyn all her life. Actually, she's a Panamaniac. We're all into trying to define *hoochie coochie* at once. Nydia, from San Juan, has been in New York one year more than Ernesto. Usually, she knows less English than him. But being a girl, this she has already picked up. She turns to Ernesto in scorn.

Hoochie coochie, Ernesto? She gives it a Puerto Rican lilt. *Hoochie coochie*—it's the same as *lovey-dovey!*

Lovey-dovey? Ernesto asks. He says the vowels very broad: What's *lahvey-dahvey?*

He makes a big gesture with his whole wiry body and throws up his hands in bewilderment. He looks at me. I don't want to stick my neck out so I look at Marva.

OK, Marva, you tell him. What does *lovey-dovey* mean?

Lovey-dovey? says Marva. She kind of sings it and thinks about it. *Lovey-dovey* is… *lovey-dovey* is… you know, Ernesto—she throws open her arms wide—*amore!*

It seems settled but I'm not. I want to go back to *hoochie coochie*, get the real deal on it. Even in this international group, no one recognized *coochie* as *coucher* and though I know *hooch* means liquor down south I don't want to sound like a pedagogue either, even though I'm the teacher, and for the same reason it seems in poor taste to say it means "fucking." So I let Marva have the last word: *amore.*

But after class I'm still curious. It's a mild April dusk, a Friday. Instead of going home I turned west and headed for what had to be the sleaziest bookstore south of Forty-Second Street, Metropolitan, on Twenty-Third Street, plus it has a great reference section. I found what I was looking for. *Dictionary of American Slang.* Sure enough. It was in there. Sure enough in the twenties in New Orleans the hoochie coochie was a dance. And it's like a lot of words down there, like *to jazz* meant "to ball." Music! But still it didn't say anything about fucking.

Then I wrote a story about this, called "AMORE," and read the story at the Ear Inn on Bastille Day because I knew Ernesto was going to be there, partly to hear me read a story about him and partly 'cause he was looking for an apartment.

The Ear Inn is on Spring Street almost by the river. During the week during the day, it's a bar for dock workers and truckers, but at night it turns into a restaurant and Saturday afternoon there's a poetry reading series.

Because I was reading, I nervously came early. When I walked in there was only one person at the bar. He was a man. A big guy, much too burly and big and tough-looking to be a poet or a poet's friend, who must never have worked on Saturday before or ever thought about anyone reading their writing aloud in public before, especially in a bar.

Before the reading we were alone at the bar. He came on to me some and offered to buy me a drink which I refused, I thought, rudely. So I was sure he wasn't going to stick around for the poetry reading but after it was over, there he was. I saw him get up in the front of the bar and come over to me.

You were right, he said, with a drawl I hadn't noticed.

Right about what? I said, warily hostile from before.

About *hoochie coochie*, he said.

What about it? I said, still on guard against a possible come on but I was wrong.

It's Cajun.

It's Cajun?

I was impressed. He nodded.

Yup.

What's it mean in Cajun?

It's from *hoocher et coocher*.

That's Cajun?

Yup. It means drinkin' 'n' fuckin'...

(You know, Ernesto, *amore*.)

Trick or Treat

I

She, Annie Wright, can't stand him, Bruce, so much it's a pleasure. She always couldn't, from the very first moment he laid his slimy thyroid eyes heavily upon her. She was sitting in the Pink Teacup with Neil. Then he was selling Christmas trees on Hudson and Christopher and fruit at Union Square the rest of the year. The trees were a beat. They were small. And the fruit was probably hot but she can't leave his huge bulging eyes alone completely not even tonight. Not even after tonight, probably. They're dark and really big and his face is really small. It makes him look like he's fastened onto things, women, you, later it would be Matthew's turn, with them. Now it was June, the waitress behind the bar.

The other waitress works tables. She has blond leather hair. Her name is Minerva. Even before Bruce's big fight with the bartender, Annie Wright could tell Minerva didn't like them, her included, especially after she chose to stay out front with the boys and not go downtown with the musicians, an act which gave her less class and more action.

On his way out Chino looked at her coldly. She shook the ice in her glass at him.

I haven't finished my drink.

He went for his other drum. She went to the bathroom. When she came out he was gone. She went over to the bar.

He left, Neil said.

Oh, said Annie Wright.

Buy you a drink?

I'll have a vodka on the rocks.

He ordered it and then he and Sherwood continued their conversation.

The waitress is a honey, Sherwood said.

Maybe it's the color of her hair, Annie Wright volunteered.

Yeah, Neil said, she could earn good money. Ever since Neil has been working for Bruce, managing Bruce's whorehouse, which calls itself the New York Pets, he walks different and talks about women in a new cold-cash way. Annie Wright turns away in disgust and studies the selections on the juke box through the drink Neil just bought her.

Neil brings Bruce up to Eric's with him that night to hear Chino's band. It is Halloween. And when they come through the swinging doors at midnight you can see they're going to be doing more swinging than listening to music, that they're already loaded and gonna be buying.

Annie Wright turns and surveys the scene. Bruce is making goo-goo eyes at waitress #1, June, the one behind the bar. Neil and Sherwood and Annie Wright take seats at a table for two across the aisle from the guys from Sal Anthony's. The chairs block the aisle.

Minerva, the waitress, is furious, of course. She glares at Annie Wright. She has to bend over to get around Sherwood, which gives Neil a good look at her breasts and an even better chance at sizing and pricing her up and down, and Sherwood's still trying to get over. It's like it's a compulsion.

I bet you just washed your hair, Sherwood says as she swings it out in front of them while she wipes off the tiny table. There are icicles in her eyes though it's only Halloween. She's making no bones about it's none of his business. She asks Annie Wright to move.

This is a table for two.

Annie Wright slides in next to Matty but can't look at him tonight because she could tell that Sherwood must have told him she said she thought he was cute. Her eyes on the plate, she takes a piece of his pecan pie on her fork. Matty confides it's his very first piece of pecan pie but she's too uptight, especially in front of Sherwood, to be flirtatious and ask how it was. She can't even tell how she likes it and she's had lots. He's only eighteen.

Time to order another drink, she tells herself, if only to cut through the nuts and sugar in my mouth.

I'll have another vodka, Annie Wright says to Minerva. Sherwood says everyone on the Upper East Side is geographically displaced but tonight Annie Wright feels like a hick up at Eric's, a music club / singles bar / restaurant on Eighty-Eighth and Second, like they're the kind of bunch of rowdy downtown freaks waitresses love to hate. Anthony Jr. asks Annie Wright if she goes out with Sherwood. She laughs. Sherwood turns pink.

No, I live with Chino.

The drummer?

Where is Chino?

He went downtown. Sheryl was taking a cab. He had to get his drums home.

All of a sudden Matty looks past Annie Wright and then back to Sherwood and says with great urgency,

Your friend Bruce is in trouble.

They all look around.

Bruce is standing by the bar with his legs spread wide apart to balance himself and waving his arms and screaming ugliness at the bartender. The bartender, like we said, is at least seven feet tall. Like Sherwood says later, retelling the story, the fuckin' guy's suspenders are a foot wide.

Now Matty is just a kid. He doesn't even know Bruce, but he knows Neil, and in a flash of energy and loyalty, almost like he's on skates, he's up there beside Bruce and Sherwood and Neil are right behind him. Matty, the college boy, does the reasoning and Neil and Sherwood the restraining and eventually the bartender cools off and returns to the far end of the bar with waitress #1 tailing him.

Neil and Sherwood aren't afraid to manhandle Bruce as much as is necessary. They've had years of practice. Annie Wright shudders, remembering the time Sherwood gave a Christmas party on Horatio Street and Bruce was so out of it on a combo of ludes and alcohol that in the middle of the dance floor he tried to get his date who was another one over six feet tall to go down on him. Luckily he realized that he was too messed up to pull off anything but his pants and he put them back on.

He's like that tonight—sloppy, surly, a WASP on downs— but when Matty comes to his rescue so quick it mellows Bruce out and he gets this equally sloppy big smile on his face. He keeps saying,

He shaved my life... he shaved my life, shaking his head, spilling with feeling, and though he can hardly sit up insists on buying everybody a last round even though Matty isn't drinking and Annie Wright doesn't really want another drink.

She had ordered one vodka from the waitress in the back room during the first set. That waitress, who worked the tables where the live music was, was not as foxy as the two in the front part, the bar. She wore flat shoes, a skirt, had a big ass, and was friendlier to the musicians than the customers. Annie Wright leaned forward. Bruce was leaning forward too, looking her way, leering without meaning to. She shuddered. His eyes rolled and popped. Then she raised the glass to him and drank it down. She had ordered that fifth vodka after finishing Matty's pecan pie. She knew if she ordered another she'd be dead drunk.

I'll have another vodka, she says.

Minerva takes the order, glaring, and brings the drinks but fortunately before Bruce even tries to bring his glass to his lips, he rises carefully, takes Matty by the collar of his Lacoste shirt, and tells him to come outside with him. At first Matty looks scared and so do we, but Neil reassures us so we drink our drinks.

After ten minutes they come back in. Then Bruce veers off to the left to use the pay phone and Matty comes back to the table. He looks like he can't decide whether to laugh or cry.

What happened? Sherwood says.

Come on, man, what'd he say to you? Neil said.

Well, he kept thanking me for saving his life. Only he was saying "shaving" but I knew what he meant. He said he would do anything for me now. I said I didn't want anything. He said he had a proposition for me. He wanted to give me a job working for him. He said he would pay me $800 a week.

Shit, muttered Neil. That's what he pays me.

No shit, Sherwood says. To work in his whorehouse?

What did you say? asked Annie Wright.

There was silence. We were all waiting and wondering. Matty seemed so quiet. He and his big brown eyes were even wider than usual. He paused, and shrugged.

I told him I had to go back to college in the morning— Annie Wright smiled fondly. Neil and Sherwood laughed.

—but I'd think it over for when I graduate.

When Bruce gets off the phone he is much soberer. He grabs Neil and they go downtown 'cause Bruce wants to kill someone. It's all happened so fast. Sherwood offers to drop Annie Wright in a cab and Billy and Anthony Jr. go visit their mother with Matty.

At one, Neil goes to work. Bruce comes in and Neil asks him about the fight with the bartender up at Eric's and Bruce gives him his version.

Me and the waitress were making goo-goo eyes at each other. I ask her for another Rémy. She says that's three dollars. I say I don't think I can't pay for it, just to see if she'd buy me one. She knows I can pay for it 'cause I paid for the first round with a hundred but she goes down to get the bartender and complains I won't pay for my drink so I get mad. And all of a sudden I look around and there's this kid, what's his name?

Matthew, Neil says. Matty. He goes to school in New Paltz. He works at Sal Anthony's with Sherwood and the others on holidays. The other boys are Anthony's kids but he treats Matthew like another son.

Great guy.

You were crazy to offer him that job, Neil snarls.

He shaved my life, Bruce says simply. Neil looks away. Bruce gets up, still unsteady, but sobered, and departs.

Graveyard shift in a whorehouse on Halloween. Neil gets to play a lot of guitar and read a lot, he says. The phone rings once.

That's how New York Pets works. Bruce puts ads for each of the girls in *Screw* magazine and other places. Then a guy calls up and if his credit card checks out over the phone, the phone girl gives him the address. Neil once told Annie Wright if she was so interested in the place someday she could come up and work the phones. But she never did. Neil answers the door and lets the men in and out. The girls take their own money. Because of a legal technicality money can't change hands unless the guy is undressed. Kissing is extra.

At a quarter to two, Cassie Wright, the youngest and prettiest of Bruce's "ladies," as he calls them, runs out of her room. She is crying.

What the fuck happened to you, says Neil, all heart.

"I came!" she sobs.

II

Everyone I knew knew I was writing something about that night up at Eric's, because I couldn't stop talking about it. And I knew, even as I began to type the first draft, that Neil and probably Sherwood were going to get on my case for putting all that stuff into a story, though I hoped that including all of Sherwood's humorous remarks and exaggerating Neil's dedication to the guitar would help. But it didn't.

I was not hitting on the waitress, Sherwood said.

Neil had quit working for Bruce by the time I finished the first version of the story almost four months later. Now he was living at his mother's in Flushing and reading a lot of natural philosophy and science books. Darwin at the moment. He had a lot of free time and spent a lot of it at Sherwood's loft over on Tenth

Avenue. Naturally he smelled the story out which was lying around, unread by Sherwood, just waiting for him.

Neil read it immediately, with great anticipation because I told him I was finally writing about all the great stuff he had been feeding me about the whorehouse. He barely had time to get over his initial reaction of being insulted that I hadn't given him his own personal copy when he saw why. Within minutes he was speeding downtown, sweating and red-faced from drugs and rage. He rang my bell hard.

Neil, I said, surprised. What a surprise!

Hello, he muttered.

Vito's not home, I said, keeping the door half-open, thinking he wouldn't want to come up.

Good, he said and pushed the door open wide so he could step through. I got something I want to talk to you about.

My heart began beating rapidly.

Oh? What? I asked innocently.

He didn't say anything but followed me up the stairs.

You gained weight, he snarled.

We went into the kitchen and sat down. He took some papers from his pocket, his canary-yellow application to join the Y. He had gained weight too, living at his mother's. His hands shook. I noticed the sweat at this point. He began to talk about the Y but I couldn't concentrate. I could see the white pages of my story underneath. Finally, he dropped the yellow sheets and it was out in the open. But he paused, making me wait, before growling

How could you write such a piece of shit? He fumbled through pages looking for a place to begin. My insides curled up like oysters in stew. What do you mean?

In the first place, it's so sloppy. I mean, it's just plain bad writing. Like here. Here it says quote like we said the bartender was seven feet tall. End quote. So I go back, thinking I'd missed something to find out where before you said how tall the bartender was and it wasn't there.

Oh that, I said, and relaxed a little. This wasn't going to be so bad.

Oh that, that was just careless. I did have something in earlier, but I took it out and I forgot to change it and then when I noticed it in later I decided it was too much trouble to change it, so I left it the way it was.

You should revise more carefully.

I like to leave the mistakes.

That's so motherfuckin' jive, man. I can't believe you call yourself a writer with that theory.

Some people don't believe in editing.

Yeah? Like who?

Like Jack Kerouac. Burroughs. I tried to pick his favorites. It didn't help.

I mean, I entrusted you with that information about the girls and Bruce's place and the whole setup. You know, I expected you to do something great with it, something worthy of it. This—he picked up the pages of my story and waved them—this is a piece of shit!

I'm sorry, Neil.

Like you say quote because of a legal technicality money can't change hands unless the guy is undressed. Unquote. It's not just some legal technicality. There's a reason, you idiot. Don't you understand anything?

I forgot the reason, I said.

You forgot the reason! He stomped over to the window and glared out into space.

Please, Neil. Tell me the reason. I forgot. I'm sorry. I'll change it. I can change it.

The reason is in case the guy is a cop.

In case the guy is a cop?

Yeah. If he's a cop he has to be wearing his badge to make an arrest. And if he's undressed...

I get it, I get it, I said, sheepishly. I did feel like a jerk.

And another thing. I didn't say the chick was crying, he said and banged his fist down on the table. I said she was pissed.

I gulped. I could have sworn you said she was crying.

No, man, she was fuckin' pissed. He hit the table again so hard I instinctively stood up.

Wanna beer?

No.

That was a surprise. I never knew him to refuse a drink.

No, motherfucker. Sit down. I'm not through. I got a lot more to say.

I obeyed.

In the fourth place, I didn't start walking funny since I started working for Bruce. I was walking funny 'cause I was limping. Remember I hurt my knee? Don't you fuckin' remember anything? I was using a cane for a month.

Inside my face felt like mashed potatoes. Cold mashed potatoes.

And I didn't start talking about women in a cold-cash way since I started working for Bruce and I wasn't sizing and pricing the waitress up and down.

I noticed he had the fuckin' story memorized but I didn't say it. He was waiting for me to speak.

You did say she could earn good money, Neil... I remember. We were standing by the jukebox with Sherwood. You bought me a drink. It was right after Vito left.

Yeah, that's another thing. What the fuck did you mean it would give her more class to go downtown with the musicians. He was still quoting from memory. I mean, I came all the way uptown to see the man, to talk to the man. I didn't come up there to hear the band. And he runs out the minute he finishes, doesn't hang out, nothing. What kind of class is that?

Now he looked down at the story. Actually, he said, I liked that part where he left, where she shakes her ice at him coldly. I liked that. That's good. The rest is shit.

He dropped the pages onto the table.

I clutched myself again. My stomach was in knots. I never should have let Neil see it. I never should have let any of them see it. I never should have written it. Maybe.

You know how Vito hates to be around Bruce when he's so fucked up.

I'm talking about me. He hadn't seen me in weeks. I came all the way up there.

He was tired after three sets. He had his drums to get home. Sheryl was taking a cab.

You don't think I wouldn't have paid for his cab? Another thing. Sherwood wasn't hitting on the waitress.

Come on now Neil, here I felt like I had a firm case, you know he was. Saying things like I bet you just washed your hair, and like that.

He was just doing that for your benefit.

My benefit? I was very confused. What do you mean, my benefit? I was starting to think maybe I didn't understand anything.

You girls are all so fuckin' stupid, Neil growled.

I still don't know what you mean for my benefit?

You know what I mean.

I hung my head.

And why the fuck did you make it Halloween? It fuckin' happened in August.

It did?

I know because I quit working for Bruce right after that. After Labor Day.

Oh, I remember. It was August. I had just come back from France with my mother. But I didn't start writing it till October, the end of October. It was Halloween. Actually, I was still working on it Thanksgiving and I changed the holiday to Thanksgiving but it didn't feel right and besides I wanted it to be Halloween so I could call it "Trick or Treat."

That's so motherfuckin' jive. Why do that kind of jive shit?

I'm sorry.

He was by now really red. He was sweating. He was shaking from pure venom. Me, I felt like I was dying or something, and there was no let up.

Why not call Vito Vito. What is this Chino shit? You called me Neal.

Yeah, but I spelled it different.

What about the rest of those crazy names. Annie Wright, Cassie Wright, Minerva. I mean, really.

Well Cassie Wright is supposed to sound like Carrie White, you know the movie, Carrie?

Well, how come she has the same last name as Annie?

We're supposed to be sisters.

That's ridiculous. You don't have a sister! And Minerva, what

kind of a bullshit name is that. Who could relate to some fuckin'
Greek Goddess.

Roman, I said.

I explained I'd drawn those names out of a hat in an exercise in my class at SVA, to each pick five and then write a
Halloween story and since one of the names I picked was Neil,
I thought to tell the story of Bruce's fight with the bartender
that night so I could use the stuff about the girls and so I made
myself Annie Wright, a name I had used once before in a story,
so I put it into the hat and by chance also drew it back out so
it seemed like fate and the waitress Minerva and I called the
hooker Cassie Wright, all of us put upon by the guys that night.
I almost changed Minerva to Minnie, to make clearer Annie's
identification with the waitress exhausted from working late on
a holiday and Cassie, the half-fictitious hooker, but it was too
close to Minnie Mouse. But I was beginning to see why the
guys all hated it.

Why the fuck didn't you tell me this was just an exercise for
school. I thought this was the real story you were writing about me.

It was like all of a sudden he relaxed or had suddenly gotten
a new nervous system.

I wanted to say but it wasn't just an exercise, it was the real
thing, but I wanted the assault to stop more. He was not cool but
he was almost calm and I wanted him to stay that way. I was beat.
He seemed almost happy. I told him he was right about the
ending. His was better. The whore wasn't crying she was pissed.
I would change it. It should have been quote:

At a quarter to two, Cassie Wright ran out of her room
screaming.

"What's the matter," Neil says, reaching down for his gun.

He did carry a gun as part of his job. In the beginning I remember he was afraid he would have to use it so he kept it in the bathroom wastebasket and hid himself in the bathroom. Later, he began walking around with the wastebasket with the gun in it. Now he's really gonna kill me. Leave it at:

At a quarter to two, Cassie Wright ran out of her room screaming.

"What's the matter," Neil said, all heart.

"I came," she said. She was pissed.

Lovers Slash Friends

I

We were lovers/friends but I'm afraid that writing about him will make him come back into my life again if he isn't dead. Every time the phone rings I imagine it's him. But then I'm easily spooked. It's only been a couple of days since they sewed me back up and sent me home from the hospital. No sewing really. I have stainless steel staples, fifteen of them. I'm on two-every-four-hours painkillers. Really floating by this time, floating and scared. Soon to be scarred, home alone. V's out of town. I start to work on my story about that time in July '84 that Russell came to town and lost it—and suddenly I'm losing it too. I scare myself and take two more but all the time I'm nervous that he will come here, that by writing about him, he'll appear. I'll have made him come here, all my fault, like that other day, four years ago... Flashback: Vito screams, "Of course he'll come here. You never know what people like that will do..." Crystal knob, defective-Paralyzer-canister scene. No—start with the old "July 7 was a disaster" bit. No. Start with "It starts with phone calls."

II

When you interview show biz types and ask how did it start they always say: with a phone call. It starts with phone calls. Life/death. It started with Russell's first phone call. But really it started with Rose's. The fourth of July. Excitement. Anxiety. So close. Both have an *x* in them. Ted's dead, Rose said. Oh no! Oh shit. I can't go on. I haven't the heart. I just typed this whole story onto the word processor I just rented. The first thing I wrote, then tried to save it and pushed the wrong key and had my first wipeout. I was tired and wanted to watch TV. I don't really know yet how to stop working in the middle of something. I do know if you just shut it off, you lose everything. So I tried to save it and instead the machine started emitting these sharp loud beeps and at the same time little exclamation points coming on the screen in time to the beeps and I freaked. I shut the machine off and when I tried to start it again there was nothing.

III

July 7 was a disaster. It went from bad to worse, the way bad seems to generate bad, like somehow news of Ted's death led to my getting caught at school, which resulted in Russell's first phone call, which started the whole terrible episode. When Rose called, it was Monday morning, I was going out the door, looking crisp and feeling on target, heading for my last class of the summer. According to Rose, Ted Berrigan died on the fourth. The great poet exploded. I'd always joked with Ted that he was the only person older than me so I couldn't help feeling I would be next. I picked up Ted's *Sonnets* and a tape I had of him reading at the Ear Inn with Greg Masters and took it to school. I put it on in class, real cool, or thinking to be until I broke down, my voice broke anyway, leaving me feeling crazy the way it does when anything breaks in an institutional setting like school.

SVA no longer allows drinking at school functions since the law was changed to twenty-one, but then, especially since it was traditional to have wine at art openings and SVA is one student art opening after another, it was not uncommon for drinking, usually moderate, to occur at school but moderation was not the theme of the day. So we, Jane and I, got caught, each doing something different but something we had done a zillion times before without incident, by the worst school guard: Nick. Jane and I hated Nick to begin with. He kept *Playboy* centerfolds and sometimes photos of female SVA models on his wall. It made the female students of his office mate, who ran the literary magazine, very nervous. Jane and I had plotted multirevenge but never done it. But maybe he knew how we felt. Moreover, Nick looked like the only reason he left the Latin American country he came from was because they wouldn't let him be dictator. Plus this time across the hall were three middle-eastern students, I remember Jane said her students brought rum in juice jars, which is why she got in trouble along with me. They had, in their drunkenness, balled up a huge roll of plastic wrap, lit it, and dropped it out the window. Probably, Jane, always the smart one, said, they were reenacting the raid on Entebbe. The flaming ball of bubble wrap fell and landed right on the head of some guy who lived on Twenty-First Street and he went nuts. Though unharmed, he came roaring upstairs to the eighth floor where he surmised, correctly, the flaming missile had come from, and got Nick the guard and they came looking for the culprits. Of course, ultimately Nick was responsible for security and discipline, so he was in trouble too, scared for his job at this point and just as enraged as the other guy. They opened all the doors. Most of the classrooms were empty, until they came to the one on the end which was empty, except for three big innocent-looking students wearing yarmulkes and hanging out the window. My door was the last they opened. Thank God Jane walked in when she did, a minute or two before.

"Sarah, let's take a walk," she said sternly, sweetly, slightly slurred. Slurred but firm. So I was in the bathroom being yelled at by her—are you crazy, etc.—when Nick the guard walked in on my students. They were so zoned at that moment that they were actually sitting quietly—a little too quietly—and listening to someone reading aloud but something gave them away so when I returned, Jane and I found Nick and this strange man with the almost burned head screaming at them. They suddenly all looked very young and pale and upset, even Paul and Anthony the ex-marine and also Jane's three Israeli students. Nick then screamed at me and Jane and said we'd better clean up, the party's over, and he was going to call the president of the school David Rhodes and tell him that we had been derelict (my word) in supervising our students and we should be fired so we were only charged with neglect (being absent from the classroom) and not intent, which in my case involved a felony, but still, getting caught is always a terrible shock.

Needing more alcohol like a hole in the head, or anywhere, actually, where there never was a hole before, Jane and I then went to Caramba, to have frozen margaritas. We had planned it the day before and we wanted to act normal, like nothing had really happened, like though Nick said he was going to tell the president, and have us fired—I could see the *Post* headlines already—see my mother seeing them—the six o'clock news—he really wouldn't tell, a typical tequila dream. David Barr was a waiter there then, so Paul and Laura came too. After two margaritas, I moved from Jane's table to Paul's. I remember Jane said "Go ahead, that boy seems to have a calming effect on you." But after four margaritas I wasn't calm. I was drunk. I staggered home, hysterical, miserable, ashamed. The phone was ringing as I came up the stairs. I figured it was the president of the school already calling to say you're fired and I'm reporting you to the police. But I was wrong.

Hello.
Hello. It's me.
Russell?
Yes.
How you been?
I been fine. Perfect.
I'm so glad.
Guess where I am?
Sacramento.
No.
At your cousin's house in Santa Barbara.
No, guess again.
I have no idea.
Sixth Street.
You're here?
Sixth Street and Second Avenue.
I can't believe it.
I'm in a restaurant with my boss and two other people. The two are going back tomorrow and me and my boss are staying

here to hook up the computers at Time-Life into this international network. The program's called WHISPER but I'm not allowed to tell you what the letters stand for. I've been here for five hours.

When can I see you.

It's 10:26. You know I can't.

You mean you don't want to.

How long are you gonna be in town.

As long as it takes. Tomorrow?

I'm busy till five. You can call me after five.

(Silence). It's not that important.

Click

Hotel Warwick.

Russell Parker please.

Ringing 404.

That's all right, I'll call back.

Click

Hello.

Hi.

Why are we having so much trouble?

You sound angry.

I am angry.

Why are you angry.

'Cause you're angry.

I'm not angry.

You know you are.

I was angry but now I'm not. I got home late Friday and I tried you Saturday.

You didn't try hard enough and now I'm angry.

Are you alright?

I'm flying.

I thought so.

It started to happen just as soon as I landed in New York.

It's funny. I can hear it in your voice.

It's not funny.

Are you gonna be OK?

Are you coming up here?

Now?

It's 10:04. It's impossible. I'll come tomorrow for lunch.

Let me think. You can't just walk in here you know. You have to work at Time-Life. I can't sign you in because I'm working for someone else. And M's not here tomorrow.

M?

Would you believe, she works here, as a temp. I walked by her desk, she didn't even recognize me at first, then she did a double take, and twisted around, like she'd seen a fuckin' ghost, man.

Unbelievable. How is M? Is she still married to Bill?

M hasn't got a kind bone in her body. That's why I left her.

Maybe I should wait to come on a day when she's there though.

You sure are trying to put this off.

Click

Hotel Warwick.

Russell Parker please, room 404.

Hello?

Hi. How are you feeling.

Fine. Fine.

You getting ready to go to work?

I'm making my way over there.

Listen. I can't come today. I forgot I have to go to unemployment. Today's the first time and I have to go to Section C and sometimes they keep you all day.

Come here. They have unemployment in the basement of Time-Life.

They do?

Yes. Junk unemployment.

Click

Hello?

Hi. Where were you?

Know what time it is? Vito'll kill me.

Where were you today?

I was at unemployment all day. I couldn't come.

Come now.

It's 2:00 a.m., Russell. You shouldn't call so late.

You shouldn't hang me up.

I'm sorry. I'll come tomorrow. Where can I meet you?

Don't bother. I don't trust you anymore. You still live at 65 Greene?

Please don't.

I'll see you tomorrow.

Don't come here.

At your house.

Click

So the next day at breakfast I decide I must tell Vito that Russell is in town. It was a matter of his safety.

Vito…

What?

You remember Russell Parker?… More coffee?

Eh.

Do you?

That fuckin' maniac from Sacramento?

He's in New York.

What's he doing in New York?

Muffin?

Tell me.

Interfacing some international computer network up at Time-Life.

I thought he was crazy. He got better?

That's just it. He did. He learned about computers in six months. He's a genius. He called me a few days ago and said he was in New York. He sounded fine and I was going to have lunch with him—

You were going to have lunch with him?

Yes, and then I didn't talk to him for a few days and I called him last night—

You called him?

Yes, and he sounded totally crazy. It seemed to happen in just a few days. He said it was from being in New York, the excitement I guess, you know like on that program about herpes and how it said sometimes a very good fuck will bring on an attack, an outbreak of herpes, the concept of stress includes something the doctors call "happy stress." I mean, I'm sure nothing will happen, I mean, I know he won't come here but maybe you shouldn't answer the door if the bell rings and you're not expecting anyone, OK?

This is not the time to break off with people like this.

I'm sure he won't come here.

Of course he'll come here. You never know what people like that will do. I'm leaving.

Please, don't.

I'm going to the library to look at *Billboard*.

Wanna take a walk to the Village?

I wanna stay home and work on this story. I mean, I guess it would be nice to take a walk.

Sarah! You're driving me crazy. I'm leaving.

Get me a book.

Don't answer the door.

Bye…

Vito is gone less than a minute when the doorbell rings and I lose it completely. Why didn't I go with him? It's Russell coming to get me. I run in all directions away from and then back to the door. I can't stand it. My insides are coming out. I feel trapped inside. It rings again. I have to see. I tiptoe downstairs and peek around the window. I see a long tall shadow and the shadow of eyeglasses frames. Russell is a long tall man who wears glasses. I lose it some more and tiptoe back upstairs and lock the door. Something's ticking. I check the door to make sure it's locked. The phone rings. I hit the ceiling. He must have gone to the corner to call. It rings ten times. I'm climbing the walls.

I thought I had heard my landlord shouting before at someone. It must have been at Russell for ringing my bell so much I have to see. I run down fast and open the door cautiously.

A bolt of light and heat hits me, a blast of empty street. I dash across and knock on the landlord's door. No answer. I'm frantic. Who will help me if Russell comes back? If he's calling me from the corner. If he's watching me from the phone booth. I knock again. No answer. I try the old crystal doorknob. Nothing. I give it a turn. Still nothing. I give it a little tug and the knob comes off in my hand. I panic some more and run back up the stairs holding this cool ancient crystal doorknob for dear life and lock the door again. I wish I had a Paralyzer. The buzz-saw across the way buzzes. I think it's my bell. I run back to the door and check it. I'm not sure which way it goes. How can I defend myself. Try to find the Paralyzer. Black wet fear dripping down the stairs, a dead boy, a stain, running away, mad images. The bell rings. Then I hear the door open. I scream Don't. But it was too late.

The doorknob started to turn. In my terror and confusion I had turned the police lock the wrong way. The door had been wide open all the time. I heard the sound of his foot kicking against the bottom of the door. It sounded like he was wearing boots. In an instant I flashed on our whole erotic life together, the boots, the bruises, the power he had over us, the wild feeling we had for him, so deep it could be shared. In the summer, season of sleevelessness and shorts, it got so you could tell by the freshest bluest bruises whom he'd been with the night before. Until that night. The first blackout. Strange, I remembered it was strange. No subways but lots of busses. No lights but the phones worked. Is M there? He wouldn't answer. Just come over. Streets black—doubt. Unfamiliar. Sinister. Russell thought the blackout was Manson's Helter Skelter.

You been living in California too long, I said sarcastically. I think Bloomingdale's blew the power.

You been living in New York too long, he sneered.

We didn't know till much later that the whole Eastern Seaboard had been on a four-stage alert.

I laughed nervously.

Let's go to bed, he said.

In a flash I knew you must be up there. I remember the flash of white, him stepping out of his clothes. Sharing a cigarette, three on a match. You looking away involuntarily from both of us. By weaving his fingers in between yours and mine he moved yours down. He slid my hand in between his and yours and he took his away and I took yours.

You're so soft, you said.

I remember the way he had of taking my arm and (Ow!) twisting it behind my back so I had to flip over on my stomach... (Ouch!) Then he did me in the ass and I liked your hearing me. It was exciting watching you and not nearly as threatening as I would have thought. Not threatening at all. Being there beside you was like we were neither rivals nor lovers. We were one. Afterward we lay on our backs, him in the middle. He still had his boots on. You and I stared at the cracks in the ceiling, looking very solemn and somewhat blown away, maybe wondering how it would be without him. He looked from one to the other, from you to me and said,

It looks like Mount Rushmore.

Always did like a guy with a snappy comeback.

That was years ago but he was still wearing those same boots, though it was July. The door opened all the way and I saw that he did have a knife. A kitchen knife. My favorite kind. It's called a "boner." I raised the Paralyzer. He raised the knife. Our eyes widened more then narrowed down. I pushed the button. Nothing happened. He twitched, then froze. I pushed again. Nothing was happening. How come it always works for Veronica Hamel on *Hill Street Blues*? Canal Street fucking junk. I threw it away and pushed past him, past the knife, and ran downstairs. At the bottom lay V, my beloved, hacked to pieces, his library books spotted with blood. One had been for me. Oh what a sweet man. Now he was dead and it was my fault for courting disaster. In shame, I let myself fall over his body, the blood already thickening, the body stiffening and cold. I heard the heavy boots on the stairs coming to get me, as I was lying on the corpse of my mate. I caught a glimpse of Russell's dick, big and hard flopping up to his stomach, only it was big and kind of gray, like it was covered with sticky cobwebs, and then it was hard and cold and looked like steel. At last, the threesome of my dreams, a Sarah sandwich, only V was lying beneath me bleeding to death and Russell was sticking it to me from behind, in a place where there never was a hole before. The phone is still ringing. It's him.

Guess where I am.

Downstairs?

No.

On the corner.

No.

Where?

Bellevue.

Oh no! What happened?

My boss brought me here. I just hope nothing happens. I don't want to lose my job.

Are you alright?

I'm fine. It's over.

It's amazing. I can hear it going out of your voice.

They put me in a straight-jacket last night.

I'll come tomorrow.

Visiting hours are two to four and seven to nine.

I'll be there.

I mean, you're the first person I called when I came to New York. You are the only person who ever writes to me. It's just that you bring out the worst in me and that's *bad*. And that's the best.

Click

Hello?

Hello. Is this Russell Parker?

What happened. Why didn't you come?

I did come. I was there. They said there was no one there by that name. They said they had a Harold Parker and a Howard Parker but no Russell Parker.

I forgot to tell you they signed me in under Howard.

I forgot your real name is Howard.

So you went home?

No. Then I went over to the psycho ward on Twenty-Ninth Street. It's from another century. There wasn't anyone around to even ask. I think the morgue is in that building, isn't it? There are no lights. I couldn't see. I even went up to the third floor, to your ward. No one even asked me where I was going. There was a big sign that said: "Visitors, beware. There are patients on elopement precautions on this floor. Open all doors carefully." (I kept thinking how my horoscope for today was avoid confrontation—how Vito would be so mad if I got killed, or if he did.) I'll come tomorrow.

Hello?

Hello. May I speak to Russell Parker, I mean Howard, please.

Wait a minute.

Hi.

Is this Russell?

No.

I want to speak to Howard Parker please.

Wait.

Yes, I'll wait.

Hello?

Hi, Russell.

This isn't Russell. This is Harold.

Harold Parker?

Yes.

Oh, I'm sorry Harold, I have got the wrong Parker. Could you get Howard for me? Bye.

Hello?

Hello.

I'm coming now.

I can't have visitors today. Why not?

I have to be observed. I spent hours with this shrink yesterday. He likes me. He's the one that can release me.

Your boss seems like an understanding guy.

He's a good guy.

You think your job is safe?

I have absolutely no idea what is going to happen to me.

Click

Hello?

Russell.

I want you to speak to a friend of mine. His name is John. Wait I'll get him.

Russell—

Hello?

Hi, John. How are you?

I'm in trouble.

Trouble?

Yeah. I'm in trouble. Next time you call just ask for Led Zeppelin.

OK, John, I will. John, can I talk to Russell?

Hi.

Russell?

I'm famous around here.

Are you OK?

Yeah. I've been OK since yesterday morning. I'll be out of here soon.

Great. I'm coming to see you.

M came to see me.

How is she?

Things with M are absolutely perfect. She thought she had lost me.

I'm glad. This has been crazy—oops—I mean not seeing you yet, but I don't want to see you when you're, when you're... not... making sense.

I always make sense.

Does it make sense to say I'm the first one you called, I am the only one that writes, and that I bring out the worst in you and that's the best. Does that make sense?

Did I say that?

Don't you remember?

No.

I thought you remembered everything.

What makes you think that?

You always say it.

I do?

It scares me.

Well, you must feel safe now, with me locked up.

Click

Hello?

Hi.

Russell?

I was waiting to hear from you.

Really? Listen, I can't come tomorrow at visiting hours. I'll see you Saturday.

By Saturday I hope I might even be out of here.

Where will you go?

Back to the Warwick, unless my boss decides he wants to keep me in his custody. They're trying to reach him today. But I hope they don't, 'cause I know they'll release me by Saturday and I could go back to the Warwick. You could come there. My boss is very busy. They probably won't be able to reach him and I'm sure I'll be out Saturday. But call here first.

I can't wait.

This time put the birthmark on your tit.

What?

Last time you visited me I saw you had this little black spot of ink on your nose. This time put it on your tit.

Click

Hello.

John?

Don't call me John. Call me Led Zeppelin.

I meant Led Zeppelin. Can I speak to Russell?

He's not here.

Did they release him?

Nope. His boss took him back to California this morning.

Are you sure?

His boss came in a limo and took him to Newark Airport and they flew back in his private jet.

But it's only Saturday. Are you sure he didn't say the Hotel Warwick? Please, it's very important, John—

I told you never to call me that.

I meant Led Zeppelin.

Now I'm really in trouble.

Click

NOTES

1. Ron Vawter says Michio Kushi says cooking for yourself is healing and when I was recuperating from the slashing I noticed that it was. Like orgasm, like taking your orgasm into your own hands. It is coming, though. This story is finally coming.

2. I was gonna call it "Bad." "Bad" is bad. "Bad" is so contagious, like crazy. It's a pollutant, like twice my jealousy spurred my cat Diamonds to piss on Vito's stuff. Once he pissed inside Vito's bass drum, while V was in the studio recording. The nerve. And once he pissed on Vito's shoes. They're old shoes. In facts they're my father's old shoes, but Vito wears them a lot. When he sees

that Diamonds has pissed on them he takes his face and holds it into the pissed-on old leather for a long time screaming and yelling and then throws Diamonds out the window and closes it and locks him out of the house and so now I'm mad at V for getting so mad at Diamonds and V's depressed (a) 'cause D pissed on his shoes and (b) because he yelled at D and now D's somewhere outside and won't come home and I'm bummed out 'cause we're not a happy family and Easter's depressed 'cause the window is closed and now he can't go in and out either and I wonder about what's all this fuss about a pair of dead man's shoes. Both times, though, the bad cat behavior followed my having a screaming green-jealousy shit fit. Like Ted's death upsetting me so I got caught at school, leaving me hugely vulnerable to Russell's coming insanity. "Bad." Good title. But then Michael Jackson came out with his *Bad* so then I was thinking of calling it "Bad Calls," but it felt too like the president's speechwriters and the whole media bunch's sports metaphors. Metawhores. Then I was thinking maybe "Phone Sex"…

3. What did I tell you? It's starting to happen. Last night Willa Gelber, whom I hadn't seen or spoken to in years, calls and out of the blue asks me if I remember a recipe for green spaghetti that Russell used to make. Little old flame of jealousy. When was that little runt eating with him? She never told me. She was a sweet little sixteen, then, though, so I swallowed my anger. It was with cottage cheese, she said. It was not. Originally it was ricotta, I said nastily. And it was my recipe not Russell's. He got it from me. I used to make it for him *all* the time. One night I couldn't get ricotta and used cottage cheese. That was in the days when it wasn't the East Village and you couldn't get anything at night on

Second Avenue, except at Met Foods. It's ricotta and chopped spinach. You sauté the spinach in olive oil and garlic, add the ricotta (with an egg yolk in it) very slow so the cheese doesn't curdle. Turn off, add lots of parmesan cheese and nutmeg. And it wasn't originally for green spaghetti. I made that part up to color-coordinate with the green sauce back when I was married. I was into monotones, I guess. But it was when Willa said his name, Russell, the way it just dropped into the conversation and lay there, ticking, though for my ears only, like a bomb, made me feel it was beginning. I better change his name from Russell to Patrick so he doesn't kill me.

4. Wait a minute. I think I did dream about Patrick last night. (Did I mention that I'm changing Russell's name from Russell to Patrick? Patrick Parker. Patrick in honor of my old friend Pat Gillen who just died and her son Patrick who is in jail. At first I laughed when Maureen told me this story that after being shunted around from one max-security prison to another the last three years when they finally put Patrick in Bedford all he does is complain. Bedford is a minimum- security prison, and all Patrick can say is get me out of this fuckin' country club. Get me back to max. And I laughed till I took it up with Sherwood who said no it's true it's hell being in minimum security. No wall, so constant temptation and struggle with thought of escape, of being bad, no routine, nothing to do, no lockup, just a lot of wandering around the halls, the yard, playing softball in the yard until dark, day and night after day and night, no strict guards, you don't know where you are. Anyway so now I believe him. Still, the thought of Patrick railing at his privilege, since we all know he doesn't even ever really want to get out of jail, though maybe now that his

mother is dead everything will be different and maybe he won't have to be such a bad boy, bashing fags on Christopher Street, soccer players in Washington Square Park, a kid with his own radio in Chelsea. But the thought of Patrick screaming Lemme outta here, I wanna go back to max did provide a laugh at Pat's wake which brought up all my grief for a fellow woman (can you say that?) as well as my mother, another fellow woman, the FW par excellence, 'cause the wake was on the year anniversary of Irm's death. I never heard the expression "to be waked." I just realized now Patrick, who is really a killer, is really gonna kill me, so I better not call Russell Patrick. I'll just call him Russell.

5. Russell was my husband Robert's best friend from college, Berkeley, CA. Russell was still out in Berkeley working in the "rad lab"—the radiation lab. He had a cabin in Tahoe, played piano with his left hand and shot mice with a pistol with the right when necessary. Tall and sharp, hard and handsome, he had ocelots for pets and threw them in the garbage when they died or he had to kill them. He'd liberated a schizophrenic brother from a hospital when he was a kid himself. I'd heard about him constantly. I became interested even before I met him.

6. But the thing is, I did start to dream about him but all I remember is Jane, because Jane and the SVA disaster and Russell's first phone call from Sixth Street were the same day so they were in the same dream. Jane, sitting in a very sunny room, talking on the phone with me though we were both in the same room, and I go "we," meaning women—I think we were discussing some article I was going to write for her or we were going to write together and said "we," meaning women, and then I go

You don't mind if I say "we," meaning women, and she goes Sarah you know that's the only thing to say, I bet you think this story is gonna be about women because it's all about Jane and me and this thing we did and got caught together doing which I'm never gonna tell what it is but it isn't.

7. The night before, after the green-spaghetti incident I did have a green dream which I do remember. Wanna hear it? Sarah's recipe for a nightmare. Get slashed. Come home. Take pain-killers, watch *The Thing*, the new one, on the late late show, falling in and out of sleep and dope and dreams and skimming *Architectural Digest* bought as a treat for convalescing all about the new in color verdigris, a mutating shade of green patina. Like green spaghetti. Only it's all over the walls, it's Monica's house in Minneapolis where Vito, who lives with me, is staying while on tour. The walls are closing in and as they crumble they get greener and greener and start wriggling like green spaghetti. I guess I'm jealous of Monica Maye after all.

8. But it's not about jealousy and though it's partly about this thing Jane and I did, it's not about lesbians. For one thing, Jane has a boyfriend now but it's no secret that sometimes she has women lovers. That's what I love about her. Like Tony, though Tony once said it's like having no pier. I thought he meant no equal but he meant no place to land, but two ways in my mind is my ideal. It's so sweet and hot. By the way, here's the scoop on sugar, honey pie. It relaxes you, like orgasm. You get a spurt of serotonin (with orgasm you get endorphin—like heroin versus morphine).

9. It is happening. Writing about it is bringing it all back. Back, I shudder, I think back to life, like some dead green monster beginning to mutate only it's not the movie. Right after Willa called and asked for Russell's recipe for green spaghetti sauce, the next morning after the green dream, at the post office of course I ran into M, and of course I couldn't leave without asking her, Have you heard from Russell, only I didn't have to say it. I said, Have you heard from... Our eyes met. She shook her head. Like we didn't have to say the name. Didn't want to. Then she said how she had to have her phone changed last time and I did too and we were glad we hadn't heard from him and we wonder how he is, is he still living with his mother if she's alive if he's alive?

10. The worst thing that's happening is all this remembering and writing is making me want to call him. My curiosity has been aroused.

11. Speaking of arousal, at the gynecologist, waiting, I read an article about a woman who was epileptic and when she had seizures in her left brain she got depressed, even suicidal, hearing a radio in her head that said *goggli googli* and when she had the brief flurry of abnormal electrical activity in the right brain she became extremely aroused and very seductive with the hospital staff—two kinds of states of being, activation and arousal: activation is doing something about something; arousal is passive awareness of the world.

12. Robert, my ex, Russell's first best friend, whom I haven't seen in years, comes over yesterday, on his way to a dance concert by Tony Candido's wife Nancy. He tells me Tony, whom I haven't

thought about in ten years, heard from Russell just the other day. He's in some menial service job. I wonder what... He insists I take Tony's number. It's AL5-6789.

13. You know I really should change Russell's name to something and mine to something else so he doesn't kill us. The word processor can do it all at once. You just have to tell it and it will change it every time it occurs all at once. At least I hope it will. I'm nervous, though one of the things I like about computer writing is the constant danger of losing everything. It happened again, ya know, and the second time I had a wipeout I hadn't the slightest idea what I did wrong. Maybe I better not try to change anything.

IF YOU'RE A GIRL

(2023)

If Truth Be Told

Suddenly I find myself plunged into some new kind of deep almost bottomless grief. I feel like I'm mourning the loss of my two true loves, Val and Heather, for the first time. At last. Beautiful song. Remembering the Obamas that first night after they won. First dance. Like I'm only now (all about timing isn't it?) letting myself go to grieve. I don't know why now. What's setting it off—sometimes a sad sad song. (Because I'm listening to so much music lately, which is somehow allowing me to reach down deep to find it, to allow it to rise up. I cry every time I hear Taylor Swift's "The Lakes." Another beautiful song.) It's about time, I say to myself. Talking about Heather and Val with my dear deep old friend Anne-christine d'Adesky, about how unexpected both Heather's and Val's deaths were, so almost out of the blue, especially since the girls, Heather and Val themselves, always talked openly about how they and everyone expected me to go first. Because I was so much older. The exact numbers don't exactly matter—it's "the gap" that sounds ominous. I never felt "old," or older than my friends, or girlfriends, or even my boyfriend. Never felt like anyone's mother, though who really knows what they felt. And I could never really bring it up. I didn't even ever really think about it all that much, the age difference. Anne-christine said it was the same for her. The women she wanted were much younger than she was. She thought it had to do with "energy"—not physical energy, but their, as she put it (she's French), "joie de vivre." But I never ever talked with anybody about what that dynamic was all about. But my girlfriends talked about the age difference—all the time! It worried them, especially Val, and to be honest it wasn't so comfortable for me to talk about, except occasionally with my therapist(s). But Val especially was constantly bringing it up as a worry, a fear, a dread. Even her brother Brad talked about it with trepidation, especially since it would fall on him to take care of her, of everything. But fear of dying (unlike fear of flying, or fear of trying) was not one of my top-ten worst fears, not then, not now, if truth be told, except for those awful times, not that infrequent either, when someone, a stranger, a cab driver, a waiter, asked if she was my daughter—was I her mother? I could and often did rationalize it to mean, well, they sensed a closeness, an intimacy between us, and since we were both female, tried to explain it that way because they couldn't wrap their small minds around any other possibility. And they were awful, those awkward moments, a gut punch that took a long long while to go away. But God knows, I remember what sixty felt like. I remember how I dreaded that birthday. I fled. To the ends of the earth, or in this case the very tip of Long Island: Montauk Point, the Wavecrest Motel on Old Montauk Highway, high above the pounding Atlantic Ocean, right next door to Gurney's and much much cheaper. Heather was very considerate, made big plans, all my favorite things. She booked my favorite restaurant, Nick & Toni's in East Hampton—you usually had to wait weeks to get a reservation, especially on a Saturday night in early June! I don't know how she did it (I loved her even more for it). But she worked so hard and finally got us in, at eight no less! So sweet. Such a desperately hard worker when love was the reason, the driving force. And, speaking of driving—she insisted she would do all of it, the driving, since that had recently become a bit scary for me at night. On the way out to the Montauk Motel we stopped at the funky little video store in East Hampton and rented an old favorite, Ben Affleck and Matt Damon's first screenplay, *Good Will Hunting*, which was (conveniently for Heather) located next to the liquor store. She copped a couple of quarts of vodka. The good stuff. For the long birthday weekend. But by the time we were due to leave for the thirty-minute drive back from Montauk to East Hampton, Heather was way too drunk to drive, or even stand. She was terribly upset about having gone to all that trouble now that we weren't going to Nick & Toni's for dinner at eight or any other time. She was in complete denial about how out of it she really was and how impossible it would have been to try to pull it off. I remember feeling pulled in so many different directions, all of them bad. We ended up driving, which she still insisted on doing, and there was no arguing with her. I remember thinking to myself, "Well, if I die on the high-way, it won't even matter 'cause my life is over anyway, now that I'm already sixty." We did take it slow, and made it out to the Point to watch the lobster-fishing boats pull into the canal just as the sun was setting from the deck of one big old fish restaurant, after which she wanted to shop. Drunk shopping, like drunk dialing, is hard for me to handle. I hate to shop, even under the best of circumstances. By this time, I'd given up the idea that the night had anything to do with me, what I wanted, my birthday. My sixtieth birthday. Maybe my last one. Who knew. Or cared anymore. I sulked. She shopped, bought a few things, a present for me, then we called it a night. But only after she threw up in the bedside wastebasket at the motel and passed out. A familiar ending to a night on the town. Needless to say, there was no celebratory birthday fuck that night. The next morning—a favorite time for me anyway—was another story.

But yes, sixty is awful. Fifty isn't so bad—a kind of half time, so to speak. And then, much to my surprise, by the time you get a few decades later, it's alright. It's OK again! Somehow. And then upward and onward you just stop counting. At least I do. But sixty as I say was and will always be hell. I remember that year my dear old friend Gay from high school (really the only friend I have who is my age, though even she is four days younger than me!) was out in East Hampton and invited us to join her for some other friend's sixtieth party and we went. I remember keeping my eyes glued to Heather, who was wandering around the room full of strangers, oddly social, one drink after another, until she was very vocal—a great drunken storyteller, if a little slow and slurry in her delivery—and it was killing me, as it always did. One of these "can't take her anywhere" moments that aren't funny, although nobody seemed to notice but me. But to me they're excruciating. And enraging. Especially if you have just turned the terrible age of sixty believing with all your heart that your wonderful life was over and done with. Over period. Good thing it was a Sunday night, and everybody was either already on their way back to the city, or out there for the summer, so I could take the wheel, take us, very slowly, very carefully, back home. Or in our case, back to the Wavecrest Motel. Back to the glorious surf pounding away in the deep blackness down below.

September

I woke up this morning with a knot of gloom in my stomach. It's September! What with the academic calendar burned into my DNA practically from birth—early progressive nursery school—and then teaching practically all the rest of my life, September, not April, is the cruelest month, for sure. Summer is over. And yes, something about September 1, too. And then all of a sudden I remembered what it was—one of my favorite poems by one of the greatest poets, W. H. Auden, "September 1, 1939," which I haven't thought about in a long time, but now it's all coming back to me, leaving me utterly baffled as to how I could ever have forgotten one of the most memorable experiences of my young life. Not just the poem, not even really the poem itself, not even the very memorable line "We must love one another or die," which Auden ended up changing to "We must love one another and die," before eventually cutting the whole line, then the whole stanza, and finally deciding that everybody's favorite Auden poem about the beginning of World War II, Hitler's invasion of Poland, on September 1, 1939, should not be published anywhere, he was so ashamed of having written it. He thought it was sentimental and inappropriate. Oh yes, the whole experience is flooding back into my brain as I write. A story I must tell, before I forget it all over again.

Just like I forgot that Earth, Wind & Fire song, "September," one of my favorite songs, though I couldn't remember what it's even about, until a moment ago when it made me want to get up and dance right there and then, admittedly holding on to the dresser drawer knobs so I didn't fall. In the seventies, I was working uptown at City College, teaching freshman English—a poetry class, as I saw it. And when it came time to explicate Auden's "September 1, 1939," there was a line in the poem, "what occurred at Linz," which I could not (especially in the days before Google and Wikipedia) figure out for the life of me, so I had the thought—silly young me—to call Auden up and simply ask him. He was actually an East Village neighbor—he lived on St. Mark's Place with his lover Chester Kallman and I lived on Second Avenue and Tenth. Can you imagine? So that's just what I did.

I looked in the phone book and there he was, and believe it or not, when I introduced myself as a professor at City College— I don't think I used the word "professor"—he was thrilled because he had a date to give a reading there, but had lost the "coordinates": the date, address, directions, time, everything. He was very stressed about it, so to discover that I taught there and could find all that out, when I asked him to explain the poem to me, he immediately suggested I come by for tea.

When I did, we discussed the poem, although he told me he was actually thinking of abandoning it completely. He'd already omitted the line "what occurred at Linz," and perversely, I thought, refused to tell me what it meant because he hated the line so much. But he was happy to go on chatting about other things—the East Village, how St. Mark's Place had changed, his favorite restaurants—and after two or maybe even three hours I left, after making plans for me to pick him up and escort him uptown (I insisted we take a cab) the following week. Those really were the days. But it's a wonderful story, and I've gotten a lot of mileage out of it over the years, especially for my having the nerve, the chutzpah, the courage, to do it in the first place. It's hard to believe that I forgot about it until this morning. At some point over the years, I found out Linz was Hitler's birthplace. The line still doesn't make sense, especially grammatically. But still. I wonder. What did "occur" at Linz? For one thing, it was not quite Hitler's birthplace, but very close, the next town on the Austrian-German border in southern Austria. What else was in Linz? A huge concentration camp, Mauthausen, famous for being the camp where the Polish intelligentsia (it could have been my father or me)—artists, teachers, university professors, and, apparently, Boy Scouts—ended up being taken. It was also the very last camp to be liberated by the Allies. The prisoners at Mauthausen were engaged in slave labor in marble quarries, excavating impossibly heavy blocks, which they had to lug up the "stairs of death," as they were called, until they were too weak to live. And, fittingly, a marble plaque from this same quarry in Linz was affixed to Hitler's birth house. It read:

FÜR FRIEDEN FREIHEIT
UND DEMOKRATIE
NIE WIEDER FASCHISMUS
MILLIONEN TOTE MAHNEN

[FOR PEACE, FREEDOM
AND DEMOCRACY
NEVER AGAIN FASCISM
MILLIONS OF DEAD WARN US]

Show Them the Way

(Revised especially for today, MLK Jr. Day, January 16, 2023)

On the very first celebration of MLK's birthday as a federal holiday, I was down in DC at the Kennedy Center to write a piece for the Wooster Group who were performing there. It was noon, time for lunch, and the cafeteria was full of people rehearsing for that night's special MLK Jr. concert. I looked up and saw Diana Ross hand-feeding a giant hot dog into Bob Dylan's open mouth! What a thrill that was for me. It was January 20, 1986, not MLK's real birthday, but the third Monday of the month, the way holidays were just beginning to be celebrated. At lunchtime, when all the artists who were performing that evening were taking a break, everyone was in jeans and tee shirts and they all looked great. I always did think that that performers looked better in their sweats and 'tards than on opening night in their fluffy costumes and now a lot of dancers have learned that lesson too. And especially since 2020, when everyone wore slippers. Unless they were marching in the streets. The lines between PJs and evening dress became blurred and finally disappeared during COVID, especially from the waist down.

But on January 20, 1986, those lines were not blurred. Not at all. My second most vivid memory was the concert audience that night. That afternoon, one of the show's producers approached the Wooster Group people, who were also gathered in the Kennedy Center rehearsing their production, and asked us to be "seat fillers." You know, when some celebrity goes to pee, you jump in and take their seat so the house always looks completely full. But they took one look at us after dinner—when we were supposedly all dressed up in our Kennedy Center fanciest finery—and totally changed their minds. We just didn't fit. We were all part humiliated and part proud. Stevie Wonder was the main act that night—and not only that, he was the power, the years of effort behind getting the day recognized, the celebration of the spirit and the man. MLK was his hero, the birthday song included. And he had asked Quincy Jones, the best, to assemble the performers for the evening—people like Diana Ross, Bob Dylan (who invited Peter, Paul and Mary to join him), the Pointer Sisters, Lena Horne, Ray Charles, and many, many more. But it wasn't the singers that took my breath away. It was the audience. The beautiful African American audience who all seemed to be of one mind about what to wear (without social media to coordinate them): bright jewel tones like sapphire, magenta, emerald green, crimson, tangerine, silk and satin against skin—a tribute MLK could never have imagined, and that probably would have totally turned him on, as it did me.

The reason I was even in DC on that day so many years ago was complicated, convoluted. The Wooster Group—of which I always considered myself the groupie-in-chief, being so passionately connected to their genius and thankful that their home, the Performing Garage, was on Wooster Street, right around the corner from my loft on Greene Street—was performing, under the guest directorship of Peter Sellars, Flaubert's *The Temptation of St. Anthony*. It was a prestigious gig for them at the Kennedy Center. At the same time, Ron Vawter, one of their great actors, and I were supposed to be collaborating with filmmaker Lizzie Borden on a new piece. We'd received an NEA grant and it had to be completed that month, or the government would take back the money. We were taking it right down to the wire. The project was called *Situations of Confrontation* (Lizzie's title), and it was supposed to be about race. Our first meeting took place after Ron's show, across the street at the Watergate Hotel bar. Brilliant Ron Vawter! He said, "So tell me. What are you working on now?" I said I was transcribing all the taped interviews I'd done with Hollywood veterans who'd known my uncle Leo, the lyricist of "Diamonds Are a Girl's Best Friend" and "Thanks for the Memory." The interviews were for a biography I was presumably writing, but which more and more became just an excuse to spend as much time as possible in LA, the new love of my life. It was a love that Ron and I coincidentally shared. We'd reminisce about driving fast on the lusciously green curvy part of Sunset on the way to Pacific Coast Highway at dusk. So at the Watergate Hotel bar we pored over the transcripts of all these very old people reminiscing about their wonderful young years in wonderful Old Hollywood. Ron decided that we should get the children of various Wooster Group performers and stagehands, brilliant little twelve-year-old geniuses whose voices hadn't yet dropped, to play the aged storytellers remembering the prime of their lives. What a delightful, fabulous concept it was. And it turned into a sweet little play, too, when we performed it a month later, back in New York at the Garage. And what a thrill it was to be directed by Ron Vawter, who was loved by everyone who ever met him.

I think, among so many others, of the adorable young boy Gary Indiana, holding a crush on Ron that never really went away. I remember them popping over to the loft to drink or smoke pot after Ron's show at the Garage from time to time. I didn't even know, yet, that they'd been lovers. Not hard to picture.

Come to think of it, it just occurred to me that maybe the reason Ron got the idea to use the transcribed tapes as text for "our little play" was that the Wooster Group had used another transcription of mine for an amazing show they did, called *LSD (...Just the High Points...)*. It was my title, but Liz never gave me credit for it, or anything else really, which pissed me off at the time but there was nothing I could do about it, though I did try. In the piece, Nancy Reilly played me, listening to the tape through headphones. She even sounded exactly like me. Kind of nasal.

Just yesterday morning, a mountain climber being interviewed on morning TV was discussing her life goal of wanting to climb to the highest point in every state in the U.S, and I found out, to my delight, that there's even a name for doing that. It's called "highpointing." Now it's a verb! They keep doing that, like *tasking*. Or *gifting*. Or how an *ask* is now a noun. Val hated it when they did that. But *highpointing* is beautiful. As far as highpointing goes, that week in DC was definitely a high point. Every evening, Ron and I met in the bar of the Watergate Hotel—more than fifteen years after the famous break-in that eventually got Nixon fired—drinking and writing our little play. It was such a celebration for me, not just of MLK Jr. (free, free, free at last), but because while I was experiencing the pure ecstasy of full-on creation and joy, my mother lay dying back in her New York apartment, in the final days of her life, filling me with guilt, sadness, and terror whenever it slipped back into my consciousness, as much as I struggled to keep it down. I had to beg my mother to let me go, to leave her after months, almost every day since Thanksgiving. That Thanksgiving, when I went to see her in the hospital and share Thanksgiving dinner off hospital trays, she finally let me know about her diagnosis and what Dr. Berger had said—that she had lung cancer and three to six months at most left to live. This was if she refused all treatment, which they had both decided was the best way forward. "I don't want to spend what time I have left," she said, "bald and throwing up." I thought she was very brave. And correct.

Brave to let me leave her when she was so sick at the end because she understood how much the opportunity meant to me. I was grateful to her, too, for not making more of a fuss, not making me feel guiltier than I already did. When we'd finished, I took the Amtrak express train back to NYC, the Acela, which I loved. I settled into my seat, leaned my head against the cloudy window, and looked out at the bare winter trees whizzing by. I was relieved to be going home, happy at the thought of returning to loft life, to Vito and my cats—there were now three because Olga, my mother's big beautiful Maine Coon cat, had joined us after my mom got sick (although not for very long because when we gave her what they called a "lion cut" that summer and removed most of her long hair they discovered a big malignant tumor on her belly, and she too died). But that was later. For now, I was just glad to be going back to see her and the rest of the gang. Everything seemed to be going smoothly until just outside of Philly the train came to a screeching halt. And I sat there for a long time. Like, hours, which just increased my growing anxiety about my mother and not being able to reach her (this was in the days before cell phones). After several hours of waiting, they finally told us that a cow or a truck or something had gotten stuck on the tracks. After several more excruciating hours, we were moving again, and I was breathing normally, almost, again.

In just a few more weeks it was the beginning of the end. We all knew. Hospice asked if she wanted a social worker to visit, so she could share her feelings about dying. She almost laughed in their face. No. That was the last thing she wanted to talk about. I understood, completely. The next week the Juilliard School sent a string quartet to the apartment.

By this point they had increased her morphine and she wasn't really aware anymore. But my Aunt Berdie, her older sister, and I were wide awake and hyperaware with anxiety. Aware that the end was near. We sat together on the living room couch and listened to the beautiful chamber music and that was good. Pat, her visiting nurse, had been coming daily for a few months and took care of all of us in the most considerate, really loving and genuine way. But Pat had only recently started working for hospice, so she, like the rest of us, had never actually seen anybody actually die before. Vito came uptown for a few hours on that last day too. After he left, I went into the bedroom and stretched out next to my mother. She was breathing oddly. Then all of a sudden her teeth started shivering against each other, making a strange noise. I guess what I was hearing was the famous "death rattle" they talk about that happens just before death. Then it slowed, quieted, and stopped. And that was all. That was death. Later Pat told me a sweet thing. How my mother was so dignified and well mannered that when she died, she didn't release any of her bodily waste, like most people do when they go. Now I'm thinking of Melville's *Billy Budd*, where at the end fearless genius Herman Melville has him orgasm when they hang him. Betcha never thought of coming and shitting as the same release!

Transfiction 2

When Chris first proposed doing an expanded version of *If You're a Girl*, the first thing she asked was if there was anything in the original version I definitely would not want to include, and without a moment's thought, I said "Oh, that stupid essay I wrote, 'Transfiction.'" At the time I wrote it, I was transcribing the taped interviews for the Uncle Leo biography, and I thought the essay would be a way of exploring how I liked to combine transcribed "real" material with made-up settings, characters, situations, and conversations—real-life dialogue in imaginary settings. I called this new form (which I felt I had invented or discovered) "transfiction."

But that was almost twenty years ago, and now everything has changed, even the spelling of it. For one thing, anything with the word *trans* in it now is complicated. Would it imply that this is a new genre of romcoms for girls who want to be boys? (I love what Billy Porter said on *The View* today, to rapturous applause: "The change has already happened!")

I wrote the essay right after the Wooster Group interviewed me for that project that would become *LSD (...Just the High Points...)*. They were researching Tim Leary and wanted to talk to me after they learned I'd been his babysitter when he came east to Harvard, after his wife's suicide at Berkeley. I never knew if they really wanted to talk to me about Leary, or if they were just hoping I would bring some LSD.

Either way, it was a fabulous interview, which I painstakingly transcribed. And then Ron and I used the transcription technique again for that play we made with Lizzie Borden, casting kids to play the Old Hollywood veterans and I was cast as director, and voila!—transfiction.

But, the essay, I thought, was not so great. I don't do theory well. So when Chris asked what I'd leave out of the new book, and I said "That stupid little essay," she didn't even contradict me!

But recently she told me that another Semiotext(e) writer loved the entire book, and especially my essay. So I gave it another look over and thought maybe it wasn't as stupid as I remembered, and decided to keep it in. After that, I didn't give it another thought, until this morning, when I was listening to *The View*. The guest was Ethan Hawke. I always thought he was a wonderful actor and an interesting person. No longer a child star, he was even better looking than he used to be. He was saying that now he feels like a young old person and likes it and that's just how I feel now too. I like it a lot. Brings me real joy. Imagine that! He was talking about his latest project, *The Last Movie Stars*, a documentary about the life, the careers, and loves of Paul Newman and Joanne Woodward, which I gather were all great. Especially the loves. Their long long love. I was fascinated by his explanation of the whole process of making it—how he got a call one morning from Newman's daughter, asking if he'd be interested in the project. It sounded a little daunting, especially since Paul had, in a fit of rage or self-abnegation, burned all the interview tapes in his archive, which would have made the movie so easy. And without them, maybe impossible. But then he discovered that someone had transcribed the taped interviews and Newman had not destroyed the transcriptions. Still, Ethan Hawke wasn't sure what to do with them, or how to make the documentary. Because it wouldn't be the same without the voices, the real people, real friends of Paul and Joanne, speaking in real-time. But then of course, it was the girl—Ethan Hawke's wife and producing partner—who made a great suggestion. "Well, you're an actor," she said, "and you have all these great actor friends, all talented and brilliant and gorgeously photogenic. Why don't you have them 'play' Newman's friends, using the transcripts as scripts?" At this point my heart started to quicken. I think I actually gasped at the synchronicity of it all, like he had stolen my concept of transfiction and turned it into a major motion picture. I couldn't believe it. I couldn't wait to tell somebody. But whom? Who would even get how amazing it was for this to be happening? Ron Vawter, maybe? If only I could have told him, but Ron was dead. There was really no one left to tell who would get it. Until now, I suppose, when I can finally tell it, tell this, dear reader, to you.

The Ethan Hawke interview on *The View* ended with one more fascinating thing. Someone asked him about his twenty-four-year-old daughter, Maya Hawke, who's an actress and singer. Ethan told a funny story about how when he and Maya went to the movies a few nights before, someone came up to them, and when Ethan tried to shoo him away, saying "Not now, please, I'm with my daughter," the man said "Oh no—it was her I wanted to talk to, not you!" And all *The View* ladies laughed.

Someone else asked how he felt about Maya appearing in the nude in her latest music video, but he shied away from answering.

Then someone else asked how his wife felt about it, and he said he didn't know, which I thought was odd, that they hadn't discussed it. Maybe he just didn't want to talk about something that personal on a TV show. But I did find out who she was and then that was that.

And then the serendipity keeps happening, because that night (last night), I heard them announce on an NBC promo that Maya Hawke was going to be a guest on *Jimmy Fallon*, and though I was very sleepy, I couldn't resist finding out more about this brilliant kid everyone was talking about, who I had never heard of until that morning—yesterday morning to be exact. So I made myself stay up to watch *Jimmy Fallon* to see who Maya Hawk was and I was glad I did. She was brilliant, beautiful, charming, and unbelievably animated as only a twenty-four-year-old can be. She said she was so nervous about having to come on Jimmy Fallon's TV show that she called her mom for advice (her mom being Uma Thurman) and Maya said, her voice raised in passion and almost tears, how her mother had written this amazingly great essay about abortion—the abortion she'd had as a teenager, but kept as her dark secret until she wrote about it in the *Washington Post*—and how proud she was of her brilliant passionate mother. Then Jimmy Fallon was almost in tears as well, and thanked her profusely for bringing the whole abortion subject up on his show, and then he said "I rocked you, you know," making a little gesture of cradling an infant and rocking her sweetly back and forth, and they were almost in tears again. She had never heard that before, I guess, and was blown away with yet more emotion. As was I. The whole thing was wonderful, I can't quite explain it. It was all so real. A rarity on network TV these days. Maya was so young and yet so wise, alive. Uncynical, political, talented, and lovely, and the whole day of experiencing "meeting" them all—Ethan, Uma, Maya, the Hawke family—and feeling their emotion so loud and clear on national television, and all that serendipity, especially around transfiction, was magical.

IF YOU'RE A GIRL

(1990)

Transfiction

In Minneapolis recently I met a woman who was doing a computer animation of the visions (in word and paint) of a twelfth-century German, St. Hildegard. Hildegard didn't write or paint her visions herself. The scribes and illuminators did that. We talked a lot about scribes, a funny profession, the highest and lowliest combined, a holy calling, the words moving through you, almost like you're not there except to get it exactly right. This feeling of tapping into such an ancient spiritual activity creates excitement and mitigates against the utter boredom of doing something which is otherwise totally mechanical. There's always that tension, between feeling like a god or goddess is speaking through you, and doing the work of a machine.

LSD made me think about the value of transcribed material. Around the time that it premiered, I was working on a biography of the Hollywood composer, my uncle Leo Robin, that necessitated hundreds of hours of interviews around California poolsides. And their transcription. A seemingly mechanical process, but somehow, very exciting; it's not only the words but the voices saying the words, then you writing the words as they're spoken, that makes the voices seem like prisoners. They're trapped on the tapes and only you can release them. I think you always fall in love with the voices you're transcribing—partly because you spend so much time with them, and partly because the voice is so revealing: not thinking, misspeaking, running on, groping, speech is us. There's so much information carried in the placements of the littlest words, the tenses we favor, personal music going by at the speed of life, so fast, so hard to get it right. And, inexplicably, mysteriously, so vital to do so. Why it should make such a difference whether it's "I, um, took off my clothes" or "I took off my, um, clothes" is beyond me, which is just where I like it.

I had just begun to think about using this material in other ways when Ron Vawter of the Wooster Group, filmmaker Lizzie Borden, and I started working together on a theater piece called *Situations of Confrontation*. When Ron suggested we use my transcribed tapes for the piece, I was happy. I'd just started getting into this process. Lizzie had a script she'd written, setting New York futuristically under a dome. So I had the idea to take the California of my poolside interviews and set it adrift in the Pacific and made the drug of choice a thing called "lume," named for the luminescent phosphorescence that was all over the place in Lizzie's story.

Trying to adapt my tapes to this, I set some of the faithfully transcribed conversations, like jewels, in a totally fictional, made-up context. It's the opposite of TV docudrama, where the situation is real and the dialogue is made up. I was twisting it around the other way and liked the new spin of this tense recombination of fiction and transcription which I called, jokingly, "transfiction." The name stuck, and people talked about it like it was real and wanted to know about the process.

Since the spoken word preceded the written one, in writing this now I have to decide how to spell it. "Transfix" or "trance fiction"? Is it one word or two? Is the fifth letter an *x* or a *c*?

Are both *c*'s? "Trancefiction"? No. No. It's not that trance. "Trancfiction"? (Smile.) No, it's got to be *s*, "trans…," like *transition*, "cross," but not *x*: "transfixion." Too Christ-on-the cross. X on the *x*. "Transfiction": it's the tension between two different drives, toward fidelity and freedom. I was conscious of this tension when I was copying the *LSD* interview to disk. It was the first tape I'd worked with in which I was the one being interviewed and I had to slap my hands a few times when they wanted to change something I'd said that sounded foolish or was a downright lie.

In transfiction, you utilize this tension, you let your hands do what they want to on the keys, from being faithful down to every "um" and "er," every pause and beat of the original spontaneous spoken words, to modifying it slightly, changing plot and finally writing dialogue no one ever spoke to throw it into another world. This kind of tampering seemed dangerous, like injecting cyanide in the grapes or putting LSD in the Chicago water supply, and I liked that feeling. It captures the essence of writing. It may be the words of the gods, or of humanity, but it's always you who's ripping them off. Plato was right to banish poets from his Republic for making things up. There is always something criminal about writing: it's like B & E—breaking and entering— what the British call "smash and grab." Especially fiction: duping. There is something toxic and poisonous in lies: zap, you're transfixed. Can I help it if I wanna put back the lie in Li(t)erature, as in Li(f)e? Go ahead, Plato, make my day.

LSD (... Just the High Points ...)

Interview: Ann Rower and the Wooster Group
    with:
Elizabeth LeCompte, director, the Wooster Group
Ron Vawter
Peyton Smith
Willem Dafoe
Kate Valk
actors and members of the Wooster Group
Jim Clayburgh designer and member of the Wooster Group
Nancy Reilly
Michael Stumm
Anna Köhler
Jeff Webster
actors and associate members of the Wooster Group
Norman Frisch, dramaturg and associate member of the Wooster Group
Ann Rower, writer

LIZ. Um, what we want, then, is just for you to remember what you can about any... any images...
ANN. OK, I...
LIZ. Anything you can remember... it doesn't even need to be about him.
ANN. Yeah, I just sort of started jogging my memory and so the stuff is still coming up. I jotted some of it down. Should I read

what I wrote and we can take it from there? Some of it is a little self-indulgent.

LIZ. Honey, we're used to it. [*Laughter.*] There's a lot of that around here.

ANN. I decided to call it *LSD (...Just the High Points...)* or *Leery about Leary* [*Peyton laughs*], which I was.

KATE. We've all been wantin' to say it.

ANN. Which I was, though it might not be useful to your sense of Leary as victim of witch hunt. You could call it *King Leary*.

MICHAEL. I think we oughta call it *Leary contra Leary*.

LIZ. [*Pause.*] I like *King Leary*, I think that's great.

ANN. Yes, I thought so... That has something to do with my sense of him.

LIZ. Could be *King Leeeery*... with a lot of *eeee*'s strung out.

ANN. See... I'll just read what I wrote OK?...

They wanted to query me about Leary. That was the other title, Ron said it... but I'm glad the meeting was called off. I look so terrible today. Those unsightly bags under my eyes from too much alcohol yesterday I guess. The thing is, the fact that Leary struck me as an asshole, such a jerk, had nothing to do with the fact that people in command were so scared by his wanting to expand society's consciousness, bringing peace and harmony through LSD. Though of course it wasn't LSD. It was psilocybin. Which was typical. Certain dishonesty, something unconnected, some ability to dissociate internally that he was a prophet of LSD who didn't do it because it depressed him so much. And this is what he was trying to sell? Still, the danger he represented to others provoked hysteria and reprisals. He's probably still running. But then when I met him he was running from Berkeley to Harvard, partly to get away from the place where his wife and mother of his two kids had killed herself, partly 'cause he got a grant. He thought everyone thought he had driven her to suicide. His message preceded him, of course, to the East Coast. Mostly I heard about him from the East Side New York poets. But none of us were interested in his message. We were interested in his pills. [*Peyton chortles.*] In fact, this hurt Tim very much, I think [*giggle*]. There was a story that got back to him of everyone hanging out in Ginsberg's apartment. Allen, Peter, Jack Kerouac's ghost. Allen was cooking chicken soup and everyone was just waiting for the weird professor from Harvard with the little pink pills. Leary heard about this cartoon image and was hurt. But then everything was hurting him in those days. I met him in the early spring of '61. I did try to make the bags go away. I'd heard chamomile tea is a diuretic and an astringent but I didn't have any chamomile tea. But I bought a box of Sleepytime the other day and I know Sleepytime is mostly chamomile, which I guess is also a terrific soporific. I was going to return it because it was loose tea and not teabags but these bags, the bags under my eyes, made me desperate, so even if I didn't have to be seen by the Garage people, still it was Saturday afternoon and even if Vito was rehearsing, if I wanted to stir up any kind of action I had to do something about those bags. So I made bags out of gauze bandages and put them on my eyes and lay down and after ten minutes, which is what I read somewhere, I took them off. This interest in chemical properties of things goes way back. I shudder to think how glibly I suggested to Ron, when he asked if I knew of a good soporific tea for Jackie Dafoe, that they try valerian... I wasn't thinking who Jackie was... was a baby. That shit is strong. It has such a terrible taste. It's not as strong as some things, though. I remember looking up yohimbe, a bark suggested as a tea I was fooling around with at the time, and finding it listed in the herbal manual with a big black box around it. Well, I found out what that meant. Now even Kiehl's doesn't deal it. Weird shit. A true (meaning "local") aphrodisiac. I guess if you like being horny and nauseated at the same time... [*Kate's low, rolling laugh.*] Try throwing up and jerking off at the same time, in an outhouse, yet. Actually it doesn't sound so bad. [*Big laugh.*] I remember about that time I met an ethnopharmacologist coming down from Connecticut on the Bonanza bus and he told me the thing to do with yohimbe was to soak it in vodka, or better yet, grain alcohol, for a week and then drink it and we did. But like I said, my interest in those kinds of properties of things, that is to say drugs, goes way back. So by the time I met Leary I was already a drinker, a heavy amphetamine addict, and heavy pothead. I mean, I was ready. Anyway, the Sleepytime worked. The bags are gone. [*Laughter.*] But now I have these big hollow eyes with yellow stains under them. Those funny eyes, as Susan Leary, Tim's lovely daughter, used to say. I remember one morning in the big kitchen on the wide proper New England street. It must have been late spring, maybe May, 1961. I was squeezing orange juice (some C) for me, Robert, and Burroughs. Susan came down for breakfast. "Did you take pills?" I shook my head no. "Then how come you have those funny eyes?" That's what she called being high, "having funny eyes." It was, now that I think of it, the last morning I ever spent in Tim's house and with Tim, the last time period. That day and the evening and night before, Tim spent moving [to the more notorious Newton Center house]. It had been his last night in Newton. The reason we were there was not to babysit with the kids but with William Burroughs. Now that Burroughs is all of our neighbor, it seems hard to remember what a stranger he was that night. At the time Burroughs was still an expatriate, an exile living in Tangiers. He refused to come back to America. Until now no one, and many had tried, could even get him to put in an appearance on our shores. But Tim organized a conference on hallucinogenics. He invited everyone. All the experts on drugs were to be there. Burroughs had to be there. Tim did get him to accept. The lure was [Aldous] Huxley, who I remember was teaching at MIT that season. So Burroughs was flying in from Tangiers after a long absence, his first time in America in years, and coming directly to Tim. And Tim was moving that night. He couldn't be home. Typical. So Tim called me and Robert and asked us to be there and babysit Burroughs. Another thing that was typical. Tim had made no provisions for Burroughs's head. Here Burroughs was, ex-junkie, hash head, traveling, wisely, without anything and coming to Tim's house where there was nothing for him to smoke. We ransacked the house. There was nothing. No psilocybin. Nothing. Tim had no understanding of the drug culture he was founding at all. It bothered me. I mean, we had to fill out these questionnaires before we could take the pills. We finally found some dried magic mushrooms, and we put them in a coffee grinder and we ground them up and we smoked them. It smelled just like pot, but not much happened...

But maybe that's why Susan said, the next morning, I had those funny eyes... but like I said that was the last time I saw Tim. I don't remember much, that's for sure. And then I made a list of the things that I did remember. It's amazing, it's like a lot of holes. [*Merry laughter.*] And they're like about these six moments that I remember the most. Um... the one was the first time I met Tim. The second time was the first time I took the pills... Anyway, should I just keep on reading? Want me to talk about each of these things a little? I will... We were just focusing on the same points... [*Group mumbling.*] They had a woman, this amazing woman...

LIZ. This Chinese?

ANN. This Japanese [she *was* Chinese] woman that came with Tim and I guess was his maid, his governess, his secretary, his lover. I guess she was all these things.

LIZ. She's not mentioned in the *Unauthorized History*.

ANN. Yeah, I looked at it...

PEYTON. How much time were you involved with him, babysitting and stuff like that?

ANN. Well, I met him in January of '61 and left Cambridge in August 1961. I was involved with him probably every weekend. Or whatever, every other weekend. There was just these crazy weekends at his house. And there were always a lot of people.

MICHAEL. What were you doing in Cambridge, Ann?

LIZ. Are you recording this?

ANNIE. Ya—yep.

ANN. Oh, well, then I'll keep talking. [*Laughter.*] I had a Woodrow Wilson Fellowship, getting my master's... Harvard doesn't really give an MA, it's like a consolation prize... They enroll you in the PhD program and if you leave at the end of the year they hand you this master's thing.

KATE. Your master's in English?

ANN. Yeah, in literature, English-American literature.

LIZ. English-American, not like anything specific?

ANN. Well, my master's had nothing to do with anything specific, uh, and my PhD had to do with Renaissance literature and Faulkner... Anyway, the first time I met Tim, I was married [to

Robert Newman] and was living in Boston, 69 Revere Street, and a friend of the person I was then married to was in the math department at Berkeley and knew Tim at Berkeley and came to Boston that year. [I think Robert invited Ben to come live with us because he knew Tim and would introduce us!] I guess he came in the spring and soon as he arrived we met Tim. That was how I met Tim. Ben was sort of a math connection. When they were at Berkeley, Tim was involved, the whole psychology department I guess was involved, with the math department. They were all involved with probability theory and statistics and all this stuff. But Tim tried to be more humanist. I mean, his specialty was creativity and because he went to Harvard, he was trying to come on like he had a specialty. Trying to be very serious. Anyway, Ben took us over there this afternoon. It was a beautiful afternoon, sort of late in the afternoon. There was this beautiful sort of late, strong, winter sun. And we came in, and we met Tim. And I just remember him standing there with his arms around the kids and they all looked very depressed. They were all really very down. I guess the suicide of the wife was, whatever, fairly recent. I don't know, you could just sort of feel there was this kind of air of, you know, everything was kind of held in. And there was this little small Japanese woman, uh, who did everything. And we all went inside. This was one of these breaks when there were no pills. They would come in from Sandoz, see, come in from Switzerland, these little shipments of pink psilocybin pills... uh, and this was a dry period. Tim had this candy dish. It was amazing. Three-tiered candy dish that had these little round dishes on each level going up and they sort of swung around and they were always full of these little pink pills. Just the sound, I can still hear the sound of the pills on the ceramic, you know, on the candy dish thing. But anyway, the candy dish was empty this weekend, um, and there was this atmosphere of waiting. And so there was nothing in the house. We went into this study or whatever it was, and I remember sitting down in front of the window and, you know, there I was a sort of young newlywed and everything with newly washed hair and the sun was coming in through the window onto my hair and Tim looks at me and he says "Get the camera, get the camera." She runs and gets the movie camera. "Take it, take it, the sun's going down, hurry up." She looks through the camera and starts to shoot the sun coming through my hair when suddenly she drops the camera and it shatters on the ground. So that was my first memory, the first day. Tim sort of running around like this tyrant, uh, he was horrible to her. I don't even remember so much more specifically, but my sense of him was he was horrible to her. He was very bossy, anyway.

LIZ. Was she young?

ANN. Yeah, she seemed like she was twenty-seven or so. She was young and sort of attractive, not flashy-looking but very small and solid, compared to him being sort of gangly and all over...

LIZ. Was he considered handsome?

ANN. I guess there's a certain tweedy Irish type, um, except he wasn't really handsome. I don't think he was considered handsome. Um, but as I said, he was sort of lean and he had, he had salt-and-pepper gray hair, lean and lanky, if you like that type, but he didn't have a nice face or anything. He just wasn't attractive as a person. He had these very unattractive eyes. Maybe it was something coming out of him. As I said, he always struck me as false. That's how I always felt about him. But he was also, I think, very defended. And very hurt. He was really hurting at this point. You could tell. He didn't take psilocybin himself at that time because he was in a real depression and he was afraid that it would bum him out. And that also bothered me, the fact that that was happening and he was continuing to proselytize.

LIZ. Was this around the time... or before the time he was working with the convicts?

ANN. It was during the time. I remember, for instance, an afternoon shortly after I met him. We were over there. Tim wasn't home and we were sort of babysitting I guess. Alice, I forget her name, the Japanese woman's name that was with him, was with him. He was going to get home late. And he walked in an hour after we'd gotten there and we didn't know why he came home so early. He had given the convicts this big dose of psilocybin and brought them all into the rec room or something [*lots of everybody talking*] but he got depressed and left, sending the convicts back to their cells tripping their brains out. That was the thing. The idea of Leary pushing mass consumption and not even doing any. That really disturbed me. But anyway, the second time I met him was also hysterical. In all these scenes Leary is just in the background because that's what he was, he was just an observer. He was a scientist, a psychologist. He was giving everybody these questionnaires. It took weeks and weeks of fawning and fawning before he would give us any to take home. We would have to do it there, sit around, record our experiences afterward. It was all right. It was interesting because there was no literature on it at the time and so nobody knew what to feel or anything. I have this memory that's very clear, the first time that we took it, of all of us standing around the living room and standing with my elbow up on the mantlepiece, very casually holding myself up and feeling I have absolutely no boundaries, you know, and I just loved this woman who was standing next to me whom I had never met before. I was her. All these things... I guess we had been reading Alan Watts so it didn't come completely out of the blue. But there were no magazine articles on what it was supposed to feel like and at first it seemed to me a coincidence that it turns out everyone was feeling the same thing at that point, but that was the point. And also nobody knew how many to take. I mean, one night I took two, one night I took twenty. Well, we had no idea what we were doing. Fortunately, with these kinds of drugs, there's a point at which you take a lot, nothing else happens... Unless it hasn't happened yet. [*Laughter.*] I think that was always my experience with LSD.

KATE. I just heard this story once that a friend of mine took six hits and dove into the sidewalk. He thought it was a pool... so I only ever took one. [*Laughter.*] He just did a big swan dive.

ANN. Yeah, well, could be, could be. I never had any experience... I never tried to fly. I never had a bad trip.

RON. Did you ever see God?

LIZ. I only took one and I was [unintelligible] for twenty-four hours.

KATE. I would only ever take one hit.

ANN. Oh sure... Well I don't know if I would say I saw God, um ...but I certainly felt it in the universe. I mean, everything was, like, glowing... Is that what you mean?

RON. Ya...

ANN. But that didn't feel like a hallucination. Maybe it was, but I didn't visually hallucinate.

PEYTON. Really?

ANN. Not very often visually hallucinate. I seem to aurally hallucinate... I hear a lot of sound stuff.

KATE. I visually hallucinate. [*Laughter.*]

ANN. No, I never much… [*Laughter.*] I mean, the ceiling would move and stuff…

KATE. I am talking sheep and pigs and chickens in the air and in the sky.

ANN. With diamonds?

KATE. Serious… like everything is Peter Max drawings…

MICHAEL. Really the sound is the greatest thing about… somebody'd like slam a door upstairs…

LIZ. Then it all becomes colors.

MICHAEL. And then for the next half hour I'd hear…

LIZ. See what happened to me was sound was translated into visual images so that someone would slam a door and I would see waves of the door in colors… like vibrating.

ANN. You would be seeing what was really happening. [*Everybody talks.*]

LIZ. I would sit and look out a window and see a totally different scene than was there…

ANN. No, I did occasionally…

MICHAEL. Where is that little blue container for Christ sake?

LIZ. You know what I think it has to do with too… the different constructions of it because at the time I was taking it there were so many different kinds.

ANN. It has to do with the construction of the personality too. I'm much more aural anyway… [*pause*] but maybe not…

LIZ. Well, but maybe. I always had a feeling it had to do with what it was cut with.

ANN. It had to do with that too.

LIZ. 'Cause I knew later on…

ANN. You hallucinated less and less?

LIZ. No, I hallucinated more and more, more hallucinations of the kind where I'd look at my face and I'd see me... my skull.

ANN. That happened to me too, my face... I'd look in the mirror and I would be a hundred and three—

MICHAEL. Or you'd be green... That's the best part... when you're green.

ANN. —that could be my age now and I don't look anything like that. [*Ron laughs.*]

KATE. That doesn't sound very attractive. [*Laughter.*]

LIZ. Or you would rise and you'd be going thirty miles an hour.

MICHAEL. Well, we've gotten a little off the track.

LIZ. [*Amused*] Well, we always do.

ANN. I don't know if we have. The first time I took pills which was the second time I met Leary, which was the time I had my hand on the mantlepiece... I really felt this love just flowing out of me... And it was an amazing experience that was just so clear, but that was a culmination of what had really been a nightmarish evening. Richard Alpert was there. It was also the first time he had ever done it... and he had a toothache... [*Groans and laughter.*] And I don't know if you've ever...

PEYTON. Oh, it's horrible... I've done that.

ANN. Well, he tripped. Before he was Baba Ram Dass he had no cool or anything. He was just a grad student, a psychology grad student at Harvard. And he had this horrible experience, like eight hours of toothache. We were all somehow by Tim forced to sort of stand around him [he was lying on the dining room table] and support him... he'd be brave and moan and all... it was really terrible.

MICHAEL. Did anybody try to take his tooth out for him?

ANN. No, no, no. Especially he didn't try, but that wouldn't have done anything.

PEYTON. But I've done that.

ANN. You can get into it. You can get into the pain. What happens is you go right into it.

PEYTON. And that's all it is... and you're totally there.

ANN. You just ride into it... It seems much more with physical pain. Psychic pain it seems you can go through somehow. Anyway, there was something very ritualistic about that too. Alpert was lying out, sort of a corpse, and we were all standing around him and there were these candles, and he was moaning. An asshole. I mean, he also struck me as a real jerk.

WILLY. At this point were you a friend or a babysitter or someone that just walked in?

ANN. I was never a friend. There were just lots of people who were sort of around. You know, a group of at least ten people that were in and out, on my level, friends of friends, but that became like fixtures, who were there regularly. Babysitters.

WILLY. How, how was the... How was it presented? Huh?

ANN. Oh, it was presented very ritualistically. Tim was doing a whole number about the atmosphere. That was very important to him at that point, the atmosphere in which it was taken and that we would be supported. We would all sit down. He would build everybody up around him and everybody would take it, and then he didn't take it...

LIZ. And he wouldn't take it?

ANN. He wouldn't.

PEYTON. Would he not take it on the guise of monitoring what you were doing?

ANN. Yeah. I guess so. I guess so. But there were other people who'd volunteered to monitor.

LIZ. They used to talk about the person who would come...

PEYTON. The guide.

MICHAEL. The babysitter.

ANN. Yeah, that was a big thing for him at this point, that there would be someone who would be straight, but it was always him. He also talked about not taking it because it depressed him.

PEYTON. Maybe this was just a small, short period in his life.

ANN. Well, I don't really know. I was in B. Dalton and I looked at *Flashbacks* [Leary's autobiography] for that time period and it's sort of not there. It made me think maybe he really wasn't doing it then and so... so he didn't write about it.

LIZ. Do you remember someone called Lisa Beaverman? Somebody that was involved with him at the time...

KATE. Who did a magazine, didn't she?

LIZ. Ya, she was very involved with LSD in a serious, quote, way...

ANN. I remember hearing about her I guess.

LIZ. Seems like there was a competition between the two of them, she's very annoyed by the way he proselytized...

ANN. I don't have any specific memory of that. But, like I said, I was really only interested in the drugs, except the only other thing that was interesting at the time was that Tim was working with this amazing man [whom we did become friends with], who should have been Tim. This man, Frank Barron, was this mystic, this mystic Irish poet, also with the psychology department at Berkeley, who was into probability theory. He tested his probability theories on the tables at Las Vegas all the time he was in California. He was a poet, a genius, gorgeous, loose. He had this amazing kind of theoretical underpinning about taking drugs that also involved the idea of getting high, which was completely foreign to Tim. He was in on the project from the very beginning, but just during the time I knew him, he went to Las Vegas just one time and met Nancy, this six-foot-seven showgirl. He married her and brought her back to Tim's house. She taught me how to make great pork chops.

...I've never forgotten her. And eventually Frank got less and less involved in it and he got more and more involved with Nancy and eventually they just moved to Vegas. There was this feeling somehow that Frank should have been Tim. But that also Frank had the sense not to be Tim, because Tim had this amazing sort of ego, this irritating King Leary thing. I tried to remember about Jackie. The thing that I remembered about him is his room had shelves from floor to ceiling that were full of toys that Tim kept bringing him. He was just always bringing him home toys. [I was interested to read that Burroughs had this same memory.]

PEYTON. How old is he at this point?

ANN. It seems to me the kids were five and ten or seven and eleven. I'm not sure exactly.

WILLY. How old is he now?

PEYTON. Thirty-five.

ANN. And do you know how old Susan is?

NORM. Two years difference... She was eighteen and he was sixteen when they were busted.

ANN. Oh, I thought he was a little younger...

PEYTON. It was '61?

LIZ. He's twelve or thirteen about that time...

ANN. I have no idea. Susan was probably younger when I met her because I remember him as very small. They had this house with this big stairway. It was like this center-hall colonial New England, and I remember the kids sitting at the top of the stairs a lot looking down. Just typical kids, when parents have a party. There was all this wild stuff going on. They knew what it was all about. But Susan always thought that she could tell when people had done it. And of course we thought that that was just amazing, but obviously everyone was walking around with their pupils so dilated that of course you could tell. I wrote you a letter that you said that maybe you had lost.

LIZ. That's the one… I wanna hear more about.

ANN. Then there was this crazy, crazy weekend that I remember. It may have been building up to this big convention where Burroughs finally came. But Arthur Koestler was there and Allen Ginsberg and Peter Orlovsky and Watts and his girlfriend were there. I remember that. Koestler had never done this drug and had some kind of attitude about it. Everyone was very nervous about whether he would come, whether he would do it and all this stuff. He was very critical of it all. Maybe he had written some things that were very critical of Leary…

LIZ. Didn't he write *Darkness at Noon*?

ANN. Yeah, he did. He did. Oh, I know what it was. He didn't believe that you should get—become psychedelic [ecstatic]—by ingesting a chemical. So he was very anti. Right, that was it. He was coming from a more mystical end. He was very skeptical but he came and he did take some. And the first thing that happened was he ran upstairs and walked into his bedroom, and somehow by mistake Allen Ginsberg and Peter, who, I think, had been there for like a week already, were in Arthur Koestler's bedroom and they were, um, fucking each other and sucking each other on Koestler's bed and he got real upset…

LIZ. He was there?

ANN. He walked into the room. He took this psilocybin and he became very spiritual and he wanted to go up to his room [*laughter*] and meditate.

MICHAEL. And opened the door and bang...

ANN. That's it. And, I guess, you know, screaming and running around and sort of really, really freaking out. I don't know why I keep thinking of a comb... Allen came out combing his hair, maybe, or Arthur was looking for a comb. Anyway, it was very bizarre and then also the same weekend Alan Watts was there [Watts was a different weekend] and Watts, of course, was one of the supporters. But again there was all this kind of apprehension amongst the establishment Buddhists and Leary. You know, what was this bullshit all about? And Watts came because he was planning to get high, not with his wife but with his girlfriend. And this was supposed to be very hush-hush... He had just written, I think, *Nature, Man and Woman*. Yeah, that's the book everybody was reading at the time. And he comes in with this young thing. And everybody takes pills. And at one point there's this screaming coming from the downstairs bathroom and everybody's banging. And I come in and there's this line of people... Watts, Arthur Koestler, Allen and Peter... Tim, everybody, Frank Barron, Richard Alpert... All of them sort of there, huddled outside the bathroom door pulling on the door, "Let us in, let us in," that's the men speaking, with this woman screaming and screaming inside... Finally somebody says to her "What's the matter? What's the matter?" and she says "They're coming. They're after me. They're coming." "They're coming?" "They're coming." "Who's coming?" "They're coming. They're trying to steal my shit. They're trying to steal my shit." And finally they burst, or they pulled, the door open or she comes out... And she points to the wallpaper which has these little birds on it that she had hallucinated into these horrible vultures that were coming down, to try and steal her shit... [*Laughter.*] Anyway, that was that story.

PEYTON. This was Alan Watts's girlfriend?

ANN. Yes, this was Alan Watts's girlfriend, his secretary... And then right the next day, suddenly after I wrote that letter [about it] I must have come to see *The Crucible* or read it... No, I guess I read it because I knew you were doing it, then the scene about "the birds, the birds"... Right? [*Pause.*] Those were the specific things I could remember, except there was a lot more about the strange evening with Burroughs... It wasn't so much about Leary... Um... does any of that—

LIZ. Ring a bell? Yes, that's nice, um, a couple of things... What was the house like?

ANN. It was a very comfortable... The thing is there were two houses. There was this first house that I was in, the night that we came to babysit for Burroughs, when Leary was moving to Newton Center, then there was the house in Newton Center that was the house that became sort of infamous. There were a lot of different couples living there and it was like a commune... you know, with kids and people of all ages. Tim eventually got thrown out of it when he was thrown out of Harvard. This was the year that he really turned on all of Harvard Yard. But the first house, the only house I was really in, was a real traditional, big, spacious, center-hall colonial, very comfortably furnished. It was obviously a sublet, one of those academic sublets. Some professor who was in Tehran for a year on a Fulbright Fellowship or something had given it to him. But a very beautiful house with very opulent, dark shining woods and carpets and curtains and a big yard with trees, apple trees... [*Long pause.*] And then, as I say, I seem to remember, and then the room where Jackie put all his toys. And then the kitchen was where things happened in the house. There was this big kitchen... 'cause people were always staying over, you know, it was no big thing 'cause nobody could navigate—ya, it was very Harvard. People were always coming up to people, asking them if they were high. I'll try to, I'll just see if I can get more about the kids... partly because of the circumstances, because they were usually either in their room when I was there or I was high myself.

KATE. Didn't you have to, like, take them on outings?

ANN. No, no, I didn't. I only really started out as a babysitter but I became more of a participant in the great experiment... [*Pause.*] So I didn't have a lot of contact with the kids, they really weren't around a lot. You really had the sense that they had been hit over the head or something.

LIZ. Well, in this book Jackie talks about taking the pills he musta been eleven or twelve... taking pills randomly ...

ANN. They were just younger then, I'll have to figure out how old they really were...

PEYTON. It was '61, he musta been twelve.

ANN. [*Incredulous*] Jackie was twelve?

PEYTON. I'm pretty sure...

LIZ. According to the book I thought he was born in 1950.

ANN. Didn't seem like he was that old. Maybe he was just small.

NANCY. Hm, he's one year older than me....

ANN. Anyway it didn't seem like that was happening then ...

PEYTON. You were aware that they were taking drugs?

ANN. I wasn't aware of it anyway... Far be it from me to say it wasn't happening... Maybe that's why they were so withdrawn.

PEYTON. Ya...

KATE. This is a rude question, but how old are you?

ANN. Forty-five.

NANCY. God, you look like you're thirty-five…

PEYTON. See what drugs and alcohol will do for you? Let's go have a drink. [*Lots of talking.*]

ANN. Forty-five… If I weren't forty-five, I would not have been in Cambridge in 1961. That's all I can tell you… That's the only consolation.

LIZ. I was almost in Cambridge in 1962. I got an apartment and everything.

RON. That was the year you took off?

PEYTON. Did you just go down south?

RON. That's when they were not going to fund you for not going to school?

PEYTON. What kind of music did everybody listen to?

ANN. I don't remember anybody listening to any music… This is before music…

MICHAEL. [*Garbled*]—a little Brahms?

ANN. I don't remember any Brahms at all… I don't remember any music.

RON. What was it like after you distributed the drugs? What went on in the room? Would there be a lot of talk?

ANN. There would be a lot of talk and a lot of silence, I guess, and the talk would be about what people were…

RON. Thinking about?

ANN. Thinking about and feeling…

LIZ. Here it is, "they talked about Hindu symbolism, the Euclidean mysteries, Tantric cults—"

ANN. I don't remember that…

LIZ. —"and the ancient secrets of Tibet."

ANN. I don't remember any of that.

PEYTON. But it was clinically monitored?

ANN. Mostly it wasn't and the point is it became increasingly less and less clinical...

PEYTON. But at one point you did do it that way though, didn't you?

ANN. In the beginning he did it that way with a lot of his people that were taking it... In his house he was a little more casual and it became much looser, as I said, and eventually... he gave us stuff and we took it home [we had to con a little, say we were going to experiment creatively]. Oh, you know, we'd just come over and pick up a bottle... of fifty of 'em or whatever... I mean, it was very crazy... very irresponsible... I guess I didn't look at it that way at the time. [*Laughter.*]

NANCY. Did you take a lot of it? In 1961... how many times a week?

ANN. Oh, well, usually once. Just on these weekends, I guess, and when I had it at home... not much more than that though. That's not a lot, is it?

RON. Would you stay in the same room with everyone else... Or would you wander around?

ANN. Well, we would wander around. There was this huge house and it had this whole upstairs with all these bedrooms and then it had a den, and then this room with a fireplace, and then a dining room and this big kitchen and then there was outside... There was a lot of wandering around.

PEYTON. Was there, uh, sexual stuff?

ANN. Not while I was there, and it didn't feel like there would be. It was a very puritanical kind of atmosphere. I mean, Tim seemed very kind of tight-assed. And Alice... There was something about them as a couple.

PEYTON. Who was Alice?

ANN. It's just the name I made up for the Japanese woman... It probably wasn't... [*Laughter.*]

WILLY. I like it.

LIZ. That's my middle name... Here it's got a mention of Peter Orlovsky.

ANN. Now she's going to contradict everything that I've said.

LIZ. Do you remember much about Orlovsky being there?

ANN. Well... He was there a lot... I just mostly remember him as he was then...which was sort of mind-bogglingly gorgeous.

LIZ. Do you remember his brother?

PEYTON. Who?

LIZ. I just wonder who this guy [*referring to the* Unauthorized History] was...

ANN. ...That's the problem, I just don't remember—who's remembering this person, right?

MICHAEL. Oh, a troglodyte probably made it up.

LIZ. You remember John Bryan... Was he there?

KATE. In San Francisco...

ANN. He must not have been tripping... He remembers all this stuff.

LIZ. I feel like he's the kind of guy who's hiding in the bushes [*Ann titters*] with a full suit on, recording it.

MICHAEL. I've never told you but that's me and I've made it all up.

LIZ. [*Laughing*] That's something you would do.

MICHAEL. Full suit and all...

RON. It was sort of serious business, while you were there?

ANN. It was sort of serious, creative slash spiritual... He tried to get a kind of mix of poets and painters and musicians and academics, things like that... And there was a lot of "oh wow" and

the kind of interactions you would have if you got eight people together and gave them a psychedelic drug and who were used to talking a lot or who were intellectuals… It was sort of intellectual.
MICHAEL. What was Watts like?

[END OF TAPE SIDE A (*from fragment of conversation sounds like some was lost*) BEGINNING OF SIDE B]

MICHAEL. Well, there is this radio station…
KATE. "We could all get killed…
LIZ & KATE. …and we wouldn't even know it!" [*Liz laughs.*]
ANN. I don't remember that weekend, it's funny… people would get into the groups that they came with… like Peter and Allen would go off together, and Alan Watts and his girlfriend would go off together. Arthur Koestler would go to his room. I guess there was a lot of that…
LIZ. All right, I wanna know something and I want the straight dope on this. Were you ever in the sack with this guy?
ANN. With Leary? No, no, not my type, really.
PEYTON. Were you tripping there with your husband?
ANN. Huh?
PEYTON. I asked if you were there with your husband?
WILLY. Ah, here it is: [*mock quote*] "And then Ann and I ambled up [*laughter*] and went into the bedroom…"
ANN. Ahh… He was a liar… He's so dishonest… that's what I was saying…
NANCY. That's what the book implies, he was a liar…
ANN. He was… He was obviously a psychopath in many ways. I mean, he was a classic paranoid…
MICHAEL. Dr. Tim?

ANN. [*Pause.*] Ya, but again, like most paranoids, he turned out to be right... [*Uproar.*] You know, they were all after him.

MICHAEL. You paranoid yourself, Ann?

ANN. I don't know, the thing was that Teary, Teary Lim—

LIZ. Oh, that's a new one!

KATE. Teary Lim. [*Laughs.*] Lim Teary.

ANN. He talked such a big game... I mean about women. Like he was having all this sex... But I knew he wasn't taking the pills so I had a feeling he wasn't really having the sex. But he had this rap and on a certain level it didn't matter, it didn't matter and maybe it doesn't matter. He just seemed very tormented and very defended and as I said like a little king, only he wasn't little. I mean, he was kind of a big man.

RON. Did you say that you had been taking hallucinogenics before?

ANN. No, I had never taken any hallucinogenics...

NANCY. Had you taken any drugs at all? Speed?

ANN. I'd taken a lot of speed.

NANCY. In 1961, huh?

LIZ. Ya, in '61 all the people I knew were only into heroin... I mean, they hadn't heard of LSD or mescaline...

ANN. No, that was all very new. I don't think it was LSD until the Beatles... .

PEYTON. See, I thought it was LSD when I started and then psilocybin was the ultimate thing... That LSD was kind of a comedown.

RON. Well, when was LSD invented in the laboratory?

LIZ. Well, he didn't get it until '61.

ANN. It must have been later. It was right after that time.

LIZ. It was right after 'cause as I said it was psilocybin...

ANN. Yeah, I was there in the very sort of beginning of it all. Maybe that's one reason why I don't have so many sort of vivid memories... The stuff...

LIZ. ...was pretty vivid!

RON. There was a lot of CIA tests with psilocybin in '57–'58 so I know that laboratories were producing psilocybin. I don't know if it was Sandoz or where they got it from. [According to the Burroughs biography *Literary Outlaw*, even Harvard was doing LSD experiments on death and dying in the '50s, but they had to be discontinued when students freaked out.]

ANN. I remember the package, this box, this square box and all this packing stuff, this white packing stuff and all of these vials and vials of pills...

LIZ. Could he just be able to order it as if he was a doctor?

ANN. He had this amazing status, you know... There was that thing about him at that point, that he was special... It was all, like, special, and you were special to be allowed to take it... And there was this somehow unwritten unspoken agreement that nobody was going to get busted and all. But it was always threatening.

PEYTON. But he was legally given it as a...

ANN. ...as a researcher...

RON. A research psychologist.

ANN. Right. He was doing research into creativity. That was his experiment... The experiment was to give artists psilocybin and have them record their responses. And so he had this idea of giving it to thousands and thousands of people, and they all sort of came through his house.

RON. Would you characterize those weekends as good times?

ANN. Yes, I would characterize them as good times.

RON. Why? What was fun about it?

ANN. Well, you know, they were very cosmic.

RON. Would you drink?

NANCY. Ya, that's a good question.

ANN. No, I don't think anyone would eat or drink... Maybe a section of an orange or two...

RON. Then it was not a party.

ANN. No, it was not a party... But it was a party in a way... It just wasn't a wild party. Um, it was sort of a very internal party. I mean, there was all this stuff going on inside everybody's head and all. I think everybody was having a party separately.

PEYTON. What was your husband's relationship with the drugs?

ANN. Well, he was crazy about it... I mean, he couldn't get enough and the first time Tim gave us stuff to take home, um, it was like a Sunday night after we'd spent the weekend, and the next morning I had some early-morning class in Chaucer or something at Harvard, and I come home and Robert is on the floor of the closet, which had a little carpet on it, inside the closet on his knees. And he'd been there all day, he'd taken twenty of them and I'm sure felt that the world was ending. It was a horrible experience and it took a long time for it to go away. [Robert recently informed me that it was I, not he, who once spent hours on the carpet in the closet and it had nothing to do with drugs but rather the launching of Sputnik by the Russians.] I just remembered something about Robert Lowell. He was also in on this at this point. I think he was also interested in doing it but had this very fragile psyche that had already begun to disintegrate. Um, and I think he had a horrible, horrible experience with it, that I didn't experience, but I remember Lowell talking about falling apart and as I said my Robert kept doing it and sort of falling apart. But he couldn't get enough of it. He was really, my, he was my… I was a little afraid of it. I wasn't afraid of speed. But I was a little bit afraid of the tripping.

LIZ. It was packaged very differently for me… I remember the whole thing around it if you were a very good person and clear and you have no problems like what they do with cancer… you don't have to be afraid if you're really good, same thing with LSD.

NANCY. Did you stop for a while?

ANN. I left Cambridge. I came to New York.

LIZ. And "he" left Cambridge maybe a year…

ANN. …I think after the next year, '63… There was someone else there at the time. It was an amazing time. This guy Wasson… Gordon Wasson. He wrote a book called *Soma* and he did all his experiments with real mushrooms.

LIZ. Oh, ya…

ANN. A wonderful book. And my cousin Wendy [Doniger O'Flaherty] was his graduate assistant, so I also knew about him. Maybe he was involved with Tim too. So the thing is it was tremendously exciting. I mean, you asked if it was a party… It was more than a party… It was like a revolution or something. Everybody really thought, I don't know, something was happening at the time—

RON. Something thrilling?

ANN. Something thrilling and something world-shaking. On a certain level everyone believed that if you could give this to everyone it would change the world. It's so hard to get back to that feeling exactly…

LIZ. It was still happening in the late '60s, early '70s… The thing… it had gotten more religious when I came in contact with it… was with religious cults.

ANN. Well, I was thinking about this and 'specially thinking about Watts and the only thing I remember about Watts is all these people being very academic about it... How much Buddhism there was in it from the very beginning and how much that must have influenced what everybody thought they were feeling... It was sort of a chicken-and-egg thing... So I don't know if I can dredge up, try to see if more stuff floats up.

LIZ. Um, this is plenty. But if you do, let us know.

ANN. I will, I will. I'm just going to try to finish this little piece and I'll send it to you.

LIZ. Great, terrific, I have no idea where we are going with it. All I remember is one of my favorite things about whether you were more creative [*soft laugh*] under acid than you were when you were without it... and all of the painters... there was that whole genre...

ANN. Well, that all just comes right out of Tim, because that was Tim's whole idea.

MICHAEL. Well, if this isn't a superfluous question... when did acid hit NY, the Lower East Side, in... or whatever the hell it was?

LIZ. Mid-'60s... '64, '65.

MICHAEL. And where did it come from? Did they make it here?

PEYTON. California... What was this... Owsley... [*Everybody talks.*]

LIZ. Ya... remember that... Sunshine... and everybody's name was Sunshine and every shop was named Sunshine...

ANN. Ya and one year I remember I had Christmas Sunshine... It was red and green.

LIZ. Then there was something special... Spalding would remember.

ANN. Then there was Windowpane which was very beautiful acid. A lot of acid had a lot of speed in it... I think, after a certain point... I used to take it when I was crashing from speed. [*Laughter.*]

KATE. [*Incredulous*] You used to take acid when you were crashing from speed?

February 1984
33 Wooster Street, NYC

I

My mother has three sisters: Rodie, Ruthie, and Berdie. And two brothers: Leo and Nate. I have lots of cousins. Seventeen first cousins to be exact, until recently.

Now I have sixteen.

Two of the sisters, my Aunt Rodie and Aunt Ruthie, and my mother's oldest brother, my Uncle Leo, live out here in California where I'm visiting with my mother as we have every summer since my father died. Ruthie and Rodie live in the Valley—as in Valley Girl—in beautiful Burbank, and Leo lives in Westwood, which is part of LA, where UCLA is.

Today, my Aunt Berdie, the oldest sister, is flying in from Kansas City where she has lived for thirty-five years, so my Uncle Gus is driving me, my mother, Aunt Rodie, and Aunt Ruthie to LA International Airport to pick up Berdie and then all go into Westwood to have lunch with Uncle Leo and his new wife Cherie. Not that new, actually. It was almost a year, then, since their August wedding, which was shortly after Leo's eighty-second birthday.

Leo, author of such Hollywood hits as "Thanks for the Memory," and such Broadway tunes as "Hallelujah!" and "Diamonds Are a Girl's Best Friend," is the oldest brother, more like a father to the "girls," as he calls them, though by now their ages range from sixty to eighty plus.

Leo thought "pictures," as he calls them, too tacky for his baby sister Ruthie, so Dorothy Lamour got the part, got to wear the sarong. He thought pictures were too lowbrow for his brother, my Uncle Nate, who was offered a studio job when he was living in Hollywood so he could study with the composer Schoenberg who was teaching at UCLA at the time, so he sent him back East with a lifetime stipend to sit in his hotel room and compose... and decompose.

Nate is the only one of the brothers and sisters who is absent today once Berdie's plane gets in. No doubt, he's in his hotel room playing with his new organ. My cousin Gary, Ruthie and Gus's son, got it for him the time before last he came East. Gary is a musician too and it was sweet of him to get Nate this wonderful Wurlitzer as a present. Only something happened to the switch and Nate couldn't use it. When Gary came to New York with Lauren I asked Gary about it.

Can't you do something about Nate's organ, I asked him at the wedding party, the eastern division. Gary blushed and looked down at the bulge in Nate's pants.

I think it's his hernia, he mumbled.

No, I laughed, I mean the Wurlitzer.

Uncle Nate has had to live with the burden of being a misunderstood painter and composer who couldn't get his paintings shown or his symphonies played but keeps on doing it to this day in his room at the Gorham which Leo thinks he does him the favor of paying for. I guess no one believes in genius like that anymore but Leo thought Nate was too good for Hollywood.

In Hollywood Leo was known as the "President of the Sweet Fellows Club." Our sweet cat Diamonds is named Diamonds because he was found, or rather he found us, the night I went to see *Lorelei*, a recent update of *Gentlemen Prefer Blondes* which was on Broadway a few years ago. It had some new songs by Comden and Green but they were so bad that they put back most of Leo's lyrics from the original show, like "Diamonds," "A Little Girl from Little Rock," "Bye Bye Baby." "Diamonds" has great lines and funny rhymes throughout, like "stiff back or stiff knees / You stand straight at Tiffany's... / Diamonds are a girl's best friend." I bet you can just hear Marilyn Monroe immortalizing it in the movie, but it was a Broadway show long before it was a movie.

It was one of the few shows Leo did. Broadway was New York and Leo didn't want to live in New York, especially with his wife and child, especially after his son, my cousin Marsh, turned into something of a behavior problem, though one year I remember they did come and Leo sent him to Cherry Lawn, a good school for bad boys. But that didn't last long. And most of the two-to-four hundred songs Leo wrote were for movies. I remember when the movie of *Gentlemen*, as the show was called when it was in rehearsal, came out. By then people were calling them "films." The movie starred Jane Russell and Marilyn Monroe. No one in our family would go to see it because Carol Channing, who played Lorelei Lee, the artificial blond from Little Rock, in the show, and who was Leo's darling, had been passed over by Hollywood—typical!—for the movie in favor of Marilyn Monroe, who made "Diamonds Are a Girl's Best Friend" a classic. Though Sheilah Graham noted that Carol was big enough about it to stand in for Marilyn at some dinner at which Jule Styne the composer was also present. Carol used to call him Uncle Leo too.

As did Margaret Whiting, daughter of one of his main partners, Dick Whiting, at Paramount.

But actually, I read, Marilyn was miserable about the movie too, because it was Jane Russell, not she, who got star treatment by the industry. Certainly, the movie was changed from the play, which was based on a twenties novel, by making the brunette so glamorous. The idea is that the brunette is the plain sensible one, as in "gentlemen prefer blonds but they marry brunettes." But actually that idea is a complete switch from the idea that you get in all nineteenth-century romantic literature, Scott's *Ivanhoe*, even Melville (see *Pierre*), that the blond is the plain Jane, blond = bland, pale, home-hugging Anglo you marry while the dark raving and ravenous beauty the hero is allowed to have a fling with in the forest, a wild ride, is the brunette. Is Eastern, exotic, Semitic, foreign, possibly with a name like Miriam, as in Hawthorne, or Rachel, as in Scott. And, if he can't tear himself away from her to get back to the blond he left behind, the dark one dies.

But by the twenties, in Hollywood, the blond had all the flash and lure. Thanks for the peroxide! Cherie is a blond still, strawberry blond. Fran, Marsh's mother, was a honey blond. Beautiful. Ruthie's hair is reddish blond. Rodie's as red as the day she was born. Even my Uncle Leo goes to the hairdresser once a week to have his gorgeous thick grey hair washed and shaped. Cherie goes then too.

It's some little place up near some little Swiss restaurant Leo calls "the veal deal." He's still rhyming. Cherie has the diamonds now. Cherie made a career out of Leo. When Leo was married to Fran, Cherie was his accountant, I think. Even when he wasn't working on a movie or a show, which he stopped doing, possibly for Marsh, he was making a lot of money from ASCAP royalties.

Come on! Thanks for the Memory! Every time Bob Hope comes on stage, Leo gets a cut. So he needed a good accountant. And I'm sure Cherie was good. So good she has Leo now. More than diamonds to her I'm sure. Before Leo, she worked for Marilyn Monroe, when Marilyn was living on Sutton Place. I think she was in a play. Cherie said she only had one dress and never went out. One night Cherie sent Marilyn's Rolls-Royce over to pick up my mother and father and take them to the theater or something. And before Marilyn, Cherie worked for Burt Lancaster and Harold Hecht. And before that David O. Selznick.

She says she was standing there when Olivier brought his girlfriend Vivian Leigh over and introduced him to Selznick and that's how Selznick found his Scarlett O'Hara. Everyone in the family calls her Cherie, giving it the French pronunciation, though Leo pronounces it like "Sherry." But even after Fran, Leo's second wife and mother of his only son Marshall, did the perfect number of pills to kill herself or did she have a heart attack in her sleep, when they were in New York so no one would know she had a breakdown and a habit—let's hear it for Betty Ford—Cherie and Leo could not marry.

It was just because of my cousin Marsh. Cherie felt that Leo, whose interests she had at heart, was too old to have to deal with a grown son who overdosed, or got arrested or had to leave the country on the orders of his shrink every other year. And the actual reason Cherie would not marry Leo is that Leo insisted on keeping the door of his Westwood apartment open at all times of the day or night in case Marsh was ever in trouble, strung out, without keys or money, and Cherie refused to sleep with the door open. Even after Marsh had supposedly quit for the last time and was clean and about to be married to a nice clean girl, the door remained open. Though he couldn't have been clean for that long because the summer before, the first time we went to California, the actual summer my father died, we were supposed to see Marsh half a dozen times and each time Leo cancelled out for him.

Not actually the first time. The first time we went to California my father and Marshall were both alive. Marsh was nine. I had just finished my freshman year at the University of Michigan. Marsh and Leo and Fran, the beautiful southern belle, were living in style at the Maple Drive address in Beverly Hills. They were right across the street from Louella Parsons, the gossip columnist. Louella always kept her blinds half-down which seemed backward to me.

I remember one time we were sitting around Leo's pool as usual. Leo was screaming at Marsh who was misbehaving as usual. Aunt Fran had a towel wrapped around her Kentucky-thorough-bred hair recently bleached Hollywood blond, beautiful legs crossed. She always looked perfect, always looked dressed up, even in her bathing suit. Maybe it was the diamonds. Always with a drink in her hand but always seemingly perfectly sober. Maybe it was the pills. Marsh was dipping rags—rags! probably Leo's finest imported-Irish-linen handkerchiefs—in kerosene, then attaching the rags to the tips of the new arrows Leo had given him, igniting them and shooting them with the new bow, at the thatched roof of the new bathhouse Leo had just had built, one by one, until he finally succeeded in burning it to the ground, and nothing the Beverly Hills Fire Department did could save it.

So, then, it was the second time we went to California that Marshall was incommunicado for lunch or any other meal. It was at least twenty years after the first time I was there with my parents. My father repudiated, as Faulkner would say, Hollywood and all it stood for—popular culture in general—and so there was no reason to go there while he was alive, and then after he died there was because my mother's family was there, but I remember that the day we drove into Westwood to have lunch with Leo and Marsh, Marsh was not there. Leo said he was sick. Leo and Cherie were not married yet. My father had just died. We sat around in Cherie's apartment which is all light blue, even the water in the toilet bowl.

Then Leo wanted us to go down to his apartment, which was on the floor below Cherie's. He called it his "pad." It had a big grand piano in it and on the piano was the Oscar. He won it for "Thanks for the Memory." It was his third nomination that was the lucky one but I recently found out he had twelve songs up for Oscars between 1929 and 1959 when he quit writing "songs" for "pictures" in the waning days of the Hollywood musical or maybe he quit when Fran died or to spend more time with Marsh, unless that was the year Marsh was conveniently exported with his psychiatrist to Vienna. Anyway, Marsh was somewhere else that day and his absence was a gloomy presence. So we sat around and talked about songwriting.

Uncle Leo's a wonderful story teller. (I always did think there is some kind of tie-up between songwriting and prose, that lyrics like stories are kind of the opposite of poetry.) He told the story of how the censors at Paramount made him change the line in "Thanks for the Memory"—"We went to Niagara but we didn't see the falls" to "That weekend at Niagara when we hardly saw the falls." You gotta admit, Hollywood is good at the fine lines of compromise.

He told the story of when the hit show *Hit the Deck* went to London, Leo decided to fly to London to check out the English version only to find to his dismay huge English headlines about how the show was blasphemous and sacrilegious. How the exchequer threatened to close it after opening night. It turned out that the blasphemy was in the song "Hallelujah!" There was a line about the angel "Gabriel tootin' on his horn." The offending word was "tootin." Too jazzy to refer to an angel that way, I guess, for the stiff upper English. So Leo changed it to "blowin'" and the show ran. When he retold that story at the 92nd Street Y a couple of years later, the younger members of the New York audience laughed at "tootin'" for a different reason, one I'm sure Marshall would have appreciated.

I crossed the room and walked over to the piano with the Oscar on it and I picked it up and got goosebumps. It was so much heavier than I expected. At the time I was writing a lot of songs with Vito and for the first time I thought about inheriting bent, the gene for the lyrical impulse, the rhyme-scheming that runs in my mother's family which I can never share with the family and I was glad to see Leo had censor trouble too, but at least it wasn't his mother. She died young.

Actually, this whole story started out to be about songwriting. First I was gonna talk about how the best lines in a song either don't mean anything at all or were written by someone else: Vito's friend Masterelli's contribution to my song "American Cancer," "the stars are really in your eyes"; Gary Lenhart's "Isn't this my cloud / For a thousand dollars you can be perfect" 'cause he thought the song was about EST. Vito's addition to Dada Mama, "Love is the revolution / unless you're dead," is both—written by someone else and doesn't mean anything!

Then I was gonna tell how songwriting runs in my mother's family. My mother and Leo's father was a poet before he was an insurance salesman and Leo was at first a poet and then because he was at the right time in the right place, a hit songwriter. How I'd definitely inherited Leo's compulsion of corny puns, clever titles, funny rhymes, off-color double meanings. How I couldn't bring myself to tell Leo about my own efforts at lyric writing, "words for songs" as he'd call them, because I was afraid he'd ask me to recite them in front of my mother. How families have to keep certain things official secrets and have secret taboo subjects which was all I ever wrote about: sex, drugs, rock 'n' roll, money, pop, death, deviance, dalliance, and even divorce, though Leo had three wives, Aunt Ruthie, her son Gary, my mother my father and me, two spouses, and Markie Ruthie's other son, married six times.

Uncle Nate and Jessie never married, one of the many things I admire them for. When I came back from LA, Jessie, who had been with Nate, though living separately, for forty years since he picked her up on a bus, couldn't believe I hadn't told Leo I wrote songs and even made a single but I still think I did right in not giving him a copy of "Love Makes You Vicious."

It's hard enough with my mother. Like when she phones and asks what I'm doing and I say I'm working on a song with Vito, just to make conversation, and she asks, just to be supportive, What's it called?

It's called "Why Are All the People I Love Crazy?"

Ann, she says in a put-out tone. I'm hurt.

Oh Mom, I say, in a put-upon tone, it's not about you.

Well, is Vito crazy?

Mom, I say, exasperated, it's just a song.

But she knows better. My father would have died if he'd heard our pop songs. He died anyway. I love him for the way he did: beyond repair and therapy in the only part of his body he had true respect for—the left side of his brain, or what stemmed from it.

It was his theory that people became ill in the part of their body they favored the most not out of some evil fate or 'cause life is just plain cruel. No, he thought it was just that the favored faculty or part gave out first from overuse. So it was no surprise to him when his first wife who was a concert pianist developed Parkinson's disease, which makes the hands tremble out of control.

So it was no surprise to me when his stroke left my father aphasic—that is, his speech, reading, writing, comprehension, even, to my bewilderment at first, his listening (e.g., to music) were fucked up. But not his grammar and syntax. This was disturbing but not surprising. According to Noam Chomsky's theories about transformational grammar and deep syntax, we are born with the deep structures of language and the ability to transform them—say to change a statement to a question, or a negative statement, or a passive voice—deep in our genes where they are safe from the ravages of wear and tear or "cerebral accident," as the doctors call a stroke. These deep structures are called "transforms" and we all have them no matter what languages we speak. The four possible sentence transforms are, as noted, statement, question, negative, and passive.

I don't know about the ability to form the passive, though. It may be mutating out. Maybe it's the active that's passé but in any case, a lot of people in my writing class had trouble transforming to the passive. Sue wrote:

Statement: I go to the park.
Negative: I do not go to the park.
Question. Do I go to the park?
Passive: I don't really care if I go to the park.

Angel wrote his passive statement:

Death is a turn-off.

The first words to return after a stroke blasts your brain are nouns. My father's first speech therapist gave him a test:

Celine is a
a) flower.
b) novelist.
c)dog.

Dad got it right. Nothing basic to intelligence is changed, just the input and output get scrambled. The last words to return are what the aphasia specialists, the speech therapists, call the "little words," prepositions, all the words that indicate specifics: time, direction, relation. Because when he asked "Did it happen today?" he might have meant "today" or "tomorrow" or "yesterday." If a woman visitor came, he referred to her as the man's "wife" though he might have meant "wife" or "mother" or "sister" or "daughter." He would often say simply "his woman," which sounded so hip. Once he called his "doctor" his "daughter," but that was understandable. A rhyme as well as a reason. It broke my heart to hear him say "Monday, Tuesday, Threesday." He always knew when he was wrong. He would shake his head miserably. His expression would just kill me. "I can't find it," he would say. "I can't find it." So I was glad when he jumped.

I remember Chomsky's own examples of the four sentences were:

Statement: Jack loves Jill.
Question: Does Jack love Jill?
Negative: Jack does not love Jill.
Passive: Jill is loved by Jack.

I love to see the way the transformations spread the sentences out. I knew a girl named Jill who was loved by Jack. His real name was Ralph. Ralph was a junkie. Like any junkie he was always trying to kick.

We wrote one of our best songs about Ralph, called "Kickin'," about how gorgeously alive he always looked when he was just starting to kick, when all the drug poison was out of his system and just before the withdrawal started to do its own form of dirty work. His eyes would shine darkly, his face would be very white. The best line in the song, like always, was not mine, about how Ralph looked "straighter than he ever looked straight / Higher than he ever looked high." It was a great song but certainly another lyric I would have felt funny showing to my uncle Leo, certainly not now, since my cousin Marsh OD'd the night before his wedding two Januaries ago. There was no funeral, or I guess we would have gone to California twice that year.

But by August of that same year Leo and Cherie could finally get married. There was a wedding and my mother was going, though I was not. I had just been away with her in the South of France for seventeen days. I had a great trip, wrote a great song called "French Customs" entirely (almost) from Berlitz phrases: "I got nothing to declare / I'm just passing through / Give me a room that's in the back / Do these roses come in black," etc. Now there's a lyric I could have shared with the family. A neutral travel song, not even my words, just phrase book. But I had just come home and I didn't want to leave Vito so soon again to go to California for Leo's wedding, though now I'm completely sorry. Cherie had them play her favorite song of Leo's, "If I Should Lose You." He even sang it to her. Considering his advanced age, I'm sure I would have cried.

Leo and Cherie still kept their two apartments in Westwood. Westwood is where they filmed *American Gigolo*, and where UCLA is. Leo loves to be around young people. So just after we picked up Berdie at the airport, Gus drove us into Westwood to have lunch with Leo and Cherie. The freeway from LA International Airport goes past the cemetery where Marsh is buried.

I'm the only one in the family who ever goes, says Aunt Ruthie.

Gus says Leo had left money in his will to have Fran dug up and brought from Kentucky to lie beside Leo and Marsh in the mausoleum when Leo dies but I don't know now that he's married to Cherie.

Let's go, says Berdie enthusiastically. Let's all go.

Oh, you're all so morbid, Rodie says.

Psychologists say it's good to talk about death and dying, says Berdie. She's a social worker in Kansas City, about to retire. Especially if you're afraid of it.

Psychologists, says Rodie, who is scared to death of flying, don't say you have to discuss it the minute you get off the plane!

II

Then my Aunt Berdie retired from social work and became a writer. So in a mad moment I showed her this story, thinking her writing would make us sisters, 'cause she's having family problems with her novella. It's about Fanny and Max, my grandparents, her parents. Uncle Nate doesn't like her portrayal of "mama" as having sex drives. But Berdie said I certainly shouldn't let Leo see this story and should, if I insisted on showing it to my mother, take out the part about being glad Simon jumped. Finally, she suggested I should really make the ending very light, remembering how absolutely hysterical all the girls, as she called me, my mother, Rodie, Ruthie, and herself, got in Uncle Gus's car when Rodie said, about Death, "you don't have to talk about it the minute you get off the plane." She said I should end it with "How we all laughed."

III

And now it's three years later. Even in families, people can change. Rodie now flies. Berdie's writing up a storm. Nate and Jessie are finally living together after forty years because their combined rent at the Gorham was over $1,200. Leo and Cherie's building on Midvale in Westwood went condo. They each bought their apartment. Rodie moved back from Burbank to East Sixty-Third Street. And this summer the whole family, this time including Nate who hadn't seen Leo in twenty years, was together, not in sunny California August but in rainy cold New York June. It seems like a lot of people in LA are coming East from "the Coast," as Leo calls it, like the net around Hollywood is tight now and New York is the more open "town," as Leo would call it. I guess he'd call a "venue" a "room."

Berdie flies into New York at Leo's expense. Nate and Leo are reunited after twenty-five years of coast-to-coast weekly phone calls and monthly checks. The occasion for all this is Leo's having been invited at the ripe age of eighty-seven to do two performances at the 92nd Street Y's Lyrics & Lyricists series in early June. WNEW's DJs Bob Jones and Jonathan Schwartz, performing with his father Arthur Schwartz, songs Schwartz Sr. wrote with Leo. Jonathan has written a novel, I know, and sings at that Upper East Side place Woody Allen plays clarinet: Michael's. And singing were Margaret Whiting, whom Leo used to cuddle as a baby while he and her father, Dick, wrote hits. Also Julius La Rosa.

On my birthday Leo and Cherie took all of us to the Russian Tea Room for lunch. Leo always went to the RTR when he was in town. He seemed disgruntled about the table they gave us partly 'cause he was in a mood from having been stuck in crosstown traffic in a cab on the way from his first rehearsal and was thirty minutes late. We were all nervous. All trying to take our minds off his and hence the family's doubts. After all, it seemed a very long time that Leo had done anything like this, though it turned out he'd been giving interviews and tapings a lot in his last years.

But the next day Leo was grand, to use a word so corny he wouldn't touch it, probably. There was a cocktail reception for him at the Songwriters Hall of Fame, at the heart of Times Square. As you go in, the list of members is carved on the wall. The dead members list is four times as long as the living. When we walked in, Leo was standing on his one good leg, the other up on the piano bench, his pipe in his mouth, as he must have stood decades ago, for decades, writing songs, in this case listening to Arthur Schwartz play their songs on the old studio upright, or was it a grand? We met all these famous songwriters. For weeks afterward all Vito could say was "We met the guy who wrote 'Rudolph, the Red-Nosed Reindeer.'" His name is Johnny Marks. His face was half-paralyzed. Jay Gorney was there with his daughter Karen Lynn. She seemed my contemporary. We talked. She was smashed.

He wrote "Brother, Can You Spare a Dime?" She was John Travolta's girl in *Saturday Night Fever*. Not the fat one. We met

Ann Ronell, the first and still one of the only women to make it in Hollywood as a songwriter. She wrote "Willow Weep for Me" and "Who's Afraid of the Big Bad Wolf?"

The most touching moment was when Harold Arlen was wheeled in. He had just had a stroke. And Leo, who can hardly hear or see, who just had bypass surgery and is on his second pacemaker, took his leg off the piano bench and walked to the door to kiss him and I swear Harold Arlen rose slightly out of his wheelchair to kiss him back. Harold wrote "Over the Rainbow," from *The Wizard of Oz*.

The reception was all very Hollywood. Cherie's hairdresser was there. He did Leo's hair. He even remembered my mother from our last visit. He had just come in from East Hampton, visiting a friend who had just opened an inn called the Hedges. He was very sweet. His name was Jerry Sweet. Cherie was worried that no one was talking to him for a minute.

Go tell Jerry about Vito's music, said Cherie, but I was shy. She was pretty gone, but mostly on happiness.

You must be very happy today, I said.

Suddenly she straightened and looked very straight.

Tossing her head, gingerly, because she had head surgery recently, she said

Leo and I paid dearly for this happiness.

There was a long silence.

I know, I said, but I didn't.

You don't, she said. For twenty long years, we paid.

No, I said, I didn't know that.

At the Y the next night a funny thing happened and the papers picked it up. They introduced Leo's singing of "If I Should Lose You" as the song he sang at his wedding. Then the spotlight went on Cherie. She stood. Applause. Her diamonds blazed. Her eyes glowed. She later told me it was the happiest moment of her life and I do not doubt it. Anyway, then she sat down and the applause died down and Leo, in his wonderful small sure voice full of emotion and humor and fifty years of practice, sang the song he had sung at his wedding.

The *Times* and the *Post* picked it up and repeated it, implying that it had all been years ago. I thought it made a better story to tell everyone that the wedding in question had only happened recently, when Leo was eighty-two, but at my suggestion everyone in the family just glared. Typical!

And "Thanks for the Memory" is still getting Leo in trouble with the censors. It was all very hush-hush, but I ferreted it out through an in-law cousin. It wasn't easy. It was last year. At the time Leo hadn't worked in at least twenty years, what with one thing and another, Fran's death, Marsh's problems, etc. Now suddenly Frank Sinatra wanted Leo to rewrite "Thanks for the Memory" for his new album and TV special forty-five years after the original song was written for a movie. Leo was so uptight about it that no one in the family was supposed to know he was doing it until the record actually came out. Of course, we all knew but we pretended we didn't. It's that way in families. There are all these secrets that everyone knows but no one is supposed to speak about, much less write about. And these show biz types are especially superstitious. The only person Leo told was Ruthie's husband Gus, because Gus was part of the California branch of the family, hence the most immediate, because he is a man and mostly because he is Italian, so he had to know about Sinatra and, of course, Gus told Ruthie, because husbands tell wives and vice versa, and Ruthie told her son Gary, because she tells everyone everything. And, of course, Gary told Flip, because cousins tell cousins and Flip told his wife Bobbie and my cousin Bobbie told me.

But it was like pulling teeth. We all knew Leo had written something in the rewrite of "Thanks for the Memory" that had gotten him in trouble with the record people. We knew Ruthie knew. So I called her and she admitted it was true but she said it was so dirty that Leo hadn't even realized it and she refused to repeat it to me. Flip is my cousin Bobbie's husband. He works for Playboy, Inc. He couldn't get it exact because apparently there was no one of any age or place in the family who could pronounce the obscenity but it was something like "our romance has too much heart and not enough head" or something. Anyway, he changed it before anyone else heard it. I could never figure out where it would have been in the song. Frank sang it on his TV special. It had new words, very California, like "Thanks for the memory / of how we used to jog, / even in a fog, / that barbecue in Malibu / away from all the smog," etc. And the line that originally caused trouble—"That weekend at Niagara when we hardly saw the falls"—was changed again, though Leo tried to keep its original risqué flavor by making it, somewhat mysteriously, "We had a pad in London / but we didn't stop for tea," which was supposed to be a dirty joke but nobody outside the family gets it but we girls, how we all laughed!

IV

Of all the songs that Leo wrote, his favorite was "June in January" and it was seventy degrees even at 7:00 p.m. when we arrived at LA International Airport on New Year's night. Though we purposely didn't tell anyone when we were coming in so they wouldn't have to meet us, my mother's (and Leo's) youngest sister Ruthie and her husband Gus and Cherie, Leo's wife, were all waiting and understandably upset when our plane was three hours late, especially since Cherie had a 7:30 reservation at the Velvet Turtle, one of Leo's favorite Beverly Hills restaurants of late.

The reason we were so late is that our plane couldn't take off in New York because Chicago, where we had to change, was snowed in under twelve inches. And since it was January 1, a funny day to fly, going across decorated America, around mountains and trees, hills and lakes, and buildings, there were tiny holiday Christmas lights rimming everything plus all the lights of habitation, so landing in LA at 7:00 p.m. was totally, as they say in the Valley, totally beautiful. If you know how LA looks from the air at night anyway, you can imagine how it looks at Christmas. The sun was just going down but there was still kind of dark light. The air was balmy. There was a warm wind blowing. The palm trees were in black-velvet silhouette, waving and rustling. Palm trees at airports always make me smile, and they did.

Maybe it was all that and the rented car, the restaurants, all that contributed to the feeling that it was a holiday so when at the funeral Jack Leonard got up and sang on this unusually summery day in the middle of winter, January 3, to be exact, "It's June in January / Because I'm in love," they were tears of joy in your eyes, not sorrow, all the while watching Bob Hope, who had just shown up, late, running around the outside of the all-glass chapel at the cemetery where the service was being held at noon at Hillside Memorial Park, trying panel after panel, with a panicked expression on his face, looking frantically for a way in, like a Marcel Marceau pantomime character trying to get out.

Cherie's face, which had been a mask until then, broke into a smile. Hope had shown.

Because there had been a lot of arguing back and forth about whether Bob Hope was going to come. *Variety* announced that the scheduled speakers at the funeral were to be fellow lyricists and friends Hal David, head of ASCAP; Sammy Cahn, head of Songwriters Hall of Fame; Johnny Green; Arthur Hamilton, vice president of the Academy of Motion Picture Arts and Sciences; and, representing the Songwriters Guild, Alan Bergman, David Rose, Donald Kahn, and David Starling. It even mentioned that Jack Leonard was singing "June in January." But Bob Hope's name wasn't mentioned, and its absence was some kind of an affront.

And even though I didn't really expect Hope to be there, it crossed my mind in a fantasy of the funeral I had on the plane, as we were crossing over downtown Denver twinkling between the Rockies below. You can have fantasies about a Hollywood funeral. Try to picture what who will wear. And you could wonder what stars would show and how many eulogies. And how many flowers, and from whom? It was like a production. And as a production, Bob Hope's presence was essential for it to be a hit. But the night before the funeral we still hadn't heard.

Marshall Robin, who was coordinating the funeral, which was more like a combination memorial service and religious funeral, had called him on Tuesday. Finally his office called back Wednesday afternoon to say that Bob was going to try to rearrange his day and would call back by six. It was five when we got to Cherie's Westwood condo for drinks before dinner. We had spent the day at Robinson's. My mother bought pantyhose, Berdie got her hair done, I bought a can of mousse, and we had lunch, all at the department store, which is down Wilshire in

Beverly Hills, right across from the Beverly Hilton. The water in the fountain at the Hilton is blue, just like the water in Cherie's toilet bowl.

I'm waiting to hear from Bob, she said when we walked in. She glared.

The phone rang.

Maybe it's Bob.

The room was hushed. You could feel a hush on the other end. I guess partly 'cause Hope is just a big big star, like Sinatra (actually Frank did call, but was in New York, or Anaheim, or some other town and couldn't make it, though he and Leo had just recently worked together on the rewrite of "Thanks for the Memory" for his TV special) and also since the most famous thing Leo had done was written Bob's signature song, you'd have to say it would be poetic justice. And every time the phone rang everybody jumped, and it was never Bob. It was just some other condolence call.

Also having drinks were Marcie, Cherie's daughter, and now my official first cousin since Leo and Cherie's wedding six years ago, to make up for the loss of my cousin Marsh, Leo's only child who died on the eve of his own wedding seven years ago. Actually, the funeral made her seem even more like family. Cherie's brother and his wife from Seattle were there too. Their son used to be in the Turtles and now writes the music for *Care Bears*. Finally, there was the woman who does Marcie's and Cherie's nails. She does an amazing job on their nails. So good in fact that Cherie's nails are a family joke. (Example: I called Cherie that morning, which was, after all, only five mornings after Leo's death. I asked her how she was. Her voice shook. She said she couldn't pull up the covers on Leo's side of the bed which struck me as a strong and touchingly physical correlative for grief but my Uncle Gus said Oh, she probably just didn't want to break a nail.)

The argument as to whether he would or wouldn't broke down along generational lines, it seems. Cherie's brother and wife, Cherie, my mother and aunt all kept the faith. They kept saying, he'll call, he'll call. Marcie, Cherie's daughter, and I and her manicurist doubted that Hope would call back at all. I took the path of the pessimist. In Hollywood, the two paths always present themselves: Hollywood, home of the happy ending, the perfect fulfillment, or the Hollywood of which Dore Schary, one of Leo's oldest and closest friends, spoke when he said in Hollywood, when they shake your hand and look you straight in the eye and say I'm with you all the way down the line, that's when they're about to stab you in the back. The story of the big star not having anything to do with all the little stars who put him in the sky.

I tried to be realistic, knowing he hadn't been particularly friendly with Leo in the past and was everything that Leo was not. Part of my lack of faith in Hope had to do with family gossip about how only a few months before, at some ASCAP dinner, Bob had snubbed Leo though Leo and Cherie were sitting only a few rows ahead of him. After I saw the size of the huge print on the typewriter his funeral speech was typed on (Marshall Robin collected them all and sent them to Cherie who Xeroxed copies for everybody), I developed another theory: he must not have had the right glasses on.

The most tense part was when Marcie called her maid to make sure the wine for the reception, which was to follow the funeral at Marcie's Bel Air home in the hills, had been delivered. It turned out they delivered Inglenook instead of Taylor's. There was some feeling that we should let it go but Cherie was very sure she wanted everything to be as she asked for it, didn't want anyone trying to take advantage of her just because Leo wasn't here anymore. She had been that way the night before at the restaurant, when the *maître d'* tried to give her a bad table. Besides, Cherie is a Chablis connoisseur and she insisted Taylor's was better. So after Marcie got done talking in Spanish to her maid, Cherie had to call the liquor store and be mad at them and get them to change it all without holding up the line.

I said I remembered when Inglenook was first being introduced, they were giving it away free at some inn in Washington, Connecticut and Cherie's brother snapped that Inglenook isn't new. They've been making it in California for a hundred years and it's considered the best wine in the world and then Cherie snapped back at him and said it was garbage.

The phone rang again.

I can't talk, Cherie said, her voice filled with tension. I'm waiting for a call from Bob Hope. Magic words. But at 6:30 we still hadn't heard. With each passing half-hour, Cherie had another glass of wine. Marcie left, the manicurist left, the plant lady came and left at seven. At 7:15 the Mexican maid brought the dry cleaning up and said goodbye. I remembered her from last time. The phone rang one more time. It wasn't Bob again. Cherie has her pride and besides, our reservations at the Swiss Cafe were for seven. We left, without hope.

Cherie was too shaky to drive her huge Cadillac so I was appointed in our beat up rented Pronto. It had this huge rust smear on the driver's door and stood out among all these Rolls, and new Mercedes, being valet parked, though later Cherie insisted I give the guy at the Swiss Cafe ten dollars for parking it. She showed us a shortcut, the back way through old Westwood, and you could see why Leo wanted to live in Westwood, plus UCLA was there and Leo liked to be around young people. Even after his son Marsh died. True Moorish, Spanish, desert palace period architecture. But we were very late and I was driving too fast. Cherie criticized me for hitting all the bumps. Also, she was not used to being in an old car so that made her nervous. She must have missed the padding of the genuine leather interior of her white Sedan de Ville.

That was the real reason she didn't want to drive. She still wasn't that used to the car because it was new. New to her. Actually it was her daughter, Marcie's, car first. Marcie's husband Jerry wanted a certain Jaguar so he gave his Mercedes to his wife Marcie so she gave her Caddy to Cherie only their son Randy had crashed his new boat into his Datsun while hauling it and so Marcy gave Randy Jerry's old Mercedes and got a new green Porsche to match Jerry's new Jaguar and now Cherie was driving Marcie's computerized Sedan de Ville. Everything is automatic. Cherie is a great driver even when she's been drinking wine but the new car, the wine and grief was too much for her.

But it didn't matter that we were late. There was a hush as we walked in. They already knew. That was gratifying to Cherie. The Swiss Cafe on Rodeo Drive had been one of Leo's favorite restaurants. The beautiful patroness, Flora Hug, rushed over, then the piano player, an old friend of Leo's, some of the waiters, kissing, crying, extolling, fussing Cherie and us as they had fussed Leo when he was alive. She gave us Leo's favorite table. We left an empty chair and then everybody ordered the fried cheese appetizer because it was Leo's favorite, though it had been years since he was allowed to eat it. Then Flora joined us in the place we had left for Leo, and the piano player played all of Leo's songs, Cherie felt acknowledged, in the spotlight, for Leo, we all felt it and of course moved with sadness and smiling and by the loveliness of some of the songs. It was a continuous medley: "Louise" which he wrote for Chevalier. "In Love in Vain" which he wrote with Jerome Kern, for *Centennial Summer*, "Prisoner of Love," which Perry Como and later James Brown had monster hits out of, but which Leo originally composed while shaving for Helen Morgan to sing on the Russ Columbo Show, "Blue Hawaii," which he wrote for Bing Crosby, "With Every Breath I Take," "My Ideal," "Easy Living," "Hallelujah," Eddie Cantor's theme "One Hour With You," "Diamonds Are a Girl's Best Friend" from *Gentlemen Prefer Blonds*, "Love in Bloom," Jack Benny's theme song, "For Every Man There's a Woman," from Casbah, "Beyond the Blue Horizon," which he wrote for Jeanette MacDonald, "June in January," and, of course, "Thanks for the Memory."

We all listened for the moment when he'd switch to a new song—he knew them all—and we'd see who would be the first to name the new tune—my uncle Gus, a musician, for years first clarinet in the MGM Studio Orchestra, who'd played the songs, my aunt Ruthie, Leo's baby sister, a former singer with Phil Harris' band who'd sung them all, their son, my cousin Gary, who'd grown up hearing them, as had I because my mother and aunts were all into all of Leo's song's and had grown up hearing them and 'cause we all loved popular music or maybe we all were into songs because of Leo. It seemed like Leo had a lot to do with everything and now Leo was dead. It was just the first time I was to hear Leo's songs quoted, or played, over the next few days. It was hard to take but it was like you wanted to be reminded of him in this way there was such pleasure in it and they were such beautiful songs, beautiful melodies, charming and full of sentiment:

Dick Whiting, Ralph Rainger, Harry Warren, Harold Arlen, John Green, Vincent Youmans, Sigmund Romberg, Jule Stein, Jerome Kern. He even played "If I Should Lose You."

Ruthie cried, I held her hand, and Cherie told us how Marshall Robin wanted to play "If I Should Lose You" at the funeral the next day, but everyone agreed that was too maudlin, especially since it was the song Leo had sung to Cherie at their wedding. I had no idea, though, how beautifully he could sing his songs until I heard him sing it again, a couple of years ago, when Leo came east to do the Lyrics & Lyricists series at the 92nd Street Y. Actually now all the people who appeared in that series with Leo that year have died: Yip Harburg, Ira Gershwin, Harry Warren, Arthur Schwartz (Arthur appeared with his son Jonathan on Leo's program), and now Leo. But the Lyrics & Lyricists performances were a big hit and it was great to see Leo getting back to work after almost thirty years of "retirement." But anyway, you can see why "If I Should Lose You" at the funeral would have been just too much to take. A tearjerker. Not what Leo would have wanted. What Leo would have wanted was why we did everything, including not feeling angry at Cherie for our—the family's—being excluded from the *NY Times* obit, in which Cherie, her daughter, and grandchildren are mentioned but the family, the three sisters and the brother, all held together as a family by Leo, his success, his generosity, his seniority, his charisma, were not. They weren't mentioned in the *LA Times* either though they were in the *Hollywood Reporter* but no one complained and we even tried not to feel angry or hurt because Leo would have thought it petty to feel so.

I guess everyone felt that way and that's why the funeral was such a success. It had a certain lightness and even gaiety that

Cherie was worried about. She told us that someone had said that the funeral was too theatrical but she didn't ever say who. Maybe her own superego.

I tell you one new thing I learned. In Hollywood you don't wear black to funerals unless you're a foreigner, or from New York. Cherie wore some very expensive hand-crocheted pale-lilac two-piece number that had been Leo's favorite dress even though it cost almost $300. I wore an old black print that had little colored birds on it. It didn't hang well and I was wearing these lacy black stockings which I realize now were in poor taste at any funeral, East Coast or West. I must have looked frightening to Cherie, like a wraith, or evil spirit. We all must have, in our dark clothes. The only other people in black were Marcie's son's wife and her mother, who were Japanese.

But the funeral was exceptional. It just was. Everyone kept quoting these funny lines from Leo's songs. Such as:

Venus de Milo was noted for her charms
But strictly between us
You're cuter than Venus
And what's more you've got arms.

Paraphrasing Leo's own words to eulogize him:

He never was a headache
And he never was a bore

I heard the lines of Leo's not quoted much, though perhaps because they were being saved for this magic-tragic moment:

What's good about goodbye?
What's fair about farewell?

Leo was there. As if the songs were not written for love scenes but as poetry for a man's own funeral. Everyone was telling these funny stories and quoting funny lines with the same regularity as the Bible was quoted and funeral prayers were recited. It really put the *fun* back in *funeral*.

I almost expected Bob Hope to sing "Thanks for the Memory." Now that would have been something. 'Cause you don't usually hear him singing it, you just hear the band playing it. It was from *The Big Broadcast of 1938*, Hope's first movie. They did show that segment on Oscar Night this year as part of a spoof on special effects. Bob Hope and Shirley Jones leaning over their cocktails singing "Thanks for the Memory" with some building being blown up behind them. But most people don't really think of the picture when they think of Bob Hope, or even hear him singing it. They think of Bob Hope's countless entrances backed up by innumerable show bands and orchestras playing "Thanks for the Memory." But seeing even that little snatch was wonderful. Hope, the actor. And "Thanks for the Memory" is a truly great song partly because, in fact, it took the place of an entire dramatic scene. Leo used to tell the story of how there was this scene in the picture in which Hope and Shirley Jones meet years after their divorce on an ocean liner and reminisce about their sensible breakup and yet show that they still feel for each other without using the word love. But the scene wasn't working. It was Hope's first picture. He was a young comedian. So director Mitch Leisen ran into Leo and his partner at Paramount, Ralph Rainger, in the Paramount commissary and told them the troubles he was having with the scene and asked if Leo could write words for a song that could express this scene. Leo and Rainger worked for a couple of weeks and came up with the song and the many choruses of conversation necessary to take the place of the scene. The only problem was that everyone they played it for, technicians, actors, other composers who worked for Paramount, even the director, cried when they heard it. Leo was certain it would never work, but it got Leo an Oscar. And Hope his theme song.

At the funeral I thought Hope was great, once he found the door. I remember thinking all the while Jack Leonard was singing "June in January" to Joe Moreno's wonderful piano playing how awful it would be if Hope couldn't find the door and left in disgust especially since he got there too late to have his name announced at the beginning. I guess I didn't have enough faith in him, or in the power of Leo's goodness and greatness, and so Hope's showing up restored it. He waited in the back and went on last, and I thought he made a funny joke when he said "No one works alone in this business. We all stand on the shoulders of giants and Leo was a giant who came along, just when I needed a shoulder to stand on." I thought that was funny.

"I came to Hollywood," Hope continued, "and was handed a song like that for my debut. How lucky can a guy get. 'Thanks for the Memory' won the Academy Award that year and I've had a pretty exciting ride on its coattails... And you know something, the true artist doesn't care. The song is the important thing. His lyrics struck such a positive note, such hopeful themes. The feelings of joy he conveyed will lift hearts for generations to come. And if you don't believe that, just hum the lyrics of 'Beyond the Blue Horizon' a few times. I guarantee you will never need to visit an analyst."

There were loads of flowers. One in particular, a huge musical note made of white roses. Somehow the rumor got started that it was from Frank, but it turned out it wasn't. It's never enough in families. Now that Hope had shown up, they wanted Sinatra too.

After the funeral there was a reception at Cherie's daughter Marcie's house. There was another pianist there who played all of Leo's songs on the white and gold piano. It didn't seem strange to have someone playing this cocktail piano at a funeral reception, though. It seemed natural. So natural that I even asked him to play "A Rainy Night in Rio" which isn't particularly funereal (nor is "June in January") and he even sang it, we all did, my mother and aunts and cousins, struggling to remember the words, everybody chiming in with some new addition, to call Leo's songs to life again. He was wonderful, a kid named Michael Feinstein.

I heard another new Leo story from Michael. I noticed him right away. He was a dark gorgeous youngish man who came in with an oldish woman who was head of Music Education or something at UCLA but it didn't look like he was her student exactly. Anyway, Michael was not only a pianist. He was Ira Gershwin's secretary. When I walked in Michael was standing by the front door telling this story to some people and I came up just at the end when he said something about Leo and Hammerstein and Ira Gershwin and one of them looking at the other and saying "Fuck Kern."

Leo said Fuck Kern? I said. The theme of the whole funeral along with Leo's wit was his gentleness and good nature, never an unkind word and so on, so it seemed unbelievable to me that Leo said Fuck anyone, let alone Fuck Kern, let alone to Ira Gershwin or was it Hammerstein. And so he had to tell me the whole story over again, but I guess it was the emotion of the funeral and the general geographical and emotional displacement and everything but I never quite got the story straight. Something about Jerome Kern and Leo and Oscar Hammerstein and a picture called *Centennial Summer* and how hard it was to work with Kern and someone, and I don't know where Ira Gershwin fit in but the story stuck in my mind and really gave me the idea to write a book about all the great Leo stories.

The next night was our last. It was spent at another of Leo's old haunts, the Hamburger Hamlet in Century City. Cherie's diamonds were quietly sparkling, though we were all sad, remembering how much Leo had liked the fried zucchini. I remember the first time I had fried zucchini it was the night we landed in California the summer my father died. Leo and Cherie met us at the airport and Cherie drove us to a different Hamburger Hamlet, maybe in Westwood, and we had fried zucchini, in slices not strips, with this great apricot dipping sauce. They're called Zircles.

Anyway, I was reading this book on Kern and kind of tickled to find that the one reference to Leo wasn't about his being a nice guy, in fact it was the Fuck Kern story about Leo and Hammerstein and *Centennial Summer* only this time from Kern's point of view, how he got Leo Robin, known in Hollywood as "the Poet," to work with him but Leo's method was so slow and painstaking that Kern couldn't stand working with him, and fired him and replaced him with Hammerstein, after Leo had written three songs. The book noted that Leo complained (what? Leo complained?) that Kern wouldn't treat him like an equal, or ever socialize or anything, just send over his dummy lead sheets for Leo to fill in and Leo didn't like working that way. So it must have been that Leo was complaining about Kern to Ira Gershwin (Leo and Ira loved each other, and so it was Ira Gershwin that Michael Feinstein was referring to who said to Leo, Fuck Kern).

Actually the Fuck Kern story was not the first new Leo story that I wanted to write about. The first story was about his last words, as he lay in his hospital bed. Cherie said at the end he insisted on going to the Motion Picture Country House and Hospital in Calabasas rather than Cedars-Sinai Hospital. Cedars-Sinai is where he had all his pacemakers put in, but when it came time to die he wanted to go where all Old Hollywood people go. I remember years ago his driving us past and saying that's where he wanted to retire, with all the other Hollywood veterans, you could almost say veterans of the twentieth century (Leo was born in 1895 and died in 1985, almost. Actually, he died December 29, 1984).

She told me his last words were "Rodie, I have only one fish," and then he said something about "lumber." And we all tried to figure out what "Rodie, I only have one fish" meant. Guilt. Did the family depend on him too much? At one point he was very rich and he did help out a lot. Did "Rodie, I have only one fish" mean he resented giving so much? He was the oldest. As long as Leo was alive something was alright with the world, Nate always said. And now Leo was dead. And what had he meant by "lumber"? It reminded my aunt of a story about dirt. How when Leo was a little boy one day he had been playing out in the yard and got all dirty and his mother called him into the house and got him all cleaned up and beautifully dressed and all of a sudden Leo started to cry inconsolably. What's the matter, his mother asked. Put the dirt back on my face, Leo sobbed. I want you to put the dirt back on my face! And how the next night, Leo's (and my mother's and Berdie's and Rodie's and Ruthie's and Nate's) father was making a political speech when he was running for something in Cleveland and retold the story only he ended it with "Gentlemen. Do you want to put the dirt back on your face? Then vote for my opponent."

Everyone expected Nate to fall apart but when we went over to his hotel after lunch he was strong and composed. He had good color. He was calm. But quiet. Very quiet. And he didn't want to hear any details, so we didn't tell him about Leo's seemingly meaningless last words about "lumber."

What are you thinking about, Nate, Berdie said tenderly yet skillfully trying to draw him out. Berdie was a social worker, and the oldest sister. She said it quietly so as not to scare him.

I was just remembering Leo, said Nate, a little shakily. When Leo and I were little, Leo and I used to play next door. We lived next door to a lumberyard. We used to play in this lumberyard. And one time it was very windy and the wind swept up this board and it hit Leo in the face and he was bleeding and we had to run home in all this wind and Leo had blood all over his face. And Rodie and Berdie and Irma, the sisters, were remembering that time, around the same time, way back when Leo was a small boy crying his heart out for them to put the dirt back on my face, put the dirt back on my face, and on January 3, at Hillside Memorial Park, in sunny California, they did.

ARMED RESPONSE

(1995)

clink, clink, clink.

In the morning Mira returned and, miraculously, after we slept together, so did some of Aunt Cherrie's strength. She was walking again. That afternoon the three of us, Mira, me, and Aunt Cherrie, sat in the kitchen in the chairs with the pink bows and sorted pills for the week. There were three little bottles—morning noon and night—per day, seven days a week. They were all different. At night Valium and L-tryptophan were added, the only chalky white pills in the group. The L-Tryp were white footballs and the Valiums, also white, were those with the little open heart, then a new thing. The rest were peach, hot pink, aqua, yellow, baby pink, and light blue. It's just like her house, her clothes. Only no black ones, no black pills. She had black jeweled jogging suits.

Clink. Clink. Clink. Into the little glass bottles.

Aunt Cherrie caught every pill mistake. That night, after Mira and Lola had both left together, she decided that the L-tryptophan was poisoning her.

"No no," I said. "You're supposed to have it. You're not supposed to have so much Valium."

Aunt Cherrie seemed to have developed a little Valium habit. Suddenly I wondered if after finally giving up drinking (too much) and smoking after Uncle Leo's death, if the reason she seemed quite at ease the last few years had something to do with her having access to these drugs. Now they were in little bottles and someone was supposed to give them to her at the right time and in the right amount. Mira and I had decided we had to hide the Valium. Not that she didn't know what was going on. She was hardly ever wrong.

"No no," she said, "the L-tryptophan is poisoning me. It gives me fever." (The next year L-tryptophan was pulled off the market because a huge batch had caused thousands of deaths. At first they thought it was "just" a tainted batch, but it wasn't.) But at this point I thought she was trying to manipulate me into giving her extra Valium, which immediately made me manipulative. So I said she couldn't have the Valium unless she took the L-tryp. So she said OK, but when I looked again, the second little bottle contained two long white oval L-tryps and no Valium.

I wasn't worried about sleeping with Aunt Cherrie anymore. It wasn't so bad. It just took some getting used to. I just wasn't the type to sleep with people. I'm an only child. I never slept with my cousins or my best friends that I can remember, like lots of my friends did. Like they still do, when there is only one bed. The only time I slept with girls was when I "slept" with them, and at the time I hadn't done that in a while.

The first time, actually, was pretty eventful. I had never had sex before, but had been masturbating like crazy for years. Grace had presumably had teen sex with boys, but she'd never had an orgasm, so when it happened, I knew what was going on but she didn't. Can you imagine? Not only did she hoot and holler and thrash around a lot, but she made another noise, a noise of shock and disbelief. I think she uttered God's name but you could not say she took it in vain. It was a hymn of praise. I was very pleased it happened since I had a big crush on her and it was nice to please her but now I don't even remember if I came. Can you imagine that?

Anyway, I had not slept with girls, well, except one other time but that was in a car on the street, and there was no sleeping at all and, but, anyway, well, Aunt Cherrie had asked me again that day if I would sleep with her that night. By this time I didn't make an issue of it. Besides, I had no choice. I didn't want to make her beg. She was lonely, cold, old, sick. It was her last wish, or so I thought.

I slipped into bed beside her. This time I got closer to her and then put my hand on her flank. It was bony. The skin was dry and thin, not velvety or silky or satiny or even burlappy. It was like fabric, but from another planet. I moved closer and tried to curl into her like the two spoon thing because she'd said she wanted to cuddle. I tried to put my arm around her and touch her stomach. It was mushy. But she'd always told me how sexy she used to be, and I still thought she was sexy, at least until she got sick. I wondered if love is blind can it also be deaf and dumb. And why not—I couldn't think of the word for having no sense of touch? Dyspheelia? Atoucheremia? Numb. Love is numb? It sounded all right. Musta been the Valium talking. I heard her snoring and flopped over onto my side, facing away but letting my ass touch. Something felt different, though, than the night before. At first I thought it was all in my mind. Then I realized it was the egg crate.

No one who hasn't had to deal with the terminally ill even knows what an egg crate is. If there are any of you out there, I'll explain. An eggcrate is a piece of blue foam, what used to be called rubber but I guess now is polyurethane or is that what used to be varnish? Anyway it's a mat about two inches thick at its highest places but its texture on one side is smooth and on the egg crate side it's millions of little hills and valleys, just like an egg carton, and you slip it under the sheet of a bedridden person who is so sick or so downed-out on morphine or both that they can't move in bed and the eggcrate prevents them from getting bed sores. I know about this because my mother died at home of what was originally lung cancer—she'd stopped smoking thirty years before—but the cancer metastasized and went all over. She stopped eating and slowly starved to death. Somewhere in the last week she went on to morphine and was even quieter in bed and so the visiting nurse ordered an egg crate and we slipped it under the sheet of her hospital bed which the hospice program had provided so she could rest in peace until she really rested in peace. The hospice program was wonderful. One day they sent a string quartet over from Juilliard to play outside my mother's bedroom. That was also the day they started the morphine so I don't know how much of the Mozart she got, but she was smiling and my Aunt Bertie was crying so it was OK. The next day, day two on the morphine, they sent the social worker. Now I happen to know that the social workers in the hospice program are supposed to sit on your bed and discuss with you your feelings about dying. "Prepare you." She was disappointed that my mother was so out of it that this conversation could not take place. I was secretly delighted. I knew my mother. I loved my mother. It wasn't that my mom didn't want to deal with it but she sure as shit would not have wanted to talk about it, like she rarely talked about sex or money. It wasn't done. The idea is that if you talk about it, you can let go more easily and help the dying process, but my mother was a tough egg and she wasn't going to let go a moment before she had to. I did everything I could to make her death easier. I even fought off the wrath of her friends and relations who objected to my mother's decision not to have any treatment for what she knew was her own personal terminal cancer rather than dying bald and retching from chemo, which I respected, and her doctor recommended, but everyone else thought I was conspiring to commit matricide. Well, only if you spell it "mattress side." Because that I did commit.

It's funny the way it happened. My mother could not ask me directly to come and see her every day after she was diagnosed. But she told me a story about how when her mother was dying of cancer, she, my mother, then a young newlywed living in Westchester, would come in every day to be with her mother and that was my mother's way of telling me what to do. But the social worker came in and talked to me and my aunt and we cried. That was good. The best part was she told me what to do and what to expect when the big moment came and that was a big help. She said that when your mother dies you will have to call someone, her doctor, so he can come over and sign a death certificate. Otherwise the funeral home will not be allowed to take the body out of her apartment and she'll have to lie there forever. But she told us if you know someone has less than a week to live you can call the funeral home and make all the arrangements and they will call the doctor and send over the bagmen and I wouldn't have to worry about any of it. I remember that week. After school on Wednesday I called and she was still alive but breathing very shallowly. She was suddenly very active, moaning and making funny gestures with her arms, her hands in fists, pounding them on the bed. The nurse had told me that just before she went under she told her there were three men who came to sit on her bed and said that she didn't have enough money but by evening she wasn't seeing anything, there or not. I almost spent the night there, thinking it might happen, but I was afraid. I went home, leaving my Aunt and the hospice nurse in terror. The nurse was new, and she'd never seen anyone through to the end before either. The next morning I came up again. I got there around lunchtime. I could tell the nurse had not had much sleep. They'd brought a cot into my mother's room so there could be someone beside her in the night. I told the nurse to go out to lunch and I would watch her. My mother was "sleeping" and taking very shallow breaths and letting them out slowly. I sat for a long while and watched her. The room was quiet. Then I lay down on the bed next to her. We were quite close. The room was beginning to feel very full, full of her breathing, full of my feeling. I lay there beside her thinking I had never just held her or told her how much I loved her but now it seemed OK, as if my position communicated enough even though she was in no position to read me. I wanted to cry but couldn't. The nurse came back from lunch. I got up and went out and sat with my aunt. The nurse called us in and we watched as her jaw opened and shut, her fists opened and shut, and then slowed down, and then rattled and stopped.

Well, I made the call to the funeral home and set things in motion. Still I had to wait hours for the doctor but then men came with this long black-plastic zipper bag and zipped her up and took her. I went back into the bedroom and sat by the bed. Then I stripped the bed. Then I stopped dead and gasped. The egg crate was completely imprinted with her shape. I was struck dumb.

Then overcome. I fell onto my knees on the carpet and I put my head down into it, buried it in this print of my mother and vowed to keep it forever. Then I realized that it did smell, though very faintly, delicately, pleasantly almost, of urine. There was no way anyone I knew and loved was gonna let me take it home and put it on the wall as art. So I rolled the egg crate up and stuffed it down the incinerator, feeling like I was throwing my beloved mother, at long last, away.

Since then, I hadn't seen one, or thought about one, much less sniffed one until that afternoon when Lainie, on the phone, insisted that Aunt Cherrie needed an egg crate and called and had one delivered. Aunt Cherrie had a double queen–size bed. They delivered a single. We called Lainie. Lainie called the hospital-supply place and they came and took it back and brought a bigger one. A super double king–size one, for a dying giant, much too big. By now it was almost five o'clock. Poor Goldilocks. Everyone had decided that the big one would do until morning so Mira made up the bed with the egg crate sticking out about a foot on each side under the sheet before she left. I remember thinking it looked very weird, kind of like droopy cantilevered architecture or big wings. It also occurred to me that it wasn't safe but the bed seemed so big and everyone was so tired of discussing the egg crate that I let it drop.

Crash.

Sometime in the early hours I must have moved closer into the center of the bed and Aunt Cherrie, though desiring it so much, was not really used to sleeping with anyone and must have moved away from me over toward the edge. But it was not the edge of the bed anymore but the too-big eggcrate sticking out over the edge with no mattress under it to support it. She was on extra Valiums too, and she rolled over and off. I woke to hear her poor old skull cracking on the marble bed table. I rushed around to the other side of the bed and tried to lift her dead weight. I could feel the scar from my operation in my abdomen stretching and hurting, could easily imagine everything falling out as I put her back into bed.

Crash.

After Aunt Cherrie fell out of bed the second time, I dragged her to the bathroom, she was incredibly heavy and we didn't quite make it so I had to go back and scrub the white rug with Resolve (the spray) and I started feeling angry at having to clean up her shit as well as carry her dead weight around and sleep with her.

Crash.

The third time was too much for me. I was really afraid my scar would rip. I let her finish sleeping on the floor. In the morning I told Aunt Cherrie my worry and must have expressed some of my resentment. This made Aunt Cherrie have to return to the idea of the night nurse, not for herself but to be good to me. Mira couldn't come back because she had already taken another night job, so we got a new nurse. At Aunt Cherrie's son-in-law Rocky's insistence, we got a male nurse. Rocky assumed that a man would be strong, bulky, and insensitive, like himself. But instead of a moose, the new nurse, Gary, was a more of a spirit, a slender reed, more delicate than either me or Mira, almost as delicate as Aunt Cherrie, but he worked out and wasn't dying—not yet, at least, or at least he didn't know yet. He was twenty-four and gorgeous, his hair long and cruelly curly like some pale Afro from another planet. He was the most beautiful nurse of any sex in the world, a young faun from the other side of the earth.

I held the door open for him, held him with my eyes, held on to every word he spoke as we sat and chatted in the kitchen on the chairs with the pink bows, waiting for Aunt Cherrie to wake up and smell the coffee. We clicked. I am the world's best listener, east or west, avidly surfing the waves of information. And everybody knows Australian waves are perfect tens and he had done things I couldn't believe. At twelve he ran away and joined "—a circus?" I asked—can't help interrupting—

"No."

"—a band of Gypsies?"

"No. I didn't really run away. My mother had left when I was twelve and so my dad said to me one day when I was thirteen, 'I guess you might as well leave too.' He gave me bus money. There I was, a boy on a bus to Adelaide. I ended up backstage at the Olde Kings Music Hall. It was a drag review. I stayed there five years, first putting on makeup and stuff backstage, and then they let me out front. I did Dietrich."

He couldn't believe it when I told him Aunt Cherrie's husband wrote practically all of Dietrich's songs—well, not "Falling in Love Again," and not "The Laziest Gal in Town," but "Hot Voodoo," "What Am I Bid for My Apple," "I Couldn't Be Annoyed."

"My total favorite," said Gary.

"Do it."

"Not without makeup," he said.

"What else?"

"Well, I used to run around the streets of Adelaide in a little yellow tutu and everybody followed me and fell in love with me and nothing bad ever happened to me. I've led a charmed life."

"Musta been the yellow tutu," I said.

He said he got very good with makeup and then he expanded to the body. He did bikini waxes over there, in Adelaide, where male fauns are allowed to give bikini waxes to women. Not in the USA. He had the longest eyelashes I'd ever seen. He gave off the sense that he understood women, maybe not me, but women like Aunt Cherrie. He understood and admired her especially for having her hair and nails done when she was dying.

So when Aunt Cherrie woke up, Gary suggested that she have a bikini wax. She clapped her old hands together and her eyes lit up.

"I've never had a bikini wax," she said, "and I never thought I'd ever have one."

"Well," he said, "you're getting your wish."

I didn't add "your last wish," though I thought it, even though I'd thought her wanting me to sleep with her was going to be her last wish, but I was wrong.

"You don't even have to leave the house," he said. "You don't even have to leave the bed."

"I always thought that calling it a 'bikini' wax was kind of ass-backwards," I chattered, just nervous, I guess.

"Here," he said, ignoring me and handing Aunt Cherrie two pieces of peach Kleenex. "Hold them over yourself." He showed her, one on either side, one in each hand, overlapped in the middle over her crack. He worked and worked. He waxed and waxed. They waited and waited. He was a little nervous but making cheerful conversation. He'd never waxed a dying woman. Then came the time to pull it off. Somehow Aunt Cherrie's cunt hairs fused with the wax in such a way that her dying labia loosened and stuck to the tape and opened up a world to the young Gary Phillips who, though he had seen so much, and thought he had seen everything, had not seen that: eye to eye with an old gal's vagina which opened up as he pulled the wax strips back, like the surface of a distant planet in some galaxy on the nightly news and he was no astronaut. One look at that fleshscape and he bolted.

"What happened?" I said, bumping into him as I came back from the kitchen.

He looked frightened, frantic, panicked.

"What?" I repeated.

"I pulled off the wax, and it"—he gasped, the way Aunt Cherrie did when I told her somebody keyed the Jag—"it all fell out..." and he was gone.

It was the first bikini wax she got, the last he gave.

Aunt Cherrie had this painting by Henry Miller. It had been given by Henry to my Uncle Leo and all the years I visited it lay in the library, on top of various piles of miscellaneous papers. Every time I'd admire it Aunt Cherrie would mention something about wanting to double frame it and then never do anything about it. There was a notepaper clipped on it from Henry Miller saying "Dear Leo, If this one doesn't suit you, let me know and I'll make another." It was signed Henry Miller. The address on the note was c/o Jean Varda, Monterey, California, the date, 1946. It was all so famous, resonant, and exciting to me.

The painting was untitled but it looked either like a nun lying on her side or a landscape. It wasn't great great art, but it was colorful and pretty funny. It had some gold paint and nice watercolor on it and it was by Henry Miller. I had mixed feelings about Henry Miller. He was a famous writer. He was a funny great writer about sex and supposedly an important writer about sex because he challenged the censorship laws and broke them and he was free and dirty… but he was a straight man and wrote about sex like a macho pig so I despised him along with having all my other feelings. I felt the same way about Kerouac though he didn't write about sex so crudely. But similarly he was a macho pig and he was a great writer and fun to read and famous. So on this visit, as Aunt Cherrie lay dying of cancer, I hinted about the painting. I wanted very much for Aunt Cherrie to give it to me. But one morning—maybe my fifth or sixth day there during this ten-day sojourn—I brought it over to the bed and said something about it to her. She looked at it kind of crazily and said "I've been meaning to have this framed for forever."

"I know," I said, glumly, remembering she'd been saying that for years.

"Put it by the door," she gestured, "near my keys, and we'll take it in tomorrow. I want a double frame that is hinged in the middle so we can put the note signed by Henry Miller on one side and the painting on the other."

"That'll be pretty," I said, knowing Aunt Cherrie'd never live to take anything in to be framed again or use her car keys, but also knowing now that I was not going to be the recipient of the Henry Miller painting any more than I'd ever get the Jag, the diamonds, or Uncle Leo's Oscar. I wished I'd never brought it up. I put it by the door with the other things to be done, mail to be mailed, etc. I tried to justify my longing. What would it mean to anyone else? Maybe Aunt Cherrie appreciated Henry Miller. He was of her time. And he had given it to Leo. If I didn't take it, her daughter would get it. But would they? Get it? Lainie and Rocky didn't read Henry Miller. Lainie was always complaining that she didn't have time to get through the Williams Sonoma catalogue. They didn't look at art. I couldn't imagine them framing it and hanging it with all the giant portraits of their kids and animals in the family room. What would it mean to them? It was all about meaning. Why did I feel, then, so mean? I wanted it so bad.

The next day, while Aunt Cherrie was still sleeping, I took it away from the door and put it back in the study where it always was, on top of a pile of papers, to see if Aunt Cherrie would notice. Not that she would venture into her study (where I was sleeping) anymore, but I thought she might notice it was not by the door, now that she had started to come out to look at her mail and check her pill bottles. But despite this increased alertness and mobility, Aunt Cherrie never said "Where's the Henry Miller?" So on my last night, while I was packing, I slipped the watercolor into my suitcase.

No one seemed to notice. The next day, when Aunt Cherrie walked with my help toward the kitchen she started to get a bit wobbly and had to sit down in the chair right beside the door where she'd asked me to put the Henry Miller waiting to be framed. She wheezed a little, then caught her breath. My heart thumped.

"Get the paper, Annie," she said when she'd caught her breath.

Remembering to disarm the alarm, I pulled the heavy wood door open. The *LA Times* lay on the HELLO mat at my feet.

"Read me my horoscope," Aunt Cherrie said.

I opened the *LA Times* and read her her horoscope—(Aunt Cherrie's a Cancer): "Beware of relatives trying to steal your possessions, especially jewelry, works of art, and your microwave." My heart pounded even harder and I ran out of the room.

"Where're you going?"

"Be right back," I whispered. My thoughts rushed: If I go against her horoscope advice, I'll never get home. I'll never see my lover again, my plane will crash. I can't do something this bad. So I dashed back into the study, unpacked my bag, took the Henry Miller painting out and put it back, not near the door, because Aunt Cherrie was sitting right there, but back on the pile where it used to be all those years, and went back to sit with her, feeling virtuous but terribly deprived. I asked if I could take the mystery I was reading from her study.

"Take anything you want," Aunt Cherrie said.

So I went inside and slipped the Henry Miller back in my suitcase and said goodbye.

Once airborne, I was still afraid the plane would crash. I wrote copiously in my journal, looking out the window, feeling grief for Aunt Cherrie, relief for going the other way. But overcome with guilt about stealing the Henry Miller painting, that Aunt Cherrie would notice it was gone and ask about it and then maybe accuse Lola, whom I adored, of stealing it, I had decided that if my plane didn't crash, as soon as I got to back to NY I would call Aunt Cherrie and tell her that somehow it was on this pile of papers I was taking and it got mixed in by mistake and offer to send it back. Maybe this time Aunt Cherrie would say "Oh keep it," but when I got home there was a message on my machine: Aunt Cherrie had died.

LEE & ELAINE

(2002)

I had no more visitors. I knew no one. At night mine was the only light on for miles. "Aren't you scared?" people said.

Bobby told me the first night he was here alone, he took a break from working, walked into the kitchen to fix a vodka, and there was a young Latino boy standing there in just a white tee shirt and tight jeans on a bitter cold night, shivering, wanting to use the phone. Fantasy? I believed him.

Sometimes I missed the city, missed Jack, missed the cats. Sometimes I missed Iris. But he'd said who wants to go to the beach in the winter and when she'd been here, I got no work done at all. After she left, I'd drifted, disturbed, in a fog, sometimes coming out of it and bumping into a wild happiness that lasted a moment, ten minutes, a whole CD, then back to black again.

I tried working on the old book, and made some progress, but the trip to Green River Cemetery was what really got me out of bed each morning. I'd begun thinking how the artist Hannah Wilke had a lot in common with those other women in Green River I was dying to find. Hannah, like Elaine De Kooning and Lee Krasner, was involved with a power artist of another generation. She was always in his shadow, always getting betrayed, screwed, ignored by him. She was with that big, in every way, pop guy, Claes Oldenburg, for years. I imagined maybe she influenced him too, that she was already making those beautiful little sculptures, pieces of shit, or were they cocks, or little cunts, and he might have said to himself, well, if I just make the same kind of thing only instead of little, I'll make them big. And instead of using human body parts and organic material I'll use soft plastics and make giant spoons and telephones, because that'll be easier to get. Maybe Oldenburg even talked Hannah out of making giant vaginas. Who knows. I did hear she was in love with him—maybe partly because he had power and she wanted power. Supposedly she adored him and lived happily, secure and domestic, with him. Then one day she came home. It was probably late afternoon. She had bags of groceries, a bottle of wine, a nice dinner in mind. The locks had been changed. She had no idea. Oldenburg, turned out, got married that morning. To someone else.

For months after she'd put her signature bubblegum vaginas on his mailbox. They were so clean and sweet-looking, even after when she made them out of latex and ceramic. Maybe Hannah chewed all that sweet Bazooka because she was so bitter. She felt that being a woman artist kept her from getting the attention she felt she deserved. And even worse, other women artists, especially ones who used vaginal iconography, somehow ended up being more famous, though Hannah was doing her early cunt pieces while the others were still doing what Hannah called "boy art." She always felt ripped off by them, the others who were less confrontational, less obnoxious, less involved with presenting the personal female. It got her in trouble, left her isolated, unpopular with some women artists who thought Hannah was trying too hard to be glamorous, or even that she was too glamorous. This made it hard for her to be taken seriously as an artist.

Hannah was the first artist I visited in Green River Cemetery, the youngest grave and body. But the minute I saw Hannah, found her there, I started thinking about Elaine and Lee. It was like all my history and attachments to Hannah shifted, and hooked onto Lee and Elaine in a bigger way than I could understand then.

I wondered how Elaine and Lee felt about being married to their big competitive icons. But even more, I wondered how they felt about each other. How this affected their friendship? What was it like being women-artist friends? I assumed they were friends. They were always so peripheral in all the stories about those wild men and wild times, always mentioned as Pollock's wife, de Kooning's wife. Suddenly I wanted to find out about these women. Find them, period.

I turned off the car, got out, and slammed the doors too hard, a thing I do. It woke up the dogs in the house in the back of the cemetery where I parked. I'd wondered who lived there. Was the house connected to the cemetery? Two typical East End Bonac Labs wiggled over. One dog was black, one blond. I petted them before going to see Hannah, where I always went first. I was still not sure what the pull of Green River was but I was here again. Was it, like my trips to LA, the pull of dead stars?

After Hannah I went to visit Elaine. She was my second "discovery," my only other destination. Was it finding her with Iris that made her so intriguing? When I saw a picture of Elaine she reminded me of Hannah, the same delicate-boned pretty face. I still hadn't found Lee Krasner or Jackson Pollock or Frank O'Hara, and I still kept an eye out for Mr. de Kooning even though he wasn't really dead yet. Where is everybody?

Suddenly, I heard a mower in the distance, followed the sound behind me, turned around to see a man mowing the brown grass on the back hill where Hannah was. Is. The Steve Ross part. I shouted for him to stop. The Green River groundskeeper, I liked to think of him as the gravedigger like in *Hamlet*—"Alas poor Yorick I knew him..." He shut off the motor and stood there watching me as I slogged back down the hill. I wondered if he lived in the house with the dogs. It was good to see the man with the mower, alive and not sad. He was smiling. He looked like a man's man so I asked him where Pollock's grave was. In love with Pollock's big drippy paintings ever since I was a kid, I even remembered the titles—"Lavender Mist," "The Deep," "Blue Poles." I couldn't really remember what they looked like but I remembered what they felt like.

You may wonder what a girl from Great Neck was doing falling in love with Willem de Kooning's and Jackson Pollock's paintings at the age of thirteen.

"That's awfully young," Iris had said.

I think I was in love with action painting because there was no action music, no music with a beat and words my mother couldn't get. Can you imagine being a ten-year-old without rock and roll? That is if you didn't count *Slaughter on Tenth Avenue*. I counted it. So much so that when the Poetry Project asked me to read at an event called Epiphany Albums: The Album That Changed My Life that's what popped into my mind, an instinctive, embarrassingly ancient choice. Thinking about it made me feel like dancing. Then it made me feel like crying: a little girl and my father yelling at me because he came into the house when I was playing some music he thought was trash, playing it loud and dancing to it, bumping and grinding to *Slaughter on Tenth Avenue*, and he glared at me and shut off the stereo, it wasn't even a stereo yet, it was a Magnavox blond console, though we did have the first components in our town, but that was a few years later.

"What is that crap?" he growled, like I was shit.

"But Daddy," I said, "it's a ballet. You can dance to it."

"You call that dancing?"

* * *

The gravedigger took off his cap and pointed right up the hill, in between Hannah and Elaine, actually.

"Jackson," he said, his finger still out.

He called him "Jackson." Unbelievable! Like he was an old friend. Very old, I thought. And it wasn't a gravestone. It was a real stone. It was a boulder, a big tan flecked boulder I'd walked right past many times. So big it immediately made you think how much male sweat and testosterone must have gone into getting it there, unless it was already there. I didn't think so. There was a story about it I thought I'd heard. That Jackson used to piss on some boulders behind his house on Springs Fireplace Road. I wondered if this were one of those. But they were supposed to be smaller. Check.

The gravedigger and I walked up the hill to where he'd pointed. The big rock had a brass plate on it with "Jackson Pollock" scrawled on it like he did, though I heard he had a problem with signing his work on the bottoms of his masterpieces. Slate flagstones made a little terrace. The gravedigger told me that before the new part was added Jackson's stone was at the top of the hill and behind was just low woods. I pictured that kind of messy mesh that was so common out in Springs, that made it a winter bird sanctuary. All those vines and berries—protection, wild and tangled—made me think it must have looked like a living Jackson Pollock painting. Or maybe that's what gave him the idea for the drips. So originally Jackson's boulder had sat on top of the hill, looking much bigger, with only the woods descending down behind it. Now that they've been cleared, the new part sloped back and down to the gravel road and the parking spots, making the stone disappear more. Maybe Steve Ross wanted the run-off from Jackson's grave to water his flowers.

Then out of the corner of my eye I saw another stone, a smaller, yellow boulder. It's so odd the way now you see 'em now you don't, how things popped out at you the moment you weren't looking, where you'd been looking forever. This stone too had been invisible before, hiding behind Jackson's, a miniature version of Jackson's, about six feet in front of it. We walked on a few steps and looked down at the brass nameplate with the signature on it, at Jackson's foot or feet? Was it Frank O'Hara? I'd heard that.

No, it wasn't Frank. The smaller boulder placed there belonged, of course, to Lee Krasner. It said "Lee Krasner," in script, too. Then "Lee Krasner Pollock," in type, below. Her plate was like his but scaled down. Way down. On the slate in front there was a bunch of little stones. I looked back at Jackson's. Now I was calling him Jackson. I saw there were mementos on his, too. A paintbrush and other objects. A whiskey bottle. But no little stones. What's with the stones?

"Here's Lee," I said, adopting his style.

"Yep."

But I was excited. Another woman. A friend for Elaine. Maybe I should get Iris to superimpose their gravestones, make them side by side. Isn't "Side by Side" an old song about friendship?

So where was Frank? I felt too embarrassed to ask. But why? Because he was gay? Because the gravedigger might not have heard of him because he's a poet? But that is his job. To know. No. Maybe I wanted to find him myself, like I discovered Elaine. "Thank you," I said to the gravedigger.

He stood there with me a moment longer, then went back to work.

Poor Jackson. I wondered if Ruth whatsername, the pretty girlfriend of Pollock's who wrote that book about her and Jackson, was here. Was she dead? No. She's still alive, living on West Fourteenth Street in Franz Kline's loft. She'd be great to talk to. A friend of mine knew her, wanted to make a movie about Pollock from Ruth's book. Maybe she could introduce me. She was the one who didn't die in the horrendous accident that killed Jackson and her friend somewhere on Springs-Fireplace Road. Ruth's best friend Emily something came along so it wouldn't look bad for Ruth and Jackson to be out on a Saturday night. Emily died. Jackson died.

Ruth was pretty. I'd heard that Jackson used to joke about how ugly Lee was and what it was like being hitched to such an ugly woman. Did he deserve to die? For saying that? Ruth Kligman was her name, the surviving girl, an old woman now, I supposed. I should call her.

Each time I visited Green River, I found another midcentury art-world star: Harold Rosenberg, one of the two critics, along with Clement Greenberg (not here?), who championed the whole big abstract expressionist game. Which one wrote *Tradition of the New*? Who named it "action painting"? Check on that. Harold's stone was huge, covered with some Hebrew which looked scrawled on, like graffiti, like an afterthought. Funny. I never thought of these guys—or girl artists ever—as Jewish.

As I wandered I realized that the signature of the cemetery, I guess because there are so many painters here, was signatures. Flamboyant names familiar from being seen scrawled across the bottom right of so many canvases I'd seen in galleries and museums were carved here in stone. There were a number I'd never heard of but which were scrawled with as much machismo as if they all had carved their big names one last time, though Ad Reinhardt, famous for his square black paintings, had a horizontal white rectangular marble stone with his name carved in print. Simple, beautiful, the white rectangle was completely opposite to the painting he did in life.

One day when I was standing at Elaine's grave, fascinated by this big ugly green blob on her great big heavy stone, I noticed—how could I have missed it—this huge black gleaming monolith, the height of a tall human, with the signature "Stuart Davis" across it. This time I had one of those throwaway cameras with me, and I shot him. It was so buffed there was no way of getting "his" image without getting yours back at you in the frame, like it was your grave too. It gave me chills—and warm feelings too: back when he was still a nobody my Aunt Rita had bought some Stuart Davis paintings in the fifties for $3,000 a piece and hung them in their hallway in Kings Point out on Long Island. They were just the kind of paintings a teenage suburban girl in love with the city would go for. I did. Jaunty, spicy, primary color, tilted, literal, lyrical, flat, with words in them. Bouncy, with a beat, like music. (Last year Stuart Davis had a big retrospective at the Met. Then Rita died. My cousin inherited the Stuart Davis paintings, one of which sold for $350,000 at Parke-Bernet. She bought a house in Truro with it, one designed by a Japanese architect.) When he died he was out of fashion. I was proud to have loved him then while he was still a bargain.

I kept looking. I found Jean Stafford, who was married to A. J. Liebling. They were lying next to each other, now forever, matching stones. Upright, black, matte. Nice print. Only the painters seemed to have script. Still, where was Frank? As my memories stirred about Action Jackson, Frank came alive again for me too. I wanted him. One of the first poets who became an art critic in New York. Was this true? I guessed the Americans were modeling themselves on the Europeans here, the surrealists, Dada, an art-poetry movement. In fact the connection was more explicit: art and real estate. Many of the European surrealist painters, especially Max Ernst and his wife Dorothea Tanning, came to East Hampton too. They were all friends. Someone, maybe Rothko, said the surrealists gave better parties than the abstract expressionists. Perhaps the American action painters inherited some of their misogyny from the French. O'Hara gave the art-poetry thing an American twist, got a curatorial job at the Modern.

Then finally, one dark day, I found him. I literally stumbled onto him. He wasn't really near anyone else famous, he was under a bush. Poor Frank: the picture of him stumbling drunk on the beach in Fire Island, being run over by a dune buggy. Frank's stone was white and flat, lying down flat, like Ad Reinhardt's. He was also carved like Ad, print, no signature, with a beautiful quote from one of his poems. I was as moved as the first day at Hannah's. Maybe it's the words: "Grace to be born and live as variously as possible."

Baby

One of Iris's pictures of Hannah's grave didn't come out right. She needed to reshoot it. She insisted on coming back for a second visit. The next morning, we went to Green River for a little while but by the time we got back to the house, though we were hungry, the kitchen was a mess of dirty dishes from last night and more than that, cemeteries, like I said before, always made me hot.

I nixed the cuffs, though. I liked the stainless steel, the clicking sound of them closing bit by bit, tick tick tick. But I didn't like the looks of the key. It didn't look like a key. It was just a little bent piece of metal and though I tried it on my own wrist a few times and it worked, the thought of being handcuffed to the bedposts in this yellow house scared me, even if the people who owned it edited radical books. I felt a little bit old for this, but we went with the scarves. Iris had a bunch of scarves she'd stolen from an old lady she worked for who, like so many women of her generation, had a huge collection of scarves they never wore anymore. Iris pulled them out one by one like magic, bad magic, cheap magic, coming out of her sleeve, her hat, her mouth.

"Lie down," she said.

"What are you gonna do?"

"I'm gonna tie you up, baby."

Since Iris was my student, her wanting to tie me up was a reversal. Good, I thought, to flip the power. The power switch.

I was so tired of the way things were.

"Don't you want me to?"

I knew, even as Iris picked a blue scarf and a leopard one and waved them up for me to approve, that classroom teaching would never be the same.

"Yes."

"Lie down."

Iris tied my arms and legs to the bedposts. I was still in my jumpsuit, but Iris didn't undress me or say take it off like I thought and hoped she would. It was a one-piece leopard-print sweatshirt-type material. It had snaps. Iris just began to unsnap it. Pop pop pop. I felt so good, tied to the bed, without choice, chosen, legs and arms spread; I hovered above myself, seeing my fantasy of the student's experienced fingers opening the teacher's clothes, unsnapping teacher, spreading her, sliding inside the material, over her breasts, around her shoulders, down to her navel over her belly and down into her bush, which was not as bushy, of course, as it had been when she was a student herself, much to her sorrow. I returned to my body and gazed up at the face on top of me, close, intent, the curly gray hair getting curlier from dampness. I started to thrash.

"Your chest is bright pink, baby. Why are you so red? Are you feeling something?" said Iris, a nasty tone in her voice, a taunting reference to my old Lucky Strike confession that if she ever came out, if we ever had sex, that I wouldn't feel anything.

"Talk to me. Tell me what you want."

She sounded hostile. She was not playing. I wish I'd thought to say, Gag me, baby. There were plenty of extra scarves. But I kept my mouth shut. Frozen again. What was I supposed to do? A moment ago it had felt too good to talk.

"You gotta tell me what you want."

I still didn't get it. I felt like a baby. What was wrong with me? I wasn't much of a talker, never could think of a thing to say unless I had a funny story to tell. My style was so anecdotal. I couldn't think well on my feet, or, evidently, on my back.

"Talk to me."

I tried to think B-movie. "Oh, baby," I said, feeling like a fool. I forced myself by imagining Iris was forcing me.

"It feels good."

"Good what? What feels good, baby?"

"Uh," I was whispering, "to be tied up?"

"What? I can't hear you."

"It feels good to let you."

"Let me what, baby?"

"I don't know…"

"Tell me, baby."

"Explore me."

But funny how when I said it I felt a rush of lust. Iris had been right, as usual. It made a difference. Words. Then my head was rocking from side to side, my body pulling on the scarves, pulling the knots tighter and tighter. I felt so spread. Then suddenly Iris stopped.

"What? Why are you stopping?" I whimpered, could hear a little catch in my own voice between gasps.

Iris didn't answer me. She tugged at the last snap. It wasn't a real snap. It didn't really open. It was welded shut and then I realized that because of where the snaps stopped Iris could not really get a good feel any farther down without undressing me completely, and of course she couldn't get my arms out of my sleeves because they were tied to the bedposts.

It was so ridiculous. I'd assumed that Iris, though a student, would be able to teach me about the really important things I'd missed in twenty years of tame monogamy. I assumed, from how she dressed, from her paintings, her writings, her carriage, and how she talked about herself and her girlfriends that Iris was experienced, had a clear and kinky and interesting sexual agenda. But things were going wrong again.

Like with the massage oil. After Iris left, I'd pulled off the little Henry Moore plastic bottle and tried to scrub the stain off, but it stayed. And why did Iris tie me up without undressing me first? I was beginning to get annoyed, not a sexy feeling.

Iris stood up. She bolted from the room.

"Where are you going?"

"I'll be right back."

Lying there tied to the bed alone was not a turn-on.

"I'm not going anywhere."

I listened to Iris opening and shutting drawers, imagining pots and pans, once neatly stacked, being toppled and strewn.

"What are you looking for?"

"Scissors."

I felt scared. Pleasantly.

"Come back."

Iris opened the last closed cabinet. Was it the one with the bottle with the bit of booze in the bottom?

"Damn. I can't find the scissors," Iris muttered loud enough for me to hear her.

A better fantasy! I thought. Maybe Iris could just rip my clothes off even though the jumpsuit was from Bettina Riedel.

My well felt like it was starting to fill up again with the thought. But Iris returned without scissors, and with a faraway glassy look. She went down to the bottom of the bed and loomed over me, scowling.

"I'm gonna have to untie you."

All the air went out of my balloon. The whole heated scenario deflated, taking my desire with it. This was not it at all. Iris started to untie one of the scarves.

"No, no," I cried, for the first time really expressing feelings.

"No what?"

"Don't untie me. Please." I was almost crying, but not quite. "Don't."

But I couldn't bring myself to tell Iris to rip my clothes right off me and leave me tied up. I tried to say what I wanted, like she'd wanted before, but the words wouldn't come. I was mad she couldn't figure it out.

"No. Don't."

"Yes. I want to put my mouth on you. I can't reach."

The knot was really tight from when I'd strained against the scarves, in an almost frenzy; it seemed like hours ago. Where was that lust now? Iris finally got the knot loose and slipped one arm out of the jumpsuit. At first it wouldn't come but by shifting me into a really awkward and, I was sure, very unflattering position, she wrestled the arm out of the jumpsuit and tried to go down but it still wasn't loose enough so she untied one of the leg scarves, too.

I was feeling something now: disappointment. Nonetheless I tried. I closed my eyes and spread my legs open very wide, trying to pretend they were still tied to the bed. Then I opened my arms wide and grabbed on the bedposts and tried to hang on and pretend I couldn't move. Iris knelt over me and began to move her tongue around. One of my hands was still knotted to the four-poster bed. It felt good to pull against it and then it just felt good period, first there and then all over. I pushed up against Iris, my free hand on back of Iris's neck, then backed off. I breathed into it. I waited, concentrated, stopped concentrating, let go. I felt like I had, at last, without trying, told all my secrets.

Iris was on her knees. Then she rolled over onto the bed. I was all spread out, head to one side, eyes closed. After a while I opened them and looked at her.

"Now you," I said.

"Wait a minute. I want to tie you back up first," Iris said.

First I kicked and then Iris helped pull the jumpsuit from the remaining arm and leg, and left me naked at last. Then she tied me back up. Tight.

"I'll be right back."

Iris came back into the room with her regular Polaroid. It flashed. I got anxious. Iris disappeared again.

"Where are you going?" I said, pretending to be exasperated, but really I was still purring too much to care. I twisted my head and caught a glimpse of Iris hurrying down the hall disappearing into the kitchen. She was fully dressed. I lay there, wondering about it all, half-listening to Elaine, I mean Iris, thrashing about in the other room. It made me laugh. She was so ridiculous sometimes. I wiggled my toes, like a baby. They pushed up against the footboard of the wooden four-poster that was the prize auction item, the pride of Alex's downstairs decorating scheme, her latest, most costly acquisition.

I laughed. Loud enough for Iris to hear.

"What?"

I didn't want Iris to think I was making fun of her for trying to fuck me while I was tied up without undressing me first. She was very sensitive about criticism.

"What are you doing?"

"I'll be right there."

She sounded possessed, but not by lust. Maybe she was looking for the bottle of booze. I'd hid it. She'd never find it. I was pleased. I'd felt. I'd gotten wet. I'd come. I wondered if my happiness had something to do with my corny s/m fantasy not going so smoothly, that there were kinks in the kink that had to be worked out, hitches in the knots that had to be undone by the two of us together. Plus my Bettina Riedel jumpsuit was still in one piece.

"Oops!" Iris said. It sounded like she banged her head on the open cabinet door. Then she dropped a glass.

"Are you all right?" I called. I was beginning to feel something different, helplessness, even panic, as I imagined that the kitchen was now as messed up as the rest of the house. Thank goodness Alex would not be back for months. I'd have plenty of time to clean, maybe even have the floor by the bed resanded. Get a maid. The works.

"Oh no!" Iris croaked. "Oh my God! What's that?"

It sounded like the words got stuck in her throat.

"What's wrong?"

"I don't know."

She was sort of gurgling. I wondered if she'd found the vodka I'd hid.

"What?"

"It's a car," Iris choked.

My pulse rate went up too. Had she been in the process of swallowing too big a swig when she saw something? Someone?

"What kind?"

"I don't know."

"Shit."

"Big. Something in the driveway. It wasn't there the last time I looked."

"What if it's a realtor?"

"Shit."

"They're supposed to call," I said.

"I didn't even see it pull in. I was thinking about you." She sounded slurry, maybe just scared.

"Are you drinking?" I couldn't keep the rage of accusation out of my voice. How had she gotten me into this mess?

"Just a little. I almost dropped the bottle."

She was trying to make a joke, but I had no humor or sympathy. I was furious and scared. I pictured it shattered and vodka and chips of glass falling all over her and the sink and the floor and the room reeking. I wondered how long the car had been sitting there.

Iris raced down the hall to the bedroom where she'd left me tightly retied to the bedposts, yelling.

"It's people. They're getting out. There's someone here," Iris said. She did not sound cool anymore, almost begging, like she needed me to tell her what to do.

"Go see who they are," I commanded, faintly. I already knew what was coming.

Iris raced back out of the room.

"Look out the window and tell me from there. Don't leave the window. Stay near the front door."

"Three people getting out of the car, a silver-haired very butch woman from the driver's side and two very unbutch men getting out of the back seat wearing identical cable-knit cashmeres and loafers."

"Loafers? What kind?"

"Oh, God. I don't know. They're looking at the house."

Iris raced back into the bedroom.

"I told you to stay out there."

"I don't know who they are. She looks like a dyke. Maybe it's just her haircut. Her hair's the color of her car," she shrieked as she disappeared again.

Now I was sure it was the realtor.

"You locked the door?" I called out, unsure.

Iris whirled back down the hall.

"Didn't you?"

Too late. I could hear the front door opening. I felt like I was going into shock. In my mind I saw the haircut woman peeking in, waving "her" key.

"Hellllooo!" she called in a chipper crisp voice. "Are we interrupting something? I'm Sandy Cross, from Pony Realty. I'm showing the house. Mr. and Mrs. Germaine said I could come anytime, I didn't know anyone was here." She was starting to race, having an inkling that it was not a good time, perhaps. Perhaps she'd gotten a look at the debris strewn all over the house and sensed that she was not going to close any deals. Still they'd driven all that way in from the city.

"Aren't you supposed to call or something," said Iris said in a loud voice, trying to match Pony Girl's assertive tone.

I'd explained the drill about showing the house to her one time in the car.

"Well, we tried," said Ms. Pony Express, "but there was no answer."

I remembered we'd unplugged the answering machine when we came back from the cemetery, remembered how it scared me to do it, but I felt brave and excited. But I did not want Jack to call, to hear his sweet voice leaving a recorded message.

I could hear Iris babbling now.

"Well, you see, I mean, my friend, the person who's subletting the house, I'm just visiting, is sick and we just didn't get a chance to clean up and, I mean, maybe you'd better come back..."

I called out. This was my cue, but I wondered if she could hear me. The door was open a fraction which, when I realized it, scared me more.

"Iris..."

"Excuse me," said Iris. I could tell by her voice she was moving away from the front door and coming back to me. Don't leave them alone, I thought. I don't pray. My voice was silent but sharp, picturing the mystery threesome peering into the kitchen, the broken glass still on the floor, the dishes piled in the sink, the drain choked with artichoke leaves.

"Watch the glass," Iris called back over her shoulder as she ran out of the room, down the hall, and slipped back through the crack in the bedroom door. I was flailing as much as the restraints would let me.

"Iris, for God's sake, untie me."

She began to struggle with the knotted scarves. She had tied them really good this time, planning to have a second go at me now that I was naked. The knots held.

We heard the agent calling her. Iris dashed back out, slamming the door. It sounded funny to me. Sometimes it didn't catch. I heard the second click as it unlocked and opened a crack again. At least I could hear her, hear them, coming. How would that help? I heard her run back in to where the woman and the two men were. I could tell they were standing in the middle of the kitchen.

"Is there a dishwasher?"

"No, but why don't you look upstairs first, the upstairs is beautiful, it's just been added, there's a balcony and a skylight." Iris was doing a pretty good job, I thought. I didn't know if I could do better. Still, I was scared, straining to hear, pulling on the scarves. Doesn't old silk tear?

"I'll tidy up," Iris muttered to the woman with the beautiful haircut. I wondered if she got it done out here or in the city. It sounded like Iris was trying to pretend that she and this woman were in cahoots, that she walked in on people whose houses looked like this all the time with clients who just drove three hours from the city.

"Send them upstairs," Iris said.

Good girl, I thought.

The upstairs was the one room we hadn't yet had sex in and so it was still neat.

"Later," said the agent. She liked to be in control too. At least on the job.

"Isn't there this cute downstairs bedroom?" the agent asked. "Come," she said to the men, who hadn't said a word yet. I pictured them glued to the floor, probably a combination of something we'd spilled and their own disgust, not moving anywhere near the stairs where Iris was trying to steer them or in the direction, toward me, that the agent was pushing. They liked to be in control too. It was their money. I was grateful for that.

"It's fabulous. I remember that room from last summer," the agent babbled on.

I could hear her voice getting closer.

"Great for guests. Can we see it?" she said to Iris. "It has the most wonderful four-poster bed," she cooed to the boys.

"No," Iris yelped, then tried to bring her voice down an octave. "I mean, not really, not now, that's where my friend is, she's not well, like I said, that's why it's really not a good time, we didn't even have a chance to straighten up or do the dishes, as you can see. The doctor just left," she improvised. I could see her pushing a strand of hair behind her ear, a habit she had, which would look good now, like she could do a bit of light housekeeping on herself.

"Well, we'll just take a peek. Come."

I heard them start to walk down the hall, heard a shuffle of feet, almost felt the silent struggle as Iris must've stepped out to block the hallway, trying to distract them with the one piece of good art in the house.

"That's a real Sue Coe."

"The bed is to die for," the real estate agent said.

"She might be contagious," Iris shouted. "The doctor said—"

Did they hear a howl from behind the not-quite-closed bedroom door, the four-poster creaking and groaning? I couldn't help myself. The sound slipped out. I was ready to pass out. I heard Iris lurch again, throwing herself in the agent's path, then pulling the door shut and standing against it. I heard it click shut, muffling the hushed sound of leather soles twirling on the shiny hall floors as they turned back, walked, heels clicking away down the hall, and took another look around the bare living room. It had almost no furniture, just a stereo, a chair, a Duraflame log, a TV, and a filthy flokati rug.

"Very Shaker," the realtor said, a last pitch to the men. But they were already out the door.

"Bye," Iris waved.

I pictured the agent, wiggling her fingers, Iris wiggling back. I knew she'd never done that in her whole life.

I heard the car doors. That dead sound really good cars make. Then I heard Iris lock the door. My whole body was already locked up, still tied hand and foot with her silk scarves to the bedposts. It was too late to laugh. I heard her walking back toward the bedroom. First she stood in the doorway. Then she moved down to the foot of the bed where I could see her. Her eyes were glazed. We weren't really looking at each other at all. I was frozen, terrified, sunk. Why did this feel so personal, like I was undesirable? The way the men spun on the heels of their fucking Gucci loafers and waltzed out the door? Like they didn't like the house.

COOKIN' WITH HONEY

(1996)

I bought a plastic tablecloth. I was living in a box. It was cold. Lonely. I had a new apartment. I had a new life. I'd never cooked in either. Until the hot-vodka project. I sat down in the kitchen I'd never spent time in except to hang up my coat and rinse out the cat food cans for recycling to wonder about heat. How hot was enough? Was there such a thing as too hot? Everybody's different. Immigrants from India and Mexico come to America and get depressed. The *New York Times* said the depression was from being used to cayenne in everything back home and then having none here, that it has nothing to do with low US wages.

One of the people who got me through (into?) this difficult period was Mary Dorman and it would be dishonest not to acknowledge her part in this enterprise. Brunch. Bloodies. Cajun bloodies. Great. Many. Mary. The second or third stimulated us to stumble over to the bartender for the recipe. From under the bar he produced a scary-looking bottle, a cross between something on a '50s sci-fi lab shelf, fetus in formaldehyde, and an aquarium after two weeks' vacation with no care person, loaded to the top with brownish-greenish bobbing floating things. Turned out they were jalapeño peppers. A second bottle appeared, the Polish variation: garlic blobs bobbing around, long wavy sprigs like dill and scallions, with peppers and red round things. Though I am Polish, the jalapeño vodka had my name on it, and though I have never given holiday gifts, let alone made them, maybe it was because I was now so alone that when Mary suggested I make jalapeño vodka for everyone for Xmas, I agreed. Everyone? I must have wanted everyone to love me.

My concept was to use green and red peppers (since it was Xmas). I went to the pepper boutique up the block and boned up. Scotch bonnet's the hottest; red is hotter than green, sometimes. But none of the upscale downtown markets had any that night the spirit moved me, and it was too cold and too dark and too late to truck back up to Balducci's, so I ended up with plain ole jalapeños from the all-night Korean on the corner of Bleecker and Sullivan. I'd always liked experimenting, especially with volatile substances and body chemistry, and I didn't know how many to put in and I'm no Einstein. I surmised that the original bottle at the Levee (that Cajun restaurant on First and First that burned down last year—too much vodka?) was stuffed to the brim with peppers because they had to do a new one every night, a quickie, and it was so ugly and I didn't want it to be over that fast. The first time I started with a partial fifth of vodka I already had in my freezer and shoved three jalapeños down into the neck.

They wouldn't fit so I cut them in half and while I was at it I removed the seeds. I thought the seeds contained most of the heat and might float around out of control plus are unattractive when they turn brown (before I had the strainer concept). I dropped the sliced jalapeño back into the Ketel One. I waited overnight and tasted. Not enough. I waited another day and night, testing frequently. I forgot about it the next day. Friday morning I opened the bottle, took a slug, hit the ceiling. When I came down, I was in the dark about what went wrong. Too many peppers or too long? I didn't know. I needed to get the peppers out of that bottle quick. But I couldn't slide them out and when I tried to pour the vodka out the peppers stuck in the neck and blocked it. I couldn't break the bottle. Shards of glass floating around in the vodka would not be festive, though possibly attractive. My original vision of the gift was a bottle of vodka with a pepper floating in it. Now I knew I couldn't do that though I'd heard that I could leave the pepper in if the vodka were kept in the freezer. But then I would have to include an instruction sheet with my gift which seemed pedantic plus what if someone didn't read it, or lost it, or forgot? What if someone got hurt?

So I went to the wine- and beer-making store on Spring and Lafayette for professional materials: two wide-mouthed gallon jars so I could make large quantities and so I could take the peppers out; a funnel and strainer so I could pour it back into the smaller bottles; rubber gloves, which you might have a drawer full of already, and which are a must for cutting up the peppers. I had one horrible night without them. If you don't wear them when cutting up the peppers, and then you rub your eyes or other mucous membrane, you will learn there's such a thing as too hot.

The vodka? Mary thought you could use rotgut, or at any rate the cheap stuff. The pepper will cancel it out. I found that not to be the case. The better the vodka the better the final infusion. Ketel One, Stoli, SKYY (triple distilled, like Ketel One, but made by women, so Gretchen Langheld told me) were my choices. After many long nights of experimentation, I came up with the formula:

JALAPEÑO PEPPER VODKA
Process: Two jalapeños sliced and seeded per fifth of vodka times forty-eight hours. But start testing after thirty-six hours. It may be ready. Depends on the freshness of the pepper, the phase of the moon, the heat of the apartment. (No, you don't have to solarize them, like you do with flavored vinegars. You can do it in the dark.) Friday night to Sunday 3:00 p.m. might be perfect—a nice time to take a sip in any case. Keep notes as to what kind of vodka and the time and date you started the infusion on the lid with magic marker or you'll forget, especially if you've been testing.

VARIATION: GINGER VODKA
Incredibly effective. Delicate with hot foods. Use three-and-a-half-inch chunks of peeled (or maybe not) ginger, maybe just overnight. I only made a few of these so I'm not the expert but you can be. It doesn't take nearly as long. Test it in the morning. A different kind of heat. Keep tasting, I mean testing.

Presentation: At first I had put them back into the original bottles. But I didn't like the labels. And you couldn't see the color in the SKYY bottles. So I got people to give me pretty bottles and bought some more at the wine-supply store. Fifths, for the holidays. I opted for corks. Classier. I got my friend, artist Eric Holswade, drunk on one of the first batches and got him to design me a beautiful label. The label is best applied with a half-inch paintbrush and Liquitex matte medium. You brush it first on the bottle, stick the label on and brush some more over the label, moving it into place while still wet, smoothing out air bubbles with the brush. Stop worrying. It dries clear. Wish I could do that. Then you can write on it, number the editions, the kind of vodka, the date it was finished, or started, year, etc. Since the original impulse for keeping the pepper or ginger in the vodka was for ID purposes, so the bottle would speak its own name so to speak, I settled on using a real pepper or a piece of ginger, dipped in shellac, tied it to string, let it dry, and then wrapped it in green (tan for the ginger) raffia (can you believe I did this?), and wrapped that around the bottle's neck.

PS: If there is any solid food involved in any of your love feasts, but you still can't stand the thought of spirit-free, here's a cranberry salsa that will hit some girl's holiday spot.

TEQUILA CRANBERRY SALSA
2 cups cranberries
juice of a lime or to taste
6 tablespoons honey or to taste
3 tablespoons tequila or to taste
4–5 chopped jalapeño peppers to taste
1/4 cup or so chopped coriander

Freeze cranberries, then partially thaw. They're sweeter that way. Puree in food processor till almost smooth. Add to the rest of the ingredients. Adjust flavor. Cover and refrigerate overnight (or for an hour, or for days). Taste and adjust again.

Even here the question of how many peppers, how much heat, is tricky. It seems that the longer the salsa sits, the milder it becomes, so if you want super heat use more peppers and serve immediately. If you want the smoother blend, a day or two or longer in the fridge mellows it out, to my surprise. I thought it would get hotter, like the vodka. I guess it's the difference between alcohol and food.

I can advise you, but you really have to keep testing. It's basically fail-safe, because if it gets too hot add plain vodka, or more pepper and time if too tame. But the fun is getting it right. It's hard to be sure. You can try it on your friends. Sometimes you can tell by their expression. The first person I asked, Is this too hot? went Holy shit, are you trying to kill me, let me have another sip, shit, not sure, lemme have one more. By the third hit it seemed bearable. OK. Another. Better than OK. Perfect. What changed? It's confusing. About heat. But in time, you get a feel, the feel.

There's one way of being sure about the pepper vodka. It's the no-hands method, kind of tantric, especially good if it's very early in the day—this is also the hue method wherein the pepper and the vodka exchange color, when the perfect time is when the green has moved from the jalapeño, leaving the peppers an indescribable repulsive shade of greenish brownish, to the vodka, now a pale transparent shade of emerald, perfect, occurring nowhere else in nature; it's beautiful, even if nobody loves you. Alchemy? I don't know about you, but I call this cookin'.

ANIMAL SHELTER
(2015)

Can We Go Home Now

In the beginning when everything was very sexual we talked about our fantasies. She thought about having a guy for some of it. She thought about having a gun. I had gone through a lot to get away from guys so I admit that the thought of going back to them, even for a little adventure, was surprising and disconcerting, but wanting to fulfill her every wish I went out to Red Hook and talked to my friend Eric whom Heather liked—she had bought one of his great paintings, *Race Car*—and who had guns. I'll never forget his face—we were driving across the Manhattan Bridge—and his head whipped around with his mouth wide open when I explained our scenario. I thought he was going to drive off the bridge and then we were both very embarrassed but charged and he agreed to give us the gun. He agreed to more than that.

When I got home and met Heather at 103 on Second Avenue she was waiting for me at the bar drinking a martini. "Where were you?" she asked. "I was worried."

"You'll never guess what just happened," I said.

"What?" she asked.

My heart was still pounding a little. I opened the menu and said,

"Let's order some oysters."

They came. I slurped one down and told her what I had just done.

She gave me the same stunned look that Eric had and suddenly I felt like an idiot and had to call him back and tell him to forget the whole gun thing. The whole guy thing. I'm sure he was very relieved, as was I.

"So what's it like being with Heather?" my friend Amy asked. We hadn't seen each other since Fire Island. I can still see her face when I started to describe it to her. We were sitting outside at Benny's Burritos in the East Village having lunch.

"Is she a top?" she asked me.

I was a little taken aback by her candor and didn't know what to say. I remember stammering something about how we were pretty flexible in our roles and kind of traded off. She looked skeptical.

I couldn't keep myself from telling her then about how Heather sometimes went into a complete trance when we were having sex and how I found it to be a big turn-on. I thought she looked shocked and maybe even a little disapproving and suddenly I felt strange about having said anything. It made me feel creepy about the whole thing.

Sometimes it would take days for her to come back to herself. These episodes only happened a few times in the beginning— but not the very beginning. When they started I could never tell until it was too late and by then she would be gone. I'd never seen anything like it before in my life. The first time it happened was at her new apartment on First Avenue and Seventh Street. There was music playing and I could hear voices coming up from the garden below and see the laundry flapping on the line from the apartment across the way. We were on the couch and I had my hand on her leg and she leaned her head back. Then it got very quiet. Too quiet. I didn't know what was happening. She turned her head away and suddenly stared blankly into the distance. She wasn't there. I felt scared and alone. I thought maybe she was having a seizure or that I'd done something wrong. I called her name. At first she didn't answer. I didn't know what to do but in a few minutes she came back to the moment and answered me. I was overcome with relief. It didn't last very long but it took a toll. She got very fragile and started to cry like she'd been through hell and come back. I asked her what was going on and if she was all right. She mumbled, "Don't worry. It has nothing to do with you but I can't talk about it now. I have to go to sleep. I'll tell you in the morning."

In the morning, I tiptoed around trying not to wake her. I was very upset about what had happened. This was a side of Heather I had never seen before and didn't want to see. It almost made me want to run away. I remembered how she once told me about her posttraumatic stress disorder from the abuse, but I had no idea how it affected her whole life. As I started to get dressed, she saw me and motioned me to the bed. I went over and sat down on the edge feeling shy and uncomfortable.

"Are you going somewhere?" she asked.

"I was just going down to the store," I said.

"Not now," she said. "I want to talk about last night."

She explained how her therapist, Meredith, called it a "fugue state" that happens sometimes when something touches off a traumatic memory and a person disassociates from the here and now and goes far away because it's too painful. It made me feel very tender toward her and sad as well as confused and bad. Eventually I could tell when it was about to happen and could stop what we were doing and sometimes catch her before she slipped away.

Once it happened in Las Vegas when we were at the old Stardust Hotel. We thought it would be fun to stay in Sin City for a night or two before and after the Chance Event in Primm, Nevada. But things weren't as fun as we planned. American Airlines lost my luggage, which contained my manuscript from which I had to read the next day. I learned something. Never travel with your manuscript in a bag that's not attached to your body. I was in a complete panic, worried and distracted. We couldn't leave the room until the luggage had been found and delivered and I had no idea how long that would take.

That's why we were watching so much TV

The Stardust was a classic '50s hotel with modern amenities.

Probably out of nervousness Heather started fooling around with the remote. When we saw what our TV options were we decided to order some porn hoping it wouldn't show up on our bill though we suspected it would. We started to have sex and that's when it happened again. There must have been an incident in the porn that triggered something traumatic. The fugue states generally seemed to involve something anal and she wrote in *Notice* about someone sticking a gun up her ass and threatening to pull the trigger.

Fortunately there was a knock at the door. We stopped what we were doing. I turned off the TV and threw on some clothes. Heather pulled up the covers. She was halfway out of it, kind of sleepy and curled up in a ball. I went to the door and peeped out. It was the guy from the front desk. "I've got your luggage!" he said.

I opened the door wider. I was in such conflict. I was overjoyed that it had come but worried about Heather slipping away. "Do you want me to bring it in?" he asked.

"I'll take it," I said. I tipped him, shut the door, and immediately went through my bag and pulled out the story. Heather had fallen asleep as she always did after one of these episodes. I let her rest, lay down next to her, and started to read my story, "Baby," in preparation for the event the next day. I must have fallen asleep too because when we awoke it was dusk. I opened the blinds. The desert stretched far into the distance. We stood at the window side by side and watched the sunset and talked about how we might like to move to the desert.

We went downstairs for dinner and ordered sliders. I had never had them before and the waiter looked at me as if I were crazy when I asked for mine rare. I didn't realize that the food, like the menu, was prefabricated. Heather still wasn't feeling well so we headed for the elevator. I hadn't been in a casino before.

There were slot machines everywhere and I had never heard that maddening continuous sound like Philip Glass gone wrong. The lobby was full of six-foot chorus girls in feathered headdresses swaying around topless on six-inch heels. We were happy for the quiet of our room and went to bed.

We got up early the next morning and drove to the Chance Event, which was held at Whiskey Pete's Casino in Primm, Nevada, and featured Jean Baudrillard, Diane di Prima, and DJ Spooky as headliners. I remember hearing about Baudrillard running around Vegas looking for a gold-lamé jacket so he could look like Elvis for his reading. He had to settle for silver with sequined lapels.

At the end of the event, I bumped into him in the parking lot of the casino. I was a little star-struck. On the last night of the convention, he had done some dark theoretical reading in front of a rock band. He approached me and I thought he was going to say something about my reading, but instead he asked "Ou est l'autobus?" and I pointed, "Ici," and took him there. After leaving Baudrillard at the bus stop, I discovered my favorite Diesel jacket was gone—it was a kind of off-white ribbed heavy-cotton blazer and it was my all-purpose spring and summer outerwear for years. I must have left it on the hood of our rental car and I guess someone stole it. I was heartbroken and Heather spent years running around trying to replace it but for the moment we let it go and decided to explore the desert countryside.

We got into the car and left Whiskey Pete's and drove and drove and then had to stop and wait and wait in the desert heat at a railroad crossing in the middle of nowhere for almost an hour while a train carrying nuclear waste passed endlessly by. Nevada is one of the few states where it's legal to transport it. When the gates finally went up we saw a little run-down shack by the road that looked like a store in an old western. We went in and there were guns all over the wall and two big thuggy-looking cowboys in ten-gallon hats sitting with their feet up, drinking beer, giving us the eye, or maybe the evil homophobic eye, or both, and I imagined for a bit that we would never make it out alive.

Eventually we escaped with a couple of bags of chips and sodas and drove back to Primm for the Chance Event closing party. I remember being in a hot tub with Diane di Prima, an early idol. I kept my bathing suit on.

For me, Heather's fugue state colored the whole event. I had to worry about her and take care of her and keep her from feeling left out when all I wanted to do was focus on my reading.

By the next morning, Heather was more like herself and I felt relieved. We had breakfast early and made the long drive back to Vegas, passing the Hoover Dam, which was spectacular.

The whole trip was such a mix of things but staying at the Stardust was a gas. They sold cinnamon buns the size and shape of women's breasts with so much white icing poured over them that between the size and the amount of cream the whole thing was obscene. They were delicious and I couldn't resist bringing one back to New York City in my suitcase. I kept nibbling on it for weeks till it was impossibly stale.

I know most of what I know about Heather from her writing and don't really know if it was fiction, just as she didn't really know for sure what had happened to her and what was happening sometimes. Like my cat, Buzzer Rower. When he becomes aggressive it's also like he changes from a pussycat to a vicious beast. You can see something shift in his gaze. He turns predatory. The Prozac is helping but he's still part wild. Like Heather. I don't really know what happened to her in her early days or what was done to him either. And there's no way to find out. The two wounded animals in my life.

IF YOU'RE A GIRL

(2023)

Attica! Attica!

It's a medical cliché that surgeons have terrible bedside manners. Well, let me tell you about my surgeon, who is my new crush. She's incredibly sexy, a brilliant storyteller, wise and reassuring, smart and beautiful in every way. How often do you actually want to go to the doctor? Just this Tuesday morning, I had an appointment at the Center for Men's Health of Langone (still wonder about the name) to see her about my increasingly enormous, increasingly worrisome umbilical hernia, and to discuss whether to finally have surgery. "We can fix that" was all she said when I expressed my concerns. I don't know how the subject changed, but we got to chatting about the couple she was treating. They were in their very late seventies. They still had sex daily, mostly nightly, as they always had, but they complained to her that it was taking longer than it used to, and asked if there was something she could do to help them fix the problem. Our first reaction was mutual amazement. Mixed with a bit of amusement. But most of all we were both profoundly impressed. "In their seventies?" I asked again in disbelief. "Their late seventies!" she reiterated. "How do they do that? I'm always so tired at the end of the day. I could never do that! And definitely not every night!" "And is there a surgery for that?" I asked, suggestively. She laughed. That led me to tell her the story of my second abortion, the legal one, when I asked the gynecologist afterward how long I had to wait before having sex.

The first abortion was illegal and I had to fly to Puerto Rico to get it, but the second one was in a respectable New York City hospital. The guy involved behaved beautifully, it was better than any sex I had with him. He was my colleague in the English Department of Baruch College and we'd become friends. Just friends—but it was the early '70s. Seventy-one, to be precise—I only remember because it happened the same time as the Attica Prison Riot.

Governor Nelson Rockefeller, whom we used to like, wouldn't even travel to Attica to see what was going on, let alone to negotiate. He just sent in the army with instructions to shoot, kill, and end the riot. More than thirty inmates, including the brilliant and eloquent Sam Melville, as well as a few guards, were killed. They brought Sam Melville's body in an open coffin to Washington Square Methodist Church, to be laid out in state, and a bunch of us were enlisted to stand guard over the body in case anyone tried to swoop in and kidnap him for revenge. I was given the 3:00 a.m. shift, which worked for me, since I was a speed freak and never slept anyway. Do you remember the scene in *Dog Day Afternoon* where Al Pacino stands on the sidewalk outside the bank he's just robbed, crazed and pumping his fist in the air to taunt the cops, chanting "Attica, Attica!"? Or what about John Travolta in *Saturday Night Fever*, emerging from the bathroom with a towel around his waist and scaring his grandma by joyously chanting "Attica, Attica!"?

Steve, my friend from Baruch College, who was usually gruff, was so sweet during the legal abortion. Unlike the man involved in the first, who was even my actual husband but so freaked out about the whole thing, so scared to come with me to PR, that he claimed we couldn't afford two plane tickets—asshole. Steve came to the hospital with me and waited until the end of the procedure so he could bring me back home to my sixth-floor walkup on Bleecker Street later that day. A real gentleman, he insisted on paying for half.

But back to Dr. Mary Anne: Just as I was leaving, she said "Do you have any questions?" I did have a question. One I'd been rehearsing for days, out of fear and embarrassment. It was actually one of the reasons I went to see her that particular day. I was expecting a visit from a special old friend, a genius former student from decades ago who was coming up to NY. I couldn't help thinking about him—not fantasizing, but just enjoying thinking about his writing and beautiful paintings. We'd recently reconnected after eight years and I couldn't help wondering what would have happened if, after spending a lovely long afternoon together on his fifty-seventh birthday, he had actually come here the following weekend as we'd planned. He was going to stay at my apartment—it was his idea, partly to save money—and what if we'd ended up sharing my big queen bed, which has been empty since Val died in 2020? One of the frequent images of my fantasy repertoire was of him having to climb over me getting into bed so we could take a lovely, chaste, afternoon nap.

"Naps, naps," he'd sweetly texted a few days before, "I love naps!" But before we had our nap, I asked him to slide over me so he could be on the inside (in case I had to get up to pee, which I often did) and he said "Of course"—this is all in the fantasy, by the way, but as he was sliding over, he had to pause, or maybe he didn't exactly have to, but he did pause long enough to be momentarily on top of me and I could feel his weight and I could feel he was—let me remind you again, in my fantasy—hard for a moment when he was on top of me, just passing through, so to speak… So I had to ask Dr. Hopkins my question: "What would happen in this case, considering the size of my enormous hernia, which I sometimes imagine exploding?" "Well," she said, "when you get home, just turn over and lie on your stomach. If it doesn't hurt or feel uncomfortable in any way, it should be fine if someone approximately your weight was to lie on top of you." "Even if I was on my back?" I asked, just to make sure, and she nodded, "Yes."

When I left her office, I wasn't even embarrassed. She didn't seem to think twice about my question, which she must have gotten a million times before. But the whole thing, what with my fantasy and his impending visit, and her answer to my explicit question in her nice, low voice—the whole thing was almost arousing. How often does that happen at the doctor's? Maybe it's because she doesn't wear a white coat, just a green sweater and jeans, her long brown hair tied back in a casual ponytail.

Later that day, he did come to visit and brought a nice chilled bottle of expensive Veuve Clicquot champagne, a perfect beverage, especially in the afternoon. We had an amazing conversation—he's brilliant, a genius with language and a great painter, too. We talked about everything under the sun, as we always did. It was beautiful and profound. We got a little giddy from the drink, and discussed his wife of twenty-three-years' out of control drinking, which had gotten to be a terrible problem for him.

I tried to advise him, having had some experience being crazy in love with a mentally ill drunk for years, until she eventually quit drinking, and then finally quit living entirely, after I suggested we take a short "break" for a week.

But somehow even that part of the conversation didn't spoil my pleasure in seeing him. Just before he left, I got my nerve up and asked a question I'd been wanting to ask ever since he'd told me a funny story a few months before about stopping during the last night of his cross-country motorcycle trip. He was dancing with someone in a hotel bar who said, at the end of the night, after he'd invited her up to his room, "You know I'm a boy?" I'd always wanted to ask him what he did with the boy. "That's an awfully personal question," he said, and I nodded. He didn't answer explicitly. Instead, he went off on a meditation about occasionally finding people of any gender attractive, if the mood and time were right. He seemed to enjoy speculating and theorizing about attraction. In the course of talking about desire, he anecdotally mentioned something about not caring if someone had a big cock, that it was not so much anything like that with a boy. So now I knew something I'd occasionally wondered about: Did he call it a "cock" or a "dick"? And then he asked me if I called it a "cock" or a "dick." I said I didn't have much occasion to discuss male anatomy, since I'd switched to girls quite a long while ago.

"I used to call it a 'cock' but lately I seem to like calling it a 'dick.' Like I used to call it a 'cunt,' but now I prefer 'pussy,'" I answered. I'm intrigued by the way the language changes with the times and cultural shifts. Even in novels and especially song lyrics, for more than a decade I've noticed everyone, especially girls, singing about fucking again, or even just using "fuck" for emphasis, like Taylor Swift's "Snow on the Beach"—weird, but fucking beautiful. Not to mention Beyoncé's tribute to the queer community, which features the most obscene back-up vocal: "motherfucker / motherfucker / motherfucker." Dua Lipa can get pretty raunchy all by herself, but teamed up with Megan Thee Stallion has written one of the filthiest lyrics I ever heard, all about their "sweetie pie." My OT (occupational therapist) calls this kind of language "cursing," which seems old-fashioned and wrong. I finally figured out how to get Alexa not to play the "clean version" in place of the "explicit version," which I love because I'm a great believer, in every situation and especially for women, in what my brilliant ex-student calls, in a recent poem, "The glamor of CHOICE."

Crush

The first day I met him his name was still Cathy. He might have thought of himself as Hilary's boyfriend, but I don't know if anybody else did. But what did I know? At this point. I remember the first time, that first day, especially the momentous unforgettable ending, which was when the crush probably started. Crush at first sight you could say, though it sounds completely silly. Everything about it seems silly. There doesn't seem to be a language for it, a way to discuss—let's just call it "crushing seriously." Is there another word for it, the way it happens? It's magical. But cheap magic! How it works!

Partly because it was such an incredible October blue-sky day when we went to Hilary's memorial someplace north of the city, maybe Connecticut. There was a whole line of people waiting for us to get there, to meet us, to meet Val, especially Cathy, I bet. It was like a receiving line at some official function, made even more dramatic and comical by the fact that our entrance was grand in a funny way, because Val and I were both side by side in matching wheelchairs, pushed by two of the few male guests at this event. The only other man was Hilary's brother Andrew, who did most of the burger-flipping.

Luis and Jamie, our boys, our two wheelchair pushers, our attendants (really more like our nurses), were both very hungry but too shy to ask for food because they felt so out of place in this crowd of so many sad gay women. I too felt shy and a little out of it. I didn't know anyone except Val, who went off to mingle the minute we got there. And Cathy, too, probably felt out of it. She didn't really know anyone either, although a few people, like Jan, Hilary's ex, the person who called Val to tell her that Hilary had committed suicide, had probably heard of Cathy as Hilary's girlfriend. Not yet boyfriend? At least not that I knew. Cathy was probably just as relieved as I was that Val never went up to visit Hilary in person, much as Hil entreated. She had flirted often and hard but to no avail. I was deeply touched by Val's exceptionally fierce loyalty. She was a very moral person, a rare trait these days! She didn't want to hurt me or make me any more jealous than I already was, although Val and Hilary hadn't seen each other for nineteen years.

But back to that day, that beautiful, life-changing, blue day.

Val and Hilary broke up almost twenty years before they reconnected. It was a bad, hard, breakup, full of hard feelings and hurt, especially on Val's end. Until Val and I fell so instantly and deeply in love on April 23, 2009, I don't think she'd had real love in her life since Hilary. Everyone used to say so.

And then, late one freezing-cold night at the end of 2019, just before COVID, Val and I were both taken by ambulance to St. Luke's Hospital a few blocks north of our apartment, where we were both diagnosed with RSV. At the time, no one had heard of RSV. The nurse who admitted us let us share a room because we'd asked for it. She'd assumed that we'd just met at the hospital that night—that we'd picked each other up in the waiting room, as if that were a thing, a thing people did to hook up with strangers. We thought it was hilarious and assured her we were practically married. We'd been together for almost ten years. Once they'd determined my RSV was very mild, I was discharged, and Val—although she was already deathly ill—ran out into the frigid night to find me a cab back to the empty apartment. When she returned to the hospital they put her in isolation for ten days, where no one could enter without PPE. We were all terribly worried, scared to death for her.

And so was she. Val was so sick, she genuinely thought she was going to die. So, when she discovered she'd brought an ancient address book at the bottom of her suitcase that had Hilary's old number, she forgot all the wrong things that Hilary had done and called her. Val was calling all of her family and friends, even her old agent, to say goodbye. She must have spoken to Hilary with deep, unresolved anger and love.

When Val recovered, they continued being in touch every day. Once, I was lying in bed next to Val when she and Hilary were talking, and Cathy came into Hilary's house to fix some plumbing. Cathy could fix everything, except Hilary. Hilary handed Cathy the phone and said "Val, say hello to Cathy," and that was the beginning of a beautiful, deep friendship between Cathy and Val that lasted until Val died.

I waited a little too long to inform Cathy of Val's death (Cathy was still Cathy then) —but when I finally did, and mentioned to her that my roommate Luis was going away for a few days, she immediately arranged to come down and stay with me so I wouldn't be alone, scared, and sad. Val died mysteriously during COVID and so there was no funeral, although Luis and Val's brother Brad went down to the family plot in Maryland, where Brad had arranged for her ashes to be brought. I ordered a huge bunch of red roses from the superexpensive cemetery florist. I asked Luis to leave half the roses on Val's coffin (he took a phone video of them lowering it into the grave, which I watched with fascination and passionate sorrow) and bring the other half of the roses back to me. I still have them, and they still have me. Although dried, they are huge. I never saw such big, fluffy, dead flowers. It seems like a miracle. Or some kind of message from her, or somewhere.

I think Val had a good time that day in Connecticut, if you can say that about a memorial. All those pictures. All those people. Hilary had given Val a spectacular acknowledgement in her one published book—"The immortal (if only!) Val Clarke was the biggest champion I ever had"—and Val was almost as legend to them. Still, that gathering was extremely fraught. So much feeling, so many photographs, spread out across the long, rented tables. *Who's this? Oh, I remember that time. Look how young they look.* In one Polaroid, Val is leaning back into Hilary's arms, deliriously happy and in love.

It was at the memorial where I met Cathy for the first time, just as the afternoon was coming to a close. I was wiped out from having no one to talk to for hours and finally wandered back to where Jamie and Luis were hanging out, on the edge of the crowd, probably wondering when this strange fucking ordeal would finally break up. I think no one except them really wanted it to be over because that would mean that Hilary, who meant so much in so many different ways to so many people, would really be over, gone, finally dead. I took a seat beside where Jamie and Luis were patiently waiting, our wheelchairs at the ready, waiting for Val to tear herself away.

Just as I was catching my breath, another person wandered back and plopped down in the chair across from me, looking weary and beautifully empty. It was Cathy. My eyes must have lit up, my heartbeat quickening. I was instantly, greedily, taken. I must have smiled and she smiled back, shaking her head in despair about everything—Hilary's excruciating death after recently euthanizing her beloved dog Pluto—and in one secretly choreographed second, we both reached our hands across the table. I don't know how it happened or who made the first move, but suddenly our hands were clasped together. I squeezed her hands and looked into her broken eyes. Tears were streaming down her wonderful face while I squeezed and she wept, there were no words, but I could tell it was just what she needed. I must have needed it too. It didn't even last that long—just a few moments I'll remember forever.

Cathy had been living in Massachusetts with Hilary until Hilary finally gave up, stopped trying to live. It just got too hard. Her MS was getting worse, her depression was worse, her bipolar meds weren't working. There was nothing Cathy or anyone could do to help. After having Pluto put down, Hilary put her car in the garage, closed the door, turned on the engine, and waited. The plan worked.

Soon after Hilary's death, Cathy drove to the city and stayed with us—with Val really—for a few days. Later, she wrote she would have turned to stone if it weren't for Val. Hilary brought them immediately, deeply together. During Cathy's visits, we spent most of our time reading Hilary's unpublished stories out loud and talking about where we could place them.

Hil's stories were wonderful, with imagined settings and different kinds of narrators—some were told by married women or handsome men, many of them straight. I admired this fiction, of the kind I could never write, but was never envious for a second. Cathy usually stopped at the corner and picked up wine, of which she drank a lot. These were always good times, enjoyed by the three of us, but then Val died. Cathy complained that I'd waited too long (a week, maybe two) to tell her.

But I was in shock, and Luis was pretty torn up by Val's death. He'd been so involved during her final week, especially the last morning when she passed out in the bathroom, fully dressed, leaning back against the tiled wall. The EMTs tried to bring her back, and even succeeded once or twice, but then eventually they moved her out of the apartment to the hospital, with Luis right behind them. He begged them to let him ride in the ambulance so he could hold her hand, but because of COVID they wouldn't let him. He stood outside the hospital waiting for the doctor to come out and talk to him. When he came back to the apartment where I was waiting in terror, he sobbed, "I don't think she's gonna make it." And so he left—I didn't blame him, he loved her very much—and went down to Maryland to spend a few long weeks with his wife and daughter.

When Cathy found out I was alone, she immediately came to stay, jumping in to fix things, the same way she always had with Hilary. Cathy could fix anything, from broken toilets to broken hearts, and when she came over, she did fix me in a way… the way being that I stopped being overwhelmed with grief for Val and started lusting after Cathy in a very big, terrible way.

I ordered her endless six-packs from the deli and she cooked for me. She made great fish tacos and spent quiet time sitting cross-legged and doing crossword puzzles in the big leather chair across the room while I dozed. I was still in shock. She asked me to read her something I'd written. I remember she liked *If You're a Girl*. She said, shyly, "It sounds just like you." I took that as a high compliment. My only mistake, the only line I crossed, was to read her the sex scene in "Baby," which I thought might turn her on. But after I finished reading all she said was "That made me very uncomfortable," which made me so uncomfortable I shut down too much to ask why. Maybe by that point she was beginning to seriously engage in the change process, changing her name to Cameron and getting T shots at higher and higher doses. This transition was always supervised—she was seeing a therapist and an endocrinologist, planning for top surgery, but nothing further.

But T was the thing that most intrigued me later on, as I got to know Cameron more. He was a great storyteller, and during one of our occasional late-night calls, he told me a story about going to a gay bar outside of Albany, trying desperately to get laid in an attempt to take his mind off the girl he was clearly in love with. The girl had refused to have sex with him, saying "If you were my boyfriend, I couldn't count on you to be my real friend, which I need more." I remembered it clearly, because this was the first time he'd used the word "boyfriend" and it was confusing to me. But he was so desperate to get over to the girl, he went over to three very cute, very young nurses hanging out on the back deck of the bar, and asked them each separately "Do you want to get fucked?" or maybe "Can I fuck you?" Each girl said no and acted very offended, which was upsetting to Cameron. "I mean, come on," he said. "What did they expect? They were in a gay bar, they'd have to expect to get cruised." He sounded upset, and even hornier than before.

I listened hard to this narrative and after we hung up, I was very turned on. I liked his deft use of language, his whole tone of voice, which was sexy and low to begin with, and the T just made it deeper. At this point, I thought we were close. And then I blew it. For the second time. Talking the next night, I couldn't help telling him how much I loved the story. "It was very arousing," I said, instantly feeling I'd used the wrong word—the formal word, instead of saying how it made me so hot I'd gotten myself off to it. Oh well! I keep forgetting I'm an old lady, completely undesirable to anyone of any age or gender. Funny how that is. How that happens, how you forget. God, it's so awful!

But my enduring fascination with Cameron had to do with his history around taking T. I'd had my own flirtation with the male hormone years earlier, which had nothing to do with gender per se, at least not my own, rather the gender of the new people, girls, I was starting to desire. The people I would fuck and love.

I remember sitting with Eileen Myles, my first girl crush, looking out the diner window at the Hudson River near the LGBTQ+ health center Callen-Lorde, and she was telling me about taking T. It was the first time I'd heard anyone call it that. Shortly after, there was a *Times* article about how all the ladies in London were taking testosterone because it helped them work, energized them in a new and profound way. This immediately caught my attention because I was always an energy junkie anyway, an ex–speed freak. And then I found out my oldest and dearest friend had been ordering a testosterone cream from some lab in Wisconsin and dabbing it on her thighs. I can still see her demonstrating the process, which seemed like a gentle and sweet way to do a drug.

It wasn't long before I asked my beloved internist to write me a script for T pills, which I filled at Thompson Chemists, a friendly old-fashioned pharmacy in Little Italy where everybody knows your name. And a lot more.

The first time I refilled it, Anthony, the pharmacist, was down at the other end of the counter and he called out at the top of his voice "Well, how do you like the testosterone?" I wanted the ground to swallow me up. When he came to my end of the counter, I whispered, "*I like it but, Anthony, you know, it just makes me horny and angry! All the time!*" He laughed, and said, again loud and clear, "Well, congratulations, Ms. Rower! Now you know how it feels to be a man!"

But joking aside, I liked it at first. It did what it was supposed to do. I cheated on my boyfriend with a girl, and it was excellent and easy. Smooth as silk. After a while I stopped using T because it made my face look coarse, my voice sound hoarse, and my skin broke out in acne. But they did work—they clarified my intentions away from men and toward women once and for all.

Or so I thought. You just never know, do you? After struggling to fully come out during my midlife, all of a sudden my latest girl crush started transitioning and stopped being a girl. He became—even if he still had to wrap duct tape around his tits every morning before stepping outside into the world—a man. I still had the same passionate crush, but it left me in a new, unexplored space, somewhere en route to a new nonbinary space, a place I'd never gone or even thought possible before.

And yet here I was. What next? I wish I could tell you a different story, wherein I and my new boyfriend felt free to explore all-new possible ways of loving. Or maybe we need a new word for that too. A trans comic was being interviewed on some morning show and said a brilliant thing. He was talking about how people were always criticizing the trans community for using all these different pronouns and "made-up words." And he said, "Well, you know, all words are really made-up." Ha!

But that is not how the story ends, much to my eternal disappointment. Yes. Wouldn't it have been a wonderful story if after waiting half a lifetime to come out and find such happiness being with women, especially such good sex with women—a happy ending as they say—I then, to my surprise, end up loving a man who started out as a beautiful, tough girl? What a wonderful arc, a third and unexpected possibility. I could call the story "One More Thing," the name of a song that my friend Eric texted last night. Or maybe "Saving the Best for Last."

But the truth is that Cameron and I haven't spoken for almost a year. He never returns my calls. The last time he called was just before midnight, last New Year's Eve. What a great surprise. And we just got to talking, nothing too heavy, about this and that. And on and on. I looked up and saw on the cable-box clock it was already 12:25. New Year's had come and gone. And that seemed fine too. I thought, or maybe even said out loud, "This is the best New Year's Eve ever." And then I never heard from him again. For months I was in pain, frustrated, missing him, missing his special low voice, even lower now because of the T. And then a few months ago I stopped trying to reach out. To reach him, in any way, shape, or form. And then just as suddenly and swiftly as it hit me so many years ago, the crush was just gone. Just as mysteriously as it first arrived, it disappeared. The feeling wasn't there anymore. Gone. Gone. Gone. "And then one magical night / I forgot that you existed," to paraphrase Taylor Swift, another recent crush. I must be the world's oldest "Swiftie," as my life-changing physical therapist told me we're called. But that's a whole 'nother story... dot dot dot

Dirty Old Lady

Doesn't everybody remember their "FIRST"? And how surprising they always are. You just never expect them! Though I can't say I remember my FIRST snow, or my FIRST kiss, I vividly remember my FIRST sex, which was her very FIRST orgasm as well. I also recall all too well my FIRST het sex which was with my future husband on the living room carpet of my parents' apartment in Washington Square Village. I must have been twenty, which was not that late for 1958. It was awful. Since then I have loved women and men and one in-between and then back to women (and now what?). There are always numerous semiparallel tracks of FIRSTs in my history and believe it or not even in my admittedly long life they seem to keep coming. The FIRSTs, I mean. FIRST times.

In no particular order, I am proud that Anne-christine D'Adesky, whom I always call ACD, just recently asked me to be her FIRST "Spotlight" interview subject. And because it was an online format we had to do it on Zoom which I had never done. So it was my FIRST Zoom! I was terrified, partly because I'm always terrified of technology and partly because I thought it would make me look hideous, from what I experienced seeing the few shots I'd taken of myself by accident. To this day I have never once taken a selfie on purpose. ACD set the whole Zoom thing up, sent me an invitation like you're supposed to, and with my indispensable helper Alma (who has a thirteen-year-old daughter hence is quite tech-savvy herself) at my side to guide me through the moves, it was actually fun to do and not even so unflattering as I feared. In fact I looked kinda good, I guess. I don't really know what I look like anymore. I only have one mirror, in the bathroom, and I hardly ever look up when I'm washing my face and I refuse to have a full-length mirror anywhere near my body and there's no one to look at me that way anymore, no one to murmur "You look so pretty," or "You're really still beautiful" even—except me on a very good day. Val would sometimes say it, and Heather didn't even need the "still" part. Alma compliments me once in a while, after she's just washed my hair, or she says I have good skin, which all the women on the Robin side did. She and I sometimes joke about all the Clarins face creams I splurge on, which may or may not do any good. To this day I am still so proud and joyous to have been Chris Kraus's FIRST Native Agents author she published back in 1990, my FIRST book—stories and essays called *If You're a Girl*.

Speaking of FIRSTs (drum roll please), I can't help boasting about probably the greatest source of pride (and joy) in my whole literary life. Maybe not just my literary life but my entire long and mostly wonderful life, the whole thing. Even before my books came out, long before, I was made guest editor of *The World*, the St. Mark's Poetry Project annual anthology, which was usually a poetry anthology but I asked, since I am not a poet, if I could make it an all-prose edition. As I wrote this I had no idea when that was so I googled it and to my amazement (really, I'm such a computer newbie, even though I had a computer long before anyone, and when I got my first one they called it a "portable" even though it weighed forty pounds) the newsletter said it was issue #77 of *The World*. An old old *World*. Who knew! Edited by Ann Rower, my very own name, came right up. Technology! I was flabbergasted. I couldn't believe I was even "known" in that way. Did not expect it. I was taken to a page which reproduced the typography—as if it was the old stencil itself—of the *Poetry Project Newsletter*, edited by fine poet, and my good friend, Greg Masters, announcing my call for submissions to my all-prose edition, calling for stories, essays, journal entries, plays, dream journals, and more.

And the FIRST thing I did as editor was to use my position, my "power," as an excuse to approach my favorite writer—really it was just because I was a fan, to put it mildly—and not to get him into bed, not for one minute imagining that such a thing would ever even be possible, but I had a serious age-inappropriate groupie-type crush on (beautiful punk junky that he was) the lyricist and frontman of the Voidoids, Richard Hell. I was thrilled to have a reason to meet him in the flesh—not just from the front row, or across from him at Café Le Metro on Second Avenue where all the poets hung. I asked him for some of his writing, a story, anything, which I offered to publish sight unseen, and I was thrilled when he did give me some. It was a sweet little story, a fantasy about, I seem to remember, a fawn. For the story and two nights of the best sex (as far as sex with men goes) I ever had, I gave him some of the best coke and weed I ever had—which seemed like a fair trade-off, the drugs being, if not an actual prerequisite, a fitting prelude to the lovely deed itself. Fucked me almost to death you could say. Lana Del Rey, one of my current favorite lyricists and singers, has a beautiful line: "Fuck me to death, / love me until I love myself." I love that expression—"fuck me to death." Although I shouldn't really say it. Everyone seems to think an old woman talking about sex, especially in that dirty a way, is unseemly, but what do they know? Actually most people don't know shit about being old, because most people I know are not that old. As old as me. But they will, if they're lucky as me, one day be old and still have ample amounts of lust and desire and plenty of blue talk, as they used to say, on the tip of their tongues in their otherwise scarily deteriorating old bodies. Maybe more, as unseemly it might be to the youths among us, not that they ever think about us old folk.

A little more about Richard Hell, sweet man. Back then, and for a while, we had a light friendship. Sometimes we would meet, at his suggestion, in Washington Square Park, smoke a joint sitting on a bench on the FIRST spring day. Probably he had run out of marijuana, but I didn't care. Years later, he even invited me to his wedding to Patty Smyth—the other Patti—but I was too shy to show up even though it was in the building on East Twelfth Street, the Poets' House we called it, a place I knew almost better than my own address, where so many of my friends, mostly poets, lived. Even Allen Ginsberg and his beautiful boyfriend Peter Orlovsky lived there. I remember one unforgettable and ultimately tragic terrible night—I must have been high, very very high, and on my way back home to the loft I went to the Poets' House knocking door to door and had all varieties of sex with many of them—not Richard, of course, and not Jim Brodey, but all three editors of *Mag City*, Gary Lenhart, of course, whom I was almost in love with, maybe not Greg Masters, definitely Michael Scholnick, who got his FIRST-ever blow job. It took us a while, put a lot of stress on my elbow, but after he came, he said

"You're somethin' else." I'll never forget it—afterward I had, for weeks, something resembling tennis elbow, which I called "blow job elbow" to all my friends. By the time I got back up to Gary's apartment, where I started from, he informed me that Vito had been calling all night. "Call Vito," he said. I did. "Come home" was all Vito said. And I did. But before I did I flushed what was left of my little glassine bag of coke down Gary's toilet. That was the FIRST time I ever did anything like that (the weirdest part was when I returned the next afternoon somehow the bag of coke was still floating in the toilet water. It seemed almost like a little miracle. So I fished it out and did it. But that was the day after). When I got back home to the loft, Vito said "Call your mother." I did. "Can you please come uptown" was all she said. And when I did, she said "Your father just fell out of the window." She always said "fell"—admittedly on the death certificate it did say, under cause of death, "See history of the fall," which sounded like Milton's *Paradise Lost* to me, but I knew he jumped. A very big FIRST, as FIRSTs go. My father's outrageously courageous suicide.

I was always shy with Richard. I remember going, years after, to his reading at Fales Library. His autobiography had just come out, *I Dreamed I Was a Very Clean Tramp*. Val was with me and I distinctly remember sitting there after the whole room had emptied out trying to get my nerve up to go up and congratulate him, worried that he wouldn't remember me (which looking back was crazy—not how life works), with Val next to me, imploring me to go and speak to him. Eventually everybody was gone and I was still sitting there, mute. I guess my endless crush got the better of me. His notoriety and punk fame just made me too shy. Unlike the FIRST time I called him up and asked him to "submit." There is a very special feeling you get when you're in that driver's-seat position. Ye Olde Casting Couch, East Village style. Oh God. Not Me Too. I mean Me Too NOT, feeling looking back now a little like the Harvey Weinstein of the downtown poetry scene—although as I keep saying over and over, I'm not a poet.

After I agreed to publish Richard's story, which he was actually very nervous about (having not been published in a "serious" literary magazine since he got into rock 'n' roll and became one of the best punk rockers of his "blank" generation—"Love Comes in Spurts" is genius), the other favor he asked was to also publish the brilliant work of a dear friend of his (who at this point had only published one great little Hanuman book) named Cookie Mueller. She too was thrilled to be asked and I for my part got to meet and eventually befriend her in a really gratifying way—it was really my honor to know her all those wonderful and, in the end, terrible, disease-filled years—the well-known downtown diva famed for her unique clothing which she sewed herself, and her general wildness. I fantasized that if I met her I would be then invited to all these cool parties with all these cool artists, but in the end, when we did become close, usually what would happen was she'd call me to ask my advice about writing and literary things, and never to invite me to join her and her best friend (another downtown wonder) Nan Goldin, whose fame was partly due to her taking so many beautiful pictures of Cookie and the whole downtown scene. One of her gorgeous pictures of Cookie—her head thrown way back, laughing for pure joy—graces the cover of Cookie's new, of course posthumous, anthology, which Chris just published and which won lots of prestigious literary awards and highbrow accolades—an outcome that would have shocked Cookie, had she known. Maybe she does know. I'm never sure about all that.

The last thing I will say about Richard Hell was in some ways the most unique and surprising and probably most traumatic, as well as dramatic, historically speaking, thing about Richard and me. It happened in 1991 during a book tour of Germany, East and West, soon after the Wall came down—for an East German anthology called *AM LIT*, which Sylvère Lotringer coedited with a crazy alcoholic East Berlin Stasi spy—to Berlin, Hamburg, Weimar, and back to Berlin. The lineup included Richard, Kathy Acker, Eileen Myles, Lynne Tillman, and Chris and Sylvère, of course. There are a multitude of folks and fans, young and old, who can claim to have listened to great punk music with or shot up with or no doubt had great sex with Richard, but how many of them can actually claim, as I can, that "I went to Auschwitz with Richard Hell"?

Happy Endings

A confession to make: that wasn't the whole story. There was a meditation on PT (physical therapy), what it meant to me, how it changed me, changed my body, changed my life. But then I decided to cut it. It was too embarrassing. Especially when I contemplated showing it to my real-life physical therapist. I went to great lengths to clean it up a little bit, not just for him, but for me too. To have even thought it, let alone written about it—what was that about? I wasn't sure where exploring it might lead. At first, I seriously wondered if anyone else had ever thought about it like that before. But then again, it seemed so obvious, such a cliché, so corny, that probably everyone who'd ever done physical therapy had at one time or another had those same unclean thoughts and immediately rejected them for being too silly, too juvenile, too naughty to admit to having had.

But after I finally got up my nerve to show it to him and he assured me it wasn't embarrassing at all, that it didn't change anything between us, I started to worry that I'd sanitized it too much. Is there a genre of physical therapy porn? I mean, come on. It seems so perfectly suited for it. So inevitable. So inextricably linked. Every time I think about it, it makes me giggle, especially the way I'm thinking about it. I don't mean I'm actually thinking of writing about it as a treatment or a screenplay or a funny little story, a piece of fiction, because I couldn't do a good job even if I were to try. Oh Heather, where art thou? She was a mistress of the mode, wrote about sex better than anyone I could imagine, not that I've even read any bona fide porn, or seen any porn movies or even wanted to. I know everybody's doing it these days, but it never tempted me. I wouldn't even know how to begin. The only time I ever even came close to anything like that was reading the first chapter of Heather's first novel, *House Rules*, and using it to get off. And even that wasn't easy. Not enough hands, or something.

Just yesterday morning something momentous happened—something that hadn't happened to me in a very long time, not since before COVID. I hadn't even considered it until quite recently. I wondered if my starting to think about it again had anything to do with doing physical therapy? The more I do it, the more it opens me up until I am where I am now. Addicted. To the endorphins. Not to mention how much it's improving my balance, my strength, my flexibility—all the things it's supposed to do.

But it really started to be on my mind one night, two or three months ago when I was writing in my journal at 2:00 a.m., writing about kissing of all things. And how much I was beginning to miss it. To really miss it. Miss it more than any of the other things lovemaking involves. And Val was such a good kisser.

Is there, I wonder, a relation between PT and libido? Do they enhance each other? Or maybe cancel each other out? As Freud says, sex and work (art) come from the same place, but you can't have them both at the same time. You have to choose—maybe that's why it feels like my work is going so well these days!

Like yoga—the theory more than the practice, since I can't really get down on a floor mat, though I can do certain things lying flat on the bed. Matt, my physical therapist, showed me how to do child's pose in a chair. And then there's the magic of having him count for me, all that. The first time we did a certain stretch he had put a green rubber band around my knees and then asked me to open them as far as I could. He even helped me go wider by pushing my knees apart so they almost touched the bed. It feels so good! Much to my sorrow, he never did it again, after I made some dumb little off-color joke about the position. I should have kept my mouth shut and left my legs open! Now he just counts. Which I do like, but not as much as I like his hands on the insides of my knees, opening them wider, pushing against the rubber bands to intensify the stretch.

Matt's brand of physical therapy includes bits of yoga and t'ai chi. My cousin, the renowned Hindu scholar Wendy Doniger, turned me on to a book called *Yoga: Immortality and Freedom*, by Mircea Eliade. At first, I thought I wouldn't be able to deal with it, as it was too academic. But I'm really getting deep into it. Chakra, tantra, mantra, sound, breath, rhythm, the Kama Sutra... It all interests me. Especially the chakras, the seven places in the body where different energies reside. It's very enlightened, very current... And yet, the more I look into it, the more it feels like something's missing. It's just all so het!

But what happened yesterday morning began with that late-night scribbling about kissing, which, after multiple digressions, ended with me wondering why I was even writing about it, saying *Maybe I should get a new vibrator*. And that is my habit, to go for the joke (although lately I've been trying not to, since my friend Lynne Tillman once said she thought I used satire to avoid dealing with my real feelings, which seemed useful and true, though it did sting a bit). But I did start thinking about it. I must have misplaced the old one—actually, I had two. They were huge Hitachi "neck massagers," so old you had to plug them into the wall. But that's what I'd always used for pleasure, and, I fervently believed, for good health. Physical and mental health. But then I lost touch with it, and since I went dead inside a while ago, I had not the urge to even look for it, because I had no urges at all. But writing that joke line about getting a new one made it (as writing can do) come alive. Come true.

My next move was totally predictable, a thing that girls, at least teenage girls, do—I talked about it with my best friend, the friend I can talk to about anything. Over the years—two decades at least—Kirsten and I have been through so much trauma together: Heather's suicide, Val's death. This year she graciously visited me any number of times (since I don't go out because of COVID and my mobility issues). So the next time Kirsten visited, I told her what I was thinking about for my next shopping adventure. She said she doesn't like them (vibrators, not shopping adventures), but then the conversation took another turn, and I don't think I even told her my theory that my interest in vibrators had something to do with all this physical therapy (which by now I can't live without—I don't know what I'm going to do when my insurance or funds run out, or if Matt cuts me off, moves on, moves away).

But Kirsten, who is very practical, very tech-savvy, told me I'd have to research it, see what was out there. There would be new and improved models, maybe even something with batteries. I really wanted her to help me with this part, but she didn't suggest it and I didn't know how to ask, so I told her I'd keep her posted.

After she left I was anxious to get right on it, but I didn't know where to start, so I did what I always do—I reached for my phone and called 411… Then I quickly hung up because my brother-in-law pays the phone bill and he would not only disapprove of the added expense but might see the name of the business I was trying to reach. Instead, I reached for my cell and googled Eve's Garden—a name that was buried deep in my past. I remembered visiting this ladies' toy shop in my youth, and much to my amazement a pleasant-sounding woman answered "Eve's Garden, may I help you?"

She said this so casually I lost all my shyness and just started telling her everything… How I couldn't find my old vibrator, that my partner had died, and since COVID I'd gone dead inside… I actually said those words, and she said "Um-hmmm," like she knew all about it. She didn't even ask me about what had changed, about my new needs, or my old needs returning. She just said Hitachi had a smaller, newer model called the Magic Wand Mini, complete with a rechargeable battery. She was sure it would suit my needs, and she could mail it out to me that same day.

As soon as she uttered the word "mail" I felt a shiver from root chakra to crown, imagining the package from Eve's Garden arriving—my housemate Luis assuming it was another gardening device and dutifully opening it, as he does all of our packages. So I asked Kim—I learned her name early on in our intimate phone exchange—if I could send it to Kirsten's apartment. Again, she didn't question my request, but told me it would be coming in a plain black-plastic wrapper, with a return label addressed to Lady Confidential, which, I admit, didn't seem all that subtle a disguise. But I didn't care, as long as I could set the wheels of my newly articulated desire in motion. And within a matter of days the package came as promised, and soon after, yesterday morning, so did I.

But returning to the subject of physical therapy, I started to think about this new genre, PT porn, a fantasy genre having absolutely nothing to do with my own experience, or even my deepest, darkest—not to mention silliest—fantasies that may have momentarily crossed my half-dreaming mind every once in a blue moon... I just think porn and PT would go well together. Because PT is so intimate and physical. A great combo, like nachos and cheese.

But I'm not even going to try writing these scenes. It's a special gift I don't even have. I know, because I've tried. When Heather and I were just getting together, she used to come by my house and leave letters in my mailbox. They weren't exactly love letters because they were so sexy, so excellently erotic, really pornographic, and you could tell that she knew what she was doing. She was so good that it sometimes worried me, or at least made me worry if I was being manipulated, being played. She was really a pro, in both senses of the word. She used to work the parking lot at the White Plains train station at rush hour, all the men traveling back from their jobs in the city before going home to sit with their wives and kids round the dinner table... Sex was just something Heather knew well, did well, got paid well to do after a while, and most of all, she wrote about it magnificently.

That first time I heard Heather read, at the Drawing Center in SoHo, she was reading with Rick Moody and William someone. They were both wonderful writers, but she blew them away. Heather just stood there, in her not-too-tight brown leather pants with her men's white shirt untucked and her wonderful shining hair. She stood there and quietly read, as if the words were slipping out the side of her mouth almost by accident, and I immediately fell in love.

So when we finally did get together a few years later, and she plied me with these special letters, postcoital writings meant to seamlessly continue where the fucking left off, I tried to respond in kind. But I really couldn't do it. My letters were so lame by comparison—it was really embarrassing. I keep Heather's letters tucked into my copy of *House Rules*, which is inscribed with a handwritten message: *For Ann, Because, though I didn't know it then, I must've written this for you, to make this happen—I want always to be inside you have you inside me. I still want to hear you scream, make you. Have you make me—how about now? Heather, August 9, 1996.*

I just found the book now. It has two letters in their "par avion" envelopes, but I don't want to look at them—can't bring myself to. But come to think of it, I just realized I actually have all of them on my computer, in the file called "Ann's Book," because Val wanted to hear every detail of Heather's and my so-called courtship and then some. As soon as she heard about the letters, she wanted to read them. I don't think I let her at first, but after much convincing (and Val could be very convincing when she needed to) I let her take a look at them. As soon as she read them, the first thing she wanted was to include them in what somehow had become "our" Heather book—no wonder I never could finish it—and in order to do that, the first thing she wanted was to type them into my computer.

If you think there's something a little sick about it—Val putting Heather's words into her mouth, under her fingers, literally— well, it was just not as perverse as you might think, because Val did not have a perverse bone in her body, or anywhere else. She was just that pure.

Verbatim
Journal, Dec. 22, 2022

"Do you remember that night maybe decades ago when I tried to kiss you in the back of a cab coming home from Florent?"

"Like it was yesterday," Eric says, to my chagrin.

It was not the answer I wanted. Or expected. I was definitely hoping he was too drunk to recall any of it. We were both drunk, not a thing that happens a lot for me. Otherwise it never would have even happened in the first place. Vito was in Europe. I don't know what got into me. The following is his text about it, taken verbatim from my phone:

(2:27 p.m., Nov. 23, 2022)

I just caught up with your messages, Isn't life and perspective a far out thing. I remember the cab night like it was yesterday. Seconds after I was beating myself up. Never was good at taking notice of unique opportunities, especially with human beings. I grab some but they are always so obvious. Went home with a Spanish "lady" when I was on a bike trip and she was so worrisome and finally told me as I was feeling her up on the dance floor. "You know I'm a boy..." and I said "I just wanted to know if you'd like to come back to my room, the rest is easy." But there wasn't much finesse or subtlety to our encounter, and I was unusually confident as I had been riding my Triumph solo for weeks through the Rockies and deserts with a gun and one change of clothes. Trying to be a boy and what do you know I spent my last night with a tall handsome "boy"? Let's stick to Lady! But back to the cab. I fucked up! (NOTE: Actually the phone says, because he's so prudish, "I ducked up!")

My reply:

(2:37 p.m., Nov. 23, 2002)

I was always really hoping you were too drunk to remember. I felt like a rapist. No finesse there.

It was so unpleasant. The way he turned away. Almost jerking away, repulsed. I'll never forget it. It was awful and looking back, maybe almost immediately after, just as he was supposedly feeling regret at not letting it happen, thinking he'd missed out on something wonderful, I was sure I had narrowly escaped something terrible not just impossible. It would have changed everything between us, I imagine, and I can't even imagine how it would have played out. I guess the loft was empty and we would have gone upstairs. And then what? And now what? Now I can't imagine it for a different reason, the reason being that now I might be just too old to be with anyone, what with the shape I'm in, or out of, my so-called body which I lost some time ago. Not that I was ever particularly into it or proud of it—too heavy, ass too big for the times, especially if you wanted to be a dancer in the '60s. Now it's all gone. Gone gone gone. The only thing that's really bad about getting older. At least so far. (This is the scariest journal entry I ever let myself write. I think I must rip it out of the book, something I never do, like it's a rule. But wait a minute! WHAT'S… Yes. Oh yes, I can feel it, the hand creeping up toward my body. Oh yes. Oh no. It's me. What's wrong with me? It's my hand. My jacked-up libido is gonna be the death of me… But what a way to go.)

Acknowledgements

(in order of appearance)

"I Feel Love, I Feel Love, I Feel Love, I Feel Love"
(Donna Summer)

LUIS ALVAREZ, just turned fifty, elegant in his perfectly pressed long-head doorman's uniform, at the Manchester (1905) where I live now, my personal caretaker, dear roommate, compulsive OCD cleaner, gifted natural-born Latino chef, Nuchenuche's chief playmate, and keeper of all my medicines for my own good I know!

ALMA GONZALEZ, born in beautiful Oaxaca, my perfect all-around helper in multiple ways from cleaning and wonderful healthy cooking to organizing all my papers, knowing where everything is, including taxes, takes me to doctors, bathes me, feeds Nuchenuche, mother, sister, friend. Always on the lookout for ways to make life better, late forties, always eager to improve her English, beautiful to boot.

MATT BAUER, my original physical therapist, since November 2020. "Found" miraculously, serendipitously, by Alma on a neighboring stoop up the block, a mere twenty-eight-year-old gay beauty, totally wise, inventive, original, and brilliant technique, which he described so eloquently as "chaotic but encouraging energy," as well as having a way with words, and hands, so good that ultimately his bosses promoted him and moved him to Jersey so I lost him, first person to touch me after COVID. After Val died, recommended to me most of the music I listen to to this day, spiked my blood pressure so high when he first came through the front door I sometimes had to lie down and do our workout from bed, and, significantly, always asked about my writing, thought of me as a writer, which I hadn't until he did and so made this path even possible, whom I will always, as they say, remember, never forget.

RONNIE GEIST, my first teenaged girlfriend's final longtime girlfriend, who'd died the year before, a wonderful artist, who accidentally "found" (a theme emerging here), in the apartment she and Margot shared for so many years on 117 Waverly Place, where Margot and I first had sex when we were barely fourteen, the original manuscript of the original book, this very book, *If You're a Girl*, which Margot had lovingly kept for years in her bookcase and though I didn't even remember what she was talking about, said yes (another theme) when Ronnie offered to drop it off at my uptown apartment, sight unseen (good title) in early 2022, shortly after I started physical therapy with Dr. Matt, as I called him, the next time she was coming uptown to see her son, which I discovered was bound in yellowed plastic with a title page bearing my old SoHo-loft address where I lived with a lovely man, VITO RICCI, for twenty-two years and I'd left decades ago so I could be with a girl.

AMY SCHOLDER, magnificent friend for life, "my other editor," of the High Risk novels. Fabulous queerest activist gorgeous fashionista, who came to me in 1994 after City Lights in San Fran and is miraculously still here, to me her best gift is that she courageously published Heather's greatest novel, *Notice*, after eighteen editors turned it down, "too dark" while Heather was alive, and now Chris and Hedi are republishing it with mine, is now "bi"—coastal, that is, in Malibu.

CHRIS KRAUS, original friend and editor of the first *IYAG* in 1990, destined, once I got my nerve up, who said yes (theme) to publishing with Semiotext(e) the stories Ronnie found, sight unseen, and sent the contract the next day along with one for *Notice*, Heather's beautifully sexy book which I held the copyright for, thanks to Amy, to my surprise and joy, and is making all this happen for me, to me, who never for a moment thought I'd have another book at this ridiculously advanced age, making it indubitably the best time of my life and a better book than any I could make without her, making a whole world of difference, a "hole whirled," as I like to say.

HEDI EL KHOLTI, brilliant beautiful man, Chris's partner / accomplished accomplice at Semiotext(e), great taste, great designer (e.g., my cover). He has a great "list," as they say, the only one in the world who loves *Notice* as much as I do, a deep bond forever between us, enuf said. Less is more.

ANNE-CHRISTINE D'ADESKY, all-around extraordinary girl, woman, human, world-renowned activist, from Africa to Haiti and beyond, founding member of ACT UP and Lesbian Avengers and the Dyke March, to name a few, genius innovator, wonderful prolific novelist and my own personal first neighborhood friend on East Seventh Street, walking, talking, often at the same time, a lot a lot, till she moved to SF for decades, now she's back, always a little crushed out on her tho I'm way too old I know but she changed my life just recently by publishing on (my first ever) Zoom her first of many brilliant "Spotlight" interviews which put me back out there in the world so people could know me again and get in touch as a writer which I'd stopped being it felt like forever until then a few months ago now that I have a new book about to drop into the world.

SHAUN WILSON, and then one more amazing thing serendipitously or was it intentionally happened. I just don't know about all this stuff with the universe but this is what just happened, a youngish (forties) grad student from Northumbria University in the north of England applied to Chris and Hedi at Semiotext(e) and asked if he could intern for them, being a brilliant fan of their list from way back to Sylvère (may he et cetera) and tho they don't usually say yes this time they did say yes just at the moment when they got my manuscript in dire need of somebody else's gift for editing and polishing things I'm not that good at and connected me with one of the best things in my whole long life, who fixed up my own book to perfection and taught me more, music and literature, most especially his own great novels, takes one to know one, I hope against hope is true.

RICHARD HELL, "Richard said yes," Amy texted me three little words not long ago just meaning Richard Hell sending me flying, heavenward and way beyond, cuz when we were planning my book launch for *IYAG* to be April 2024 and looking for people to read who would draw a crowd and Chris said Richard Hell, who better than a famous punk young god from the later '70s whom I was briefly but significantly connected to, with, and I'd even written about him in the first story in the first book back in 1990, "Vito in Europe," which barely scratched the surface of the true story of my deep crush from way back then, when, whose "Love Comes in Spurts" still stands as one of my favorite not to mention brilliant lyrics (poems?) of all time, still a poet today, maybe even better.

NANCY CAMPBELL, longtime gifted photographer who took the best most-beautiful-imaginable author photos of me for *Armed Response*, back in the '90s, which I couldn't find even with Alma's eagle eye and devotion tearing the whole house apart, how could someone just lose all their photos from babyhood till now—who does that?—and completely serendipitously (of course) was returning to NYC from Vinalhaven on the Cape the very next day right after I managed to get her number from the Wooster Group after all this time and called me back immediately and had her own set in her files because she's a pro and brought them to me that very afternoon, a few days ago, so I could scan them for Hedi so he could crop them brilliantly and turn them into my new blue—not pink anymore—cover, another life changing moment for me. But who is that pretty girl? Where is she now?

and NUCHENUCHE
who lies on my pages the moment they emerge from the printer whenever she gets a chance and keeps them warm.

Sources

Parts of this book have previously appeared in the following anthologies, collections, novels, and periodicals: *Animal Shelter* (2015), *Armed Response* (High Risk / Serpent's Tail, 1995), *Bomb* (1983), *Cookin' with Honey: What Literary Lesbians Eat* (Firebrand Books, 1996), *If You're a Girl* (Semiotext(e), 1990), *Lee & Elaine* (Serpent's Tail, 1995), and *More & Less* (1993). "L.S.D. (... Just the High Points ...)" was included in a performance of the same title (1984) by the Wooster Group.

ABOUT THE AUTHORS

Ann Rower is the author of *If You're A Girl, Armed Response,* and *Lee & Elaine.* She received a PhD from Columbia University in sixteenth-century English literature in 1974, and has collaborated with the Wooster Group as a writer. Rower taught writing in New York at the School for Visual Arts between 1974 and 2019.

Sheila Heti is the author of ten books, including the novels *Pure Colour, Motherhood,* and *How Should a Person Be?,* which New York deemed one of the New Classics of the twenty-first century. She was named one of the New Vanguard by the *New York Times* book critics, who, along with a dozen other magazines and newspapers, chose *Motherhood* as a top book of 2018. Her books have been translated into twenty-four languages. She lives in Toronto, Canada.